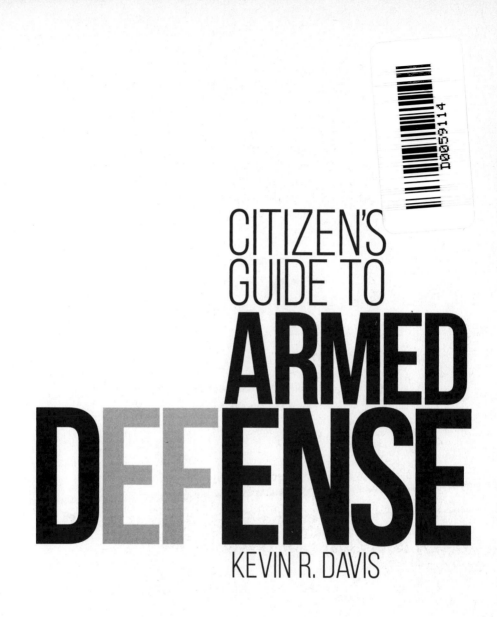

CITIZEN'S GUIDE TO
ARMED DEFENSE

KEVIN R. DAVIS

Published by

Krause Publications, a division of F+W, A Content + eCommerce Company
700 East State Street • Iola, WI 54990-0001
715-445-2214 • 888-457-2873
www.krausebooks.com

To order books or other products call toll-free 1-800-258-0929
or visit us online at www.krausebooks.com

ISBN-13: 978-1-4402-4363-9
ISBN-10: 1-4402-4363-8

Cover Design by Dave Hauser
Designed by Sandi Carpenter
Edited by Corrina Peterson

Printed in the United States of America

DEDICATION

First and foremost I would like to thank my lovely wife, Patricia. She has always been my biggest fan, supporter and promoter, as well as the cutest cheerleader I know. You hold my heart.

To my kids – Timothy, Stephanie, Aron and Emily; and the grandkids – Grant, Tayden and Caston. "Never stop learning!"

To my late parents Robert B. and Maxine S. Davis. I miss you guys but you are always with me.

To Richard Krausman, my late uncle, former Marine Sergeant and my first firearms instructor. Without his tutelage and direction my career and this book would not have been possible.

To my instructors whose training, in person, on video or in writing, kept me safe on the streets and set the bar extremely high for my own instructional standards: Rex Applegate, Jeff Cooper, Charles Askins, Evan Marshall, John Farnam, Bruce Siddle, Chuck Taylor, Mas Ayoob, Norm Evans, Ron Avery, Todd Jarrett, Bill Rogers, Clint Smith, and many, many more.

To my Brothers and Sisters of the International Law Enforcement Educators and Trainers Association. Through their friendship, high professional standards and motivation to the training mission, they have kept me motivated and focused on training. ILEETA has kept me motivated to the trainer's function over the years and for that, I am eternally grateful.

To my students – law enforcement and private citizens. You taught me much more than you'll ever know and those lessons have been included here.

To the members of our nation's military and their families, past and present. Thank you for your service, and thanks to the families for their sacrifices as well.

Finally, to our founding fathers who had the foresight to write the 2nd Amendment to the Constitution of the United States of America. The right to keep and bear arms for self-protection has kept countless citizens of this great country and their families safe from harm for over two hundred years and counting.

CONTENTS

CHAPTER ONE:

WHY WE ARM

CASE STUDY

It was seventh grade at middle school. John was a good kid from a good family. Raised in the old-fashioned way, he confronted Karlos, a thug, about some problem or confrontation they had at school. "Let's meet after school and settle this," or some other offer to meet outside the gym after soccer practice one day. I was witness as I waited for my mother to pick me up. John squared off and Karlos, who outweighed John by 25 to 50 pounds, moved in for the kill. Karlos picked John up and slammed him to the asphalt. Karlos then drew a shiv, which looked like welding rod stolen from metal shop, and stabbed John in the side.

I don't remember John's injuries, but he was bleeding from his wound. He did survive.

Years later, after I became a city police officer, I arrested Karlos for drug trafficking. After his release a few years later, he was present during an officer-involved shooting. When detectives with warrants for his arrest for breaking and entering attempted to take him into custody, a violent subject came out of the house where Karlos was hiding swinging a brush ax, a machete on an ax handle. That man was shot and killed by the two investigators (one of whom was saved from serious injury by the sleeve of his new leather coat).

I'm sure that Karlos is still in the system. Such criminals seldom get "rehabilitated." They have long ago chosen their life's path or "vocation" and wake each afternoon with only the thought of getting enough money from crime to satisfy their addictions or predilections. They kick their way into your homes in the middle of the day to commit burglary. They rob you at the ATM at night. And they break into your cars as well as commit heinous assaults and rapes whenever and wherever they chose.

There was no fair fight in the John versus Karlos match-up. Karlos was skilled in fighting and he was armed. John was thinking fistfight. Karlos was thinking felonious assault and had the street experience and the weaponry to make it happen.

Over my 35-year security and police career, I've come into countless Karlos types and personalities. They have no plan to work for a living. They only have thoughts of who will be their next victim or prey. They are exceedingly violent. Regardless of previous felony convictions, they are armed with no thought as to their actions other than to evade detection and arrest.

On-duty and off, I carry pepper spray and an expandable baton. Over the years I've had operational access to 12 gauge beanbag rounds, 37mm chemical munitions and ECW – electronic control weapons, such as the Taser.

I've pepper sprayed suspects, struck them with flashlights and batons, fired barricade penetrating rounds into locations where they were taking refuge, thrown flash-bangs in their homes and rooms to distract them, pointed revolvers,

The author has used and does carry less-lethal devices, such as these Kimber Pepper Blaster II OC control devices.

Author routinely carries two handguns off-duty – this Glock 19 with a spare magazine and a S&W MP340 in a DeSantis pocket holster.

semi-auto pistols, shotguns, sub-machine guns, M4 carbines and .308 sniper rifles at hundreds of folks.

And yes, I was involved in a tactical operation that resulted in the death of a criminal suspect firing at our police tactical team with two handguns.

I'm six feet, two inches tall and weigh in excess of 240 lbs. I have trained in the martial arts and suspect control tactics my entire career.

And I still carry at least one gun on my person while off-duty.

You see, I reached the conclusion long ago that violent crime was omnipresent and indiscriminate, that my family or I could be the intended victim of an assault, robbery or burglary at any time, in virtually any place.

This conclusion, which you may have reached as well, was fomented outside an inner-city middle school gymnasium years ago and has been reinforced by dealing with violent offenders and criminal suspects throughout a long career.

If criminal suspects don't have a second thought about attacking a uniformed police officer – and they don't – then why do citizens believe they're immune?

CASE STUDY

Even at my size, several years ago while wearing civilian clothes heading out for lunch, a crack cocaine addict and convicted felon attempted to rob me. Wearing a facemask and goggles and armed with what appeared to be a small pistol, the suspect mumbled something to me as I opened the door to an elevator lobby on my way outside. Standing six feet away, I saw what I believed to be a .25 auto in his right hand. Knowing I could not "beat the draw" or safely attempt to draw my own pistol without getting shot, I ignored the suspect and walked through the door to the stairway on my left. Once the heavy metal door closed behind me, I drew my pistol, opened the door with my foot, identified myself as an officer and threatened, in no uncertain terms, to blow the suspect's head off. After the suspect announced, "It's a toy! It's a toy!" and put his gun down on my orders, I ordered him prone and handcuffed him. I still

As I have grown older, I've gotten wiser as well. Personal insults and slights I'll let pass. Aggressive drivers tailgating me, I'll pull to the side if possible or change lanes and let them go by. Dangerous places? Well, I avoid the types of locations and places where police respond on a regular basis.

---

*"A potential high-risk environment is any place
where other people have more control
over the variables than you do."*
*~Shannon Stallard, as quoted in Eyes Wide Open,
Kristie Kilgore, Clinetop Press, 2001*

Further, I've accepted that I am not as strong, fast or agile as I once was, and realize that I don't heal as quickly as in my 20s, 30s or even my 40s. My ability to run quickly or fight as hard as I once did have diminished due to long-term sports related injuries and arthritis.

And I carry at least one gun – as well as other means of self-defense. I don't want to get involved, I'll try to be the best witness possible, but if force is necessary to protect my loved ones, myself or innocent citizens, I'm prepared to intercede.

Within arm's reach in the bedroom, this quick access safe holds a DoubleStar 1911 with Surefire X300 white light, for "things that go bump in the night."

This decision means that my life has changed accordingly. Your decision to be an armed citizen means the same thing. With the rights afforded to us by the 2nd Amendment come the responsibility to:

- know the law,
- be constantly vigilant to our surroundings and the circumstances developing around us,
- be discreet in our carry of firearms,
- be slow to anger and conservative in our willingness to display or threaten with firearms,
- be skilled in the drawing and accurate in our firing,
- be prepared for the police response and orders to disarm and submit to their custody and control,
- be educated about our legal rights and the criminal justice process post-shooting, and the liabilities – financial, political and more – to which we may be exposed, and
- understand that there may be critical incident stress which causes us and our families grief unless it is dealt with.

To be an armed citizen is to understand that continued preparation, study, training and practice are required. This decision should not be entered into lightly.

DON'T BE A VICTIM

CASE STUDY

Shaeffer, my uniformed police patrol partner, and I turned the street corner in our patrol car on a summer evening. Our patrol district was the most violent and crime-ridden in the city, filled with dopers, hookers, violent criminals, gang members and other miscreants. What we witnessed was an older male getting the living hell kicked out of him by a gang of "youths." Kicked in the head, the victim was already holding some of his teeth in his hand as he spit up blood. Once down on the ground he was continually stomped and kicked in the body and head, as is the way on the mean streets. You get knocked down or fall and they'll put the boot to you.

Shaeff and I jumped out of our cruiser and chased after the suspects. My partner caught two and I believe I caught two as well, with one or two getting away that night. EMS was called and the victim transported to the emergency room. We interviewed the arrested subjects, who readily gave up their partners who got away, and signed warrants for their arrest.

At the preliminary hearing, we met the victim in the hallway. His head was shaven and he had the most hideous

Not being a victim is comprised of many components, including armed defense.

incision line on his scalp, which was still held together with staples. The suspect's kicks and stomps had resulted in the victim's brain swelling and emergency surgery to save his life.

CASE STUDY

Neal was the 14-year-old son of a woman who was imprisoned for murder. Neal's grandmother was in prison for murder as well (another case/another victim). Neal was staying in a foster home when he was suspended from school for some stupid infraction. Angry at the world, Neal took a stolen .22 caliber revolver upstairs to the room of a two-year-old infant, also in the custody of the foster mother of the home. Holding the crib pad next to two-year-old Jamarian's head, he fired one round into the brain of the infant, killing him. In an attempt to hide his crime, he turned and fired one round out through the inside wall of the apartment causing the three boys standing outside to scatter and run.

When Shaeff and I received the call and arrived on scene, my partner went upstairs to check on the infant while I interviewed the family downstairs and broadcast descriptions of the suspects the family believed had fired into the home striking the boy in his crib.

When detectives arrived on scene and interviewed Neal, they quickly informed us that he had been the one who assassinated his foster brother. Neal was arrested and convicted and served several years for his crime (I believe it was around eight years in a juvenile correctional facility).

The epilogue to the story is that, upon his release, Neal attempted an armed robbery at a local bank. This time a security guard in line behind him drew his concealed handgun and shot Neal several times. He survived but was convicted of the attempted armed robbery and gun specs

and sent to the prison for big boys this time. Unknown if
Neal is still incarcerated at this time.

Seldom do criminals choose victims who look like they can or would fight back. Indeed, a study was done years ago by researchers Betty Grayson and Morris Stein. They filmed members of the general public walking along a city street. They then showed the film to 53 inmates incarcerated for violent crimes and asked them to rate how easy it would be to attack the person.

Women were rated as easier to victimize than men, older persons were rated as easier to victimize than younger ones. Interestingly, body posture, clothes, and whether the person walking down the street had their head down or up paying attention, were identified by the incarcerated criminals as aspects making the victims seem easier to assault or attack.

In "How the way we walk can increase risk of being mugged" (5 November 2013), BBC correspondent Tom Stafford writes that researchers at the University of Canterbury, in New Zealand, conducted a more thorough test. What the researchers found was that people could reduce their perceived vulnerability to attack by modifying their gait, posture and other body language (Victim Selection and Kinematics: A Point-Light Investigation of Vulnerability to Attack; Gunns, Johnston, Hudson; Journal of Nonverbal Behavior; September 2002, Volume 26, Issue 3, pp 129 – 158).

These studies and others clearly indicate that criminals don't want to work very hard at victimizing innocent citizens. They pick out the easiest targets – older, infirmed or disabled, and those who are seemingly inattentive to their surroundings.

CASE STUDY

A 90-year-old Stockton, California, woman was beaten and robbed in her own garage. The elderly woman found a man in the garage of her home. The suspect grabbed her and covered her mouth and nose, rendering her unconscious. After she blacked out, the suspect entered her home and stole her wallet. She was treated for injuries including a broken nose and bruises to her mouth.

Compare that case to the following.

CASE STUDY

Three teenage home invaders kick their way through the rear door of a home in Detroit. The female homeowner is armed with a 9mm carbine, she tells them she has a gun and orders the men out of her home. They tell her she's bluffing and doesn't have a gun, at which point she starts shooting. The suspects make a mad dash to exit, but one,

> armed with a handgun, attempts to reenter the house. With two young children in the home to defend, the woman opens fire once again, driving the suspects away. The event was captured on video of surveillance cameras installed after the home was burglarized a few weeks before.

You have elected, by becoming an armed citizen, to assume control over your and your family's personal safety and protection. Yes, we work in concert with law enforcement officers to maintain the peace, and if time permits and the situation allows, to apprehend suspects who threaten us or others. However, we are not naïve as to the timeliness of the police response.

Police officers love to arrest bad guys and to stop assaults or other victimization of innocent citizens before they happen. That is what cops live for. Unfortunately, as the saying goes, "When seconds count, police are minutes away." This truism is even worse in this day and age when most law enforcement agencies, especially in cities, are inadequately staffed. Proactive and preventative patrolling by police officers is essentially nonexistent. Patrol officers respond from call to call with little time for crime suppression. Further, they seldom patrol in the quieter areas of town because the trouble spots in their districts demand so much attention.

You, your family and friends cannot depend on the police to protect you or to respond in time to save you. Further, as society has withdrawn more and more behind closed doors and windows, don't expect much more than someone, anonymously because they don't want to get involved, calling 911 and reporting some kind of "problem."

In inner cities it is even worse. What you can expect in the city is that several people will whip out their cell phone cameras to record a video of the incident. Although video recording is a fairly new phenomenon, ignoring pleas for help or another citizen being attacked is hardly new.

Taking control of your safety includes keeping your head in the game and scanning for danger.

CASE STUDY

In 1964 in Queens, New York, 28 year old Catherine "Kitty" Genovese was stabbed to death near her home. Reports at the time indicated that despite her screams and pleas for help, "Oh my God, he stabbed me! Help me! Help me!" her neighbors ignored her. This bystander effect has become known as the "Genovese Syndrome." We can see multiple incidents where this has occurred.

CASE STUDY

In 2012, customers at a convenience store in Kalamazoo, Michigan, step over and ignore a male victim as he lies on the floor at the store's entrance doors for five minutes.

CASE STUDY

2011 in New York City in the Borough of Brooklyn, Maksim Gelman stabs eight victims, killing four. Aboard a subway train, he is seen by two officers riding in the conductor's cab. Gelman then stabs a passenger before the intended victim tackles and takes the suspect to the ground in full view of the officers. The suspect continues to stab the victim in the back of the head before the officers finally get involved. The City of New York maintains that it has no "special duty" to protect the victim, even though the assault took place in full view of the officers.

CASE STUDY

Just so you know that there are still some good people out there and possibly some hope for humanity, in March 2014, SEPTA (Southeastern Pennsylvania Transportation Authority) Police Officer Ronald Jones was attacked by a suspect who had claimed he had a gun. When the suspect grabbed onto Officer Jones' duty pistol, two passengers jumped in and helped restrain the suspect.

TARGET HARDENING

In loss and crime prevention, we are told about the value of hardening our businesses and homes to be less easily targeted by criminals. It is suggested that we improve the doors, locks and lighting, install alarm systems and make it harder for criminals to hide their activities by removing landscaping shrubs and trees. We are told that garages and storage sheds should be locked, serial numbers of mowers, tillers, chainsaws and other more expensive lawn care equipment recorded and inscribed with our names or other identifying marks to be more easily recovered if stolen.

These are all sound suggestions for businesses and our houses, but target hardening can be applied to our persons as well.

*When applied to the armed citizen,
being a "hard target" includes
carrying proper safety equipment.*

First of all, we should research unfamiliar places we intend to travel to or do business. If we are planning a trip to a store or business in a town or section of a city of which we have limited or no knowledge, then we spend a few minutes online checking the place out. Available to everyone are satellite maps that show parking and the general area surrounding a restaurant, store or theatre we want to visit. A web search can quickly yield news reports of crime in the district or area around our intended location. As an example, my lovely wife likes to take the grandkids to the local zoo. She knows a safe route to the zoo and also knows that I have conducted narcotics operations in many of the depressed, crime ridden housing areas nearby. She does not venture off the beaten path and has her "Spidey sense" set to a higher level when she drives back and forth. If her husband had not given her directions and warnings, she would be ignorant to the risks unless she spent some time learning the area or asking someone who had been there.

Nationally known firearms instructor Tom Givens from RangeMaster firearms training center in Memphis, Tennessee, did an excellent training DVD for

Target hardening applied to you means being aware of potential attack.

the Personal Defense Network several years ago, "Lessons from the Street." In the DVD, Givens recounted ten armed encounters his students had experienced over the last few years (RangeMaster has had over 50 involved in armed encounters). Surprising to many is the number of encounters that took place at shopping malls, which normally have hundreds if not thousands of shoppers and store employees in and around the parking areas.

What you need to understand is that thieves, muggers, carjackers, rapists and just opportunistic criminals flock to these locations as well. Why is that? Because that's where the victims, the prey these criminals seek, are located. Shoppers who are loaded down with bags, tired after trekking around the miles of mall space and inattentive to their environment, focused on everything from getting home to getting off their feet. With scant or no attention paid to what's going on, or who's around them, they sally forth to or from their vehicles.

Criminals on the other hand, are hyper-aware. Their "antennas" are up as they scan the area looking for potential victims as well as police presence. They attempt to appear innocuous and non-threatening as they maneuver and approach their intended victim. Within arm's reach they attack, assault or rob quickly and aggressively. The object is to psychologically or physically, or both, knock their victim on their heels so that they never have the time or the inclination to form a self-defense strategy. Their gun or knife will be out, displayed or threatened; they will grab, punch or kick their victim. The idea in such cases is ambush – to commit the crime as quickly as possible. Many, if not most, are under the influence of alcohol or drugs at the time of their criminal acts.

The armed citizen must also consider mentally ill subjects who wander about society. Many of the "street people" who wander about our inner city – panhandling, drinking, consuming street drugs and committing crimes – are often mentally ill subjects off their medications. Years ago when many mental institutions were closed because of the effectiveness of psychotropic medications in controlling mental illness, these subjects were reintroduced into society. On effective meds and not abusing alcohol or self-medicating with street drugs, they can be productive members of society. The problem is that these subjects oftentimes stop taking their meds and gravitate to the street, where they may experience delusions, paranoia, hallucinations and other mental issues. "In crisis," these subjects can victimize innocent citizens and may have frequent police contact. Crisis Intervention Teams of specially trained officers can help intervene, calm and direct the mentally ill to emergency mental health centers and facilities. Sometimes this requires involuntary mental commitment by force. CIT members have "kinetic energy impact munitions" (12 gauge, 37 or 40mm impact projectiles) which they can fire or the Taser, ECW – Electronic Control Weapon. If reason, de-escalation or verbal control strategies don't work, officers forcefully control the subject.

Have less lethal options available for non-deadly threats, such as this OC spray.

CASE STUDY

A long term violent and mentally ill man was seen brandishing a knife in each hand in Albuquerque, New Mexico, in 2014. When APD officers attempted to have the man voluntarily disarm over a period of two hours and he refused, they attempted non-deadly control by distracting him with a flash-bang and firing a Taser XREP – eXtended Range Electronic Projectile – round at him, which also failed. A police K9 attempted to engage the subject who raised his knives and was within several feet of the K9 handler when he was shot and killed by police.

There are also those drug-crazed subjects experiencing drug induced "excited delirium." Drug use and/or mentally ill subjects experiencing ExDS (Excited Delirium Syndrome) can become aggressive towards citizens, run through traffic, smash windows, and frequently take off their clothes due to the hypothermic effects of this condition. They can smash their way through windows and into the homes of innocent citizens. They can be very aggressive and very hard to control even for properly trained and equipped police officers.

CASE STUDY

A call of a crazed man running amuck through a quiet residential neighborhood results in two police vehicles being dispatched. As officers drive down the street, a naked man is seen running directly at the first police vehicle. Instead of stopping and calling for help, the man runs up and over the hood, roof and trunk of the cruiser. The second patrol vehicle is driven by a female sergeant who sees this naked apparition run over the marked police car in front of her, before he materializes at the driver's door of her car, banging on the window. She sees a knife in the man's hand just a second before the window explodes inward. She draws and fires killing the subject. Blood tests performed postmortem reveal the subject was under the influence of psychedelic mushrooms.

AWARENESS

Being armed, or ready, means that you have the ability to offer a more effective defense than hope or luck. Unarmed defense is more limited and dependent. When confronted with a deadly threat, i.e. a man with a knife or gun, you may be able to use deadly force to protect yourself, your family or friends. Unarmed in such a situation means that you can run away, hide or bunker, and possibly engage in empty-hand tactics against the attacker's weapon. These are dependent in large extent on your age, physical abilities and training. Certainly an armed man must have training and is always more able to defend himself if he is in good aerobic and anaerobic shape, but many a strong and fit man has been felled by a shot to the back while running away, fired from an out-of-shape and lazy armed criminal.

Awareness allows the detection and avoidance of trouble and the possible subsequent necessity of having to draw or fire your firearm.

Awareness and self-defense preparation is a lifestyle and requires constant vigilance. Certainly you can back down your "Spidey sense" when safely locked behind the doors of your domicile. That is until something happens to activate your personal warning system once again. Imagine you are sitting in your Barcalounger in your basement den, watching a ball game or your favorite TV

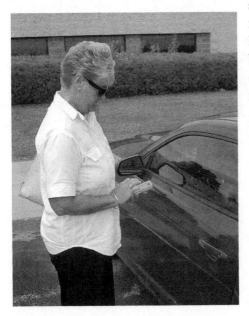

show, when you hear tires screeching and glass breaking outside. You look outside to see a male subject bail out of the passenger seat of a car that has just smashed into your neighbor's car across the street, and he is now running toward your house. Where are the other members of your household? Are the kids upstairs in their rooms or with you? Are you armed? If not, how close is your firearm? Is it loaded?

One of the worst impediments to safety and survival is the smart phone and texting. Pay attention to your surroundings. Don't be an easy victim.

Where's the phone to call 911?

Using your senses, you are aware of the sights and sounds and you quickly process these and make decisions or not.

You may be caught off guard and unprepared or never having thought about the possibility that a bad man may try to hurt or endanger you or yours. Right, now...

Awareness can be dialed up or down according to the environment, stimulus, people and activity going on around you. Last night I met my wife for dinner at a decent restaurant across town after she finished working. As I pulled into the parking lot, I surveyed the general area looking at cars and for people on foot. The car that turned into the lot in front of me and parked was occupied by a single white male, who exited his car and walked southbound to the business next door to the restaurant. About 50 years old with gray head, glasses and a full beard, he had nothing in his hands, a white t-shirt and blue jeans. I walked toward the front doors of the restaurant. A single female was walking towards me. Well dressed and not carrying anything, I held the door for her as she entered and went directly to the woman's restroom to the right in the foyer. Employees were standing around the front desk and coffee/cappuccino area. I paused and looked around the restaurant for my wife. Not seeing her directly, I asked and was told by the hostess that a single female was sitting to the right. I scanned the dining area and saw no obvious threats and ascertained that the female was not my wife. Taking a couple steps to the right of a partition, I saw my wife sitting at a booth against the wall. In the general area was a middle-aged couple directly in front of me, two booths away and what appeared to be a man, his wife and his elderly father to my left.

I was armed with a Glock 19, 9mm auto in a Raven Phantom concealment

How close is your firearm? How readily accessible?

holster underneath my short-sleeved shirt worn outside my pants. On my left hip, I had a spare 15 round mag stoked with Speer Gold Dot hollow points. In my right front pants pocket a DeSantis Nemesis Pocket holster was a Smith and Wesson, M&P340 five shot revolver loaded with .38 special Gold Dot rounds. Five spare .38 rounds of the same load were in a Bianchi Speed Strip in my left front pants pocket.

Every person who walked into our dining area or into the restaurant past me received my attention. Despite what some might consider paranoia, I enjoyed a relaxing dining experience with my wife. As we departed the restaurant I scouted the parking area once again and walked her to her car, which was next to mine. I opened and closed her door before walking around and entering mine.

This is the attention and awareness that you must have. Compare that to the standard diner or unarmed citizen who keeps his head down or buried in his smart phone the entire meal.

"Awareness repels violence, fear attracts it"
~Waking the Tiger Within, Scott Flint, 2001

I am constantly amazed of those police officers I see who don't constantly scan their environment and what comes into it. Just a couple of days ago I walked into a classroom of police officers attending in-service training. Not one looked over at me as I entered the room. Sadly too many police officers believe that "it," a violent encounter or attack, won't happen to "them." First of all, like the citizens videotaped and shown to incarcerated criminals we mentioned earlier, unaware police officers are more inviting targets. In a study conducted by the FBI and published a few years ago, Killed in the Line of Duty (Uniform Crime Reports Section; Federal Bureau of Investigation; United States Department of Justice; 1992), the story of cop killer Edward is recounted. Edward and his two associates had already performed an armed robbery prior to the traffic stop, which was for traffic violations:

As you enter and exit your vehicle, are you ready for an armed assault? Have you ever trained to shoot from inside a vehicle?

CASE STUDY

"After the officer stopped the vehicle, Edward opened the door of his car and walked back to the officer's car. Asking the officer why he stopped their vehicle, the officer responded that Edward was to go back to his car and wait there. During this verbal exchange, Edward noted that the officer was "speaking into his radio" and not paying attention to what Edward was doing. When Edward finally returned to the car in which he was a passenger, he told the individual in the backseat of the car to "get ready...something is going to happen...someone is going to get hurt."

"Edward reportedly walked back to the officer's car and stood to the side of the seated officer. Edward stated that when he arrived at the side of the car, the officer was "still looking at the radio when he was talking into the microphone. He didn't see me come to the car. He then looked up out of the corner of his eye for a fraction of a second and saw I had a gun. I shot him once in the chest and went back to the car."

Here was a police officer who lost track of the awareness level required by his job as a law enforcement officer. He entered into this traffic stop encounter with a "misdemeanor mindset" as it is known in LE. Because he stopped the subjects for a traffic violation, he thought that's all the risk they represented. Truth is, he had no knowledge about the armed robbery they had just committed or the weapons they possessed.

As he sat, inattentive behind the wheel of his patrol car, he was being sized up by a violent criminal and didn't even know it. His lack of attention indicated to Edward that he was a seemingly easy mark who offered no real threat.

Sadly many officers are lulled into a false sense of security or complacency. After nothing much happens during traffic stops and other suspect encounters, officers begin to think that nothing will happen. Former L.A.P.D. Captain Pierce Brooks was one of the detectives involved in the investigation of the kill-

Police officers are constantly distracted by the in-car computer terminals and are often texting while on the job. Heed cop murderer "Eddie's" words!

ing of LAPD Officer Ian Campbell in what would become known as the Onion Field incident. Brooks wrote the seminal book "...officer down, code three." (1975; Motorola Teleprograms, Inc.). In the incident described above, we find several of the deadly errors Brooks mentions are demonstrated by the victim officer: apathy, taking a bad position, missing the danger signs, failure to watch their hands, relaxing too soon, and preoccupation.

Oftentimes an officer, with luck, gets away with making one or two errors, but to do so places the officer's very life in the hands of a suspect.

VIGILANCE VS. APATHY

As a citizen in general and an armed citizen specifically, you cannot afford to become apathetic, develop a poor attitude or one that results in you being inattentive, lackadaisical, dismissive or unprepared. You must operate in Condition Yellow as Colonel Jeff Cooper so eloquently described the mental state wherein you constantly scan your environment for threats.

If you were behind the wheel, we would describe this mental process as defensive driving. We don't just scan or drive based on the bumper of the car in front of us. We scan the roadway ahead looking for potential hazards and threats because, as our vehicle moves forward, depending on what speed we are traveling, we will soon be in that space. Failure to maintain a clear distance to the car in front means that we fail to allow enough time and space to react and respond to threats.

We must instead stay sharp and constantly play those when/then games in our head. When that subject attacks, then I will draw my pistol as I move off the attack line toward cover. When a criminal suspect attempts to break into my

Deadly force encounters can happen anywhere, just like motor vehicle accidents. Scan your surroundings, and give yourself adequate time and space to react and respond.

home, then I will access my firearm, move myself and my family members to safety and cover, verbally challenge and order them to stop, call or have a family member call 911 and summon the police.

POSITION

You must seek a solid position that allows you to view your surroundings and people who are around you. This has become known as the "gunfighter's seat" in law enforcement and armed self-defense. If you position yourself with your back to the entrance or people, you cannot adequate evaluate them as potential threats. You want to know what opportunities for cover and concealment are in your area of operation, as well as entrances and exits. Identify other rooms you can retreat to for cover, such as the restaurant kitchen. If an armed threat suddenly appears, have you thought out where you can move and what options you have?

Properly position yourself at work or in public to minimize attacks from unseen attackers.

CASE STUDY

Terry, an off-duty police officer, and his wife are sitting at a restaurant in an adjoining city enjoying dinner when a man, armed with a shotgun, enters the restaurant and kills the bartender with a blast from his shotgun. The shooter and victim are part of a lover's triangle, and the shooter is an employee of the restaurant as well. The shooter jumps over the bar, pulls a sheath knife and scalps his victim before running out of the restaurant. Terry gives chase and fires his off-duty pistol at the suspect who is driving through the parking lot getting away.

Unfortunately, Terry's off-duty pistol is a .380 which, with the ammunition he carried at that time, had insufficient energy to penetrate the passenger compartment of the van to strike the suspect. One of Terry's rounds does cause sufficient damage to the mechanics of the engine so that the van dies on the highway soon after. The suspect simply lies in the median, puts his hands behind his head and waits until police find and arrest him.

DANGER SIGNS

Oftentimes, what police have equated as "police intuition or gut instinct" is the subconscious processing of non-verbal communication. With experience, they come to recognize postures, movements, stances, facial patterns and other non-verbal signals as clues to potential attack or attempted escape.

As an example, when dealing with street suspects my partner and I became familiar with what we called the "warrant dance." What this means is that a suspect who has warrants out for his arrest will act nervous or "dance" around. When we observed this, we would take more control of the suspect depending on the circumstances. We would have the suspect sit down or further limit their ability to attempt escape by running. Many times our "gut instinct" based on their non-verbal movements and posture would turn out to be true when we ran them for warrants. These danger signs can be missed or misinterpreted by the inexperienced.

Consider the example of an aggressive driver behind you in traffic. I'm sure you've had another driver behind you looking to pass or attempting to get you to move over to allow them to go by. If you don't comply, the driver may have escalated his actions by turning on his headlights; this may progress to closing the distance between his front bumper and your vehicle. He may veer to the left, to get you to move over and let him pass. If the driver continues to escalate, he may begin to flash his lights or beep his horn at you. As he begins to tailgate dangerously close and perhaps slips into road rage, you may see him raise his middle finger at you, become red faced and start screaming, even leaning out of the driver's window cursing at you.

This behavior may even escalate to violence such as ramming your car in an extreme road rage incident, and possibly even a physical assault if the driver runs up to your vehicle with or without a weapon.

Of course, the safest thing for you to do is to allow him to pass.

In this example we see that there has been an increasingly violent flow to the incident. The subject becomes increasingly violent as he loses control and becomes aggravated or angry, much like the mercury in a thermometer rises to indicate increasing temperature. Verbal loss of control may lead to physical loss of control and then to violence.

KEEPING UP YOUR GUARD

Just because your walk through the mall lot or the parking deck on the way into work was uneventful, doesn't mean you can lower your guard or relax too soon. Criminals are like sharks in the ocean. When sharks seek out their prey, they move in and out to see what the target's response will be. If no violent defense is perceived, the shark moves in for the kill. Criminals do the same thing. Serial killer Ted Bundy was a good-looking young man who, through a smile and friendly dialogue, could disarm his potential victims. He didn't look like a killer in his victim's eyes. What we have come to know is that there is no "look" or type to a psychotic individual or violent criminal.

Assumptions, based on appearance and seemingly innocuous behavior, are extremely dangerous. Many violent sociopaths control their voice and body language, and come across as non-threatening to disarm their prey, much like the poisonous predator in nature which appears to be harmless, thus hiding its true nature.

CASE STUDY

Troy Kell is an inmate incarcerated, at the time of this writing, in Utah's death row. Kell was in prison after he was convicted of another murder. He became a white supremacist gang leader. In the documentary 'Gladiator Days: Anatomy of a Prison Murder' we see the handsome and charismatic Kell blame the world for his troubles after he and another white inmate plan and perpetrate the attack and stabbing murder of a black inmate. Captured on prison video we see Kell brutally stab his victim 67 times in the face, head and neck as his cohort pins the victim's legs to the floor. Amazingly Kell receives numerous marriage proposals from women while on trial.

WATCH THEIR HANDS

As you scan subjects who come into your environment, you must learn to watch their hands. A subjects hands or more specifically what is in their hands are what can kill you. In our tragic story of the police officer killed by Edward covered above, we read that the suspect was able to get within arm's reach of officer with gun in hand before he was detected. Sadly far too many citizens today are more interested in their smart phones or conversations on their cells to pay attention to people around them, let alone what is in their hands.

A common street strategy for attackers is to conceal their handgun in their hand held behind the same side thigh. Approaching a victim in this way, the thug only need raise the pistol to fire or threaten you at gunpoint. Most people don't pay attention to the hidden hand whether it is held behind the thigh as in this manner, inside the front pocket of a hooded sweatshirt, under the front of an oversized shirt in the appendix area, or inside the pocket of a coat.

Most criminals do not utilize holsters. They will "Mexican carry" a handgun by stuffing it into their waistband or will put it in a pocket. In urban areas where belts are not often worn, a hand may be needed to keep his pants up as the weight of the pistol pulls them down.

CASE STUDY

Street savvy police officers understand that criminals, and even legally armed citizens who don't carry often or are not used to carrying a handgun concealed, will give physical "tells," little gesticulations and movements that experienced officers have come to recognize. These include readjusting the belt or the holster on the belt, making sure the lower hem of the concealing garment is covering the bottom of the holster, etc. Once, while working undercover narcotics on a surveillance of a dope house, I could tell from a block and a half away that a suspect was armed as he ran back and forth from a car into the house. When I broadcast the vehicle description to my uniformed partners, I told them, "The back seat passenger has a gun in the front of his waistband." When the vehicle was stopped, at gunpoint, the backseat passenger came a hair's breadth of getting shot as he had removed the pistol from his waistband and held his hand inside the car, despite the officer's verbal challenges to "Show me your hands!" Fortunately for him, he dropped the pistol to the floor of the backseat and raised his hand.

By walking toward a victim with a hand hidden by clothing or body part, the attacker is minimizing the time necessary to "get the drop" on a victim. Depending on the totality of the circumstances, such as location, environment, body language, and pre-encounter behaviors, it may be prudent to verbally challenge a threatening subject with a hidden hand. If the person refuses to stop, it may be reasonable to place your hand on your concealed handgun, draw to low ready or even to challenge at gunpoint. This does not mean that you should challenge every person with their hands stuffed into their coat pockets on a cold winter's day. It does mean that a threatening subject moving aggressively towards you with a hand behind his thigh or hidden in a coat pocket may represent a threat to you, and certainly represents a concern that must be challenged.

AVOIDING DISTRACTION

There are many potential distractions in our everyday life – children, cell phones, etc. – that are competing for our attention. We must not allow ourselves to become preoccupied with these distractions to the point that we fail to monitor our environment and potential or emerging threats.

Even the late, great Bruce Lee could have been beaten if he was sucker punched by an unseen attacker because he was busy texting. Next time you are in an urban area, or any area, watch how many walkers or joggers use ear buds or headphones. With music blaring they may get a brief respite from their everyday world, but lost in their walk or run they may not hear warning signs as a threat approaches them.

CASE STUDY

A police officer responded to a men's clothing store when the burglar alarm activated. Lulled into a false sense of security ("It'll never happen to me" and "This is just another false alarm"), he was so preoccupied by shopping for pants for himself that he didn't see the armed burglar until the suspect stepped out from behind a pillar and shot the officer with a .25 semi-auto pistol, wounding him. I ran into that officer years later walking a beat. The .38 rounds in the cartridge loops on his belt were green with corrosion. Apparently he failed to learn any lessons from his near death confrontation.

There are many reasons why we arm ourselves for personal and home defense. In a recent case out of Detroit, the white male driver of a pick-up truck pulled over to check out a young juvenile black male who he just struck with his vehicle. The juvenile and some friends were playing "chicken," stepping in front of on-coming cars and then stepping back quickly to see how close they could come. The driver pulled over in concern and was quickly attacked by a group standing in a convenience store lot where the incident occurred. The driver was beaten so severely that he was in a comatose state for nine days. A retired black female nurse lay across the victim's body to keep him from getting further beaten. The nurse had more than good intentions to stop the attack against this innocent man – she was armed with a .38 in her purse and was determined to use it if need arose.

If the victim had been legally armed and so attacked or threatened with serious bodily harm by the four men who would subsequently be arrested for the felonious assault, he would have been legally justified in threatening, displaying or using deadly force to stop the attack.

Detroit has become so violent and the police department so busy and understaffed that the Chief of Police of that city has recommended that citizens arm themselves. Liberals and firearm control advocates are aghast. Of course, they weren't there when the victim was beaten and all they could have done is call 911, not act valiantly like the armed retired heroine did.

We'll close out this chapter with an incident I experienced as a young boy. It left a lasting impression on me.

CASE STUDY

I witnessed my first shooting at the approximate age of ten. I had just walked out the front door of my parent's home in a nice quiet residential neighborhood. I heard sirens and vehicles traveling at a fast rate of speed coming down the street above our home. A large four-door sedan, a Cadillac I believe, screeched down and around the corner in front of me, lost control and blasted through the white wooden fence of our neighbors across the street. The sedan careened across the next neighbor's yard to my right and slammed into a tree. The white male driver jumped from the driver's door carrying a white pillowcase in his left hand and what looked like a P08 Luger in his right hand. My uncle had one, so the profile of the pistol was familiar to me. The suspect ran eastbound through the yard.

Another vehicle, an unmarked police car, drove up the driveway, hot after the suspect. A black male detective jumped from his car, yelled, "Halt!" stopped and fired one shot from his snub revolver, two handed, and missed the suspect.

David, an older and more knowledgeable boy and neighbor a couple doors down from my parents, yelled at me to get back. Nothing doing, heck, this was drama unfolding in front of me. The fact that I could get shot was the furthest thing from my mind!

The suspect, a bank robber who had committed an armed robbery of a bank in the city to our north, had been leading that city's police on a high-speed chase since his crime. The chase led into my city where our police had picked it up.

The robber ran east, crossed the street southbound and hid next to a storage shed in a backyard about four houses to the southeast. As he hid next to the shed a police officer walked past him, then spun and arrested him at gunpoint. Fortunately for the officer, he was not shot in the back as he failed to check the side of the shed.

I remember walking over later and looking at the suspect's getaway car. It was shot full of holes. Apparently police from both agencies had fired countless rounds at the fleeing vehicle, yet the suspect was not hit and his car kept running.

Yes, the detective missed the robber who was running away from him at an angle. Distances were probably 50 feet or more. But this was at a time (circa 1970) when police firearms training was rudimentary and based on static PPC – Police Pistol Competition. Police "tactical" training and what would become known as the "officer survival" movement was years away. The 1970s were a violent era for law enforcement, and prior to the advent and widespread issuance of modern body armor.

Sunny summer afternoons in Middle America are hardly the location where police gunfights erupt on a regular basis, but it happened on this day. I include this incident to show how random violence can be. One minute you're walking across a front lawn, the next an armed suspect is crashing into a tree in front of you and police are shooting.

CHAPTER TWO:

THE THREAT

CASE STUDY

Two 9-year-old girls in my elementary school were killed by a psychopath on 17 May 1971. We had been handed out "Glow" plastic recycle bags in school, which we were supposed to fill with recyclable materials like newspapers or tin cans. The girls had gone to a home in the neighborhood. Their murderer, 27 year old Kenneth Lykens, abducted the girls and murdered them by stabbing them multiple times. Lykens then dumped their bodies in a ditch next to a roadway seven miles away. This incident impacted me such that, 43 years later, I still recall a childhood friend and I sitting on the playground the day after the girls were reported missing, theorizing about where the girls could be. I was ten years old. Innocence lost.

Frequently my wife will look at me after an incident of severe brutality has occurred and is reported on the TV news. "Explain to me, who could do such a thing?" she'll ask. "It's evil babe. How else can you explain it? It's just evil," I'll say. Indeed, when looked at from a normal, well-adjusted person's view, we cannot fathom how or why someone would do such a thing. There may be psycho-logical terms, such as psychotic, maladjusted, paranoid, violence control issues, on and on, but in the end, does it really matter? Is it not enough that we simply accept that A) Such people exist (for whatever reason), and B) We need to protect ourselves, family and loved ones against them?

If we start looking at motive, we can begin to wonder whether somehow they are not responsible for their own actions. We can make excuses that their family, society, abusive potty training, whatever, "made" them. The truth is that, whatever race, socio-economic or single-parent household they come from, the vast majority of people who come from a similar background don't turn out to be sociopathic violent thugs, robbers, rapists or killers. Instead, the majority of folks are law-abiding, contributing members of society. Further, according to criminologists, by and large crime does not cross socio-economic or racial lines; whites are more likely to be victimized by whites, blacks by blacks, and so on.

As a street police officer in a crime ridden minority district, I found that the vast majority of citizens in the area were honest, law-abiding and supported law enforcement.

CASE STUDY

As part of our drug control strategy in one particular neighborhood during the middle of the crack cocaine wars in the early 90s, my street narcotics unit conducted drug "reversals" where undercover officers (UCs) portrayed drug dealers. When customers approached our UCs and solicited them for drugs, marked police cars and officers would swoop in and arrest them. After an evening of aggressive enforcement and one particular short vehicle pursuit, a voice called out from the darkness of the housing project, "Thank you!"

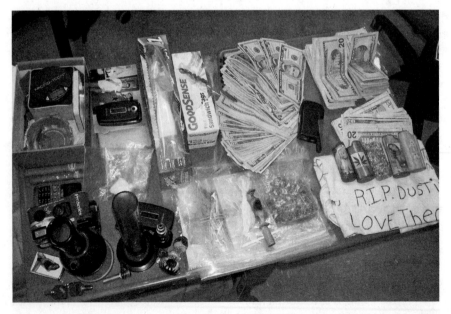

Dope and money meant guns and violence in the middle of the crack cocaine wars.

Narcotics trafficking is not a non-violent criminal activity.

These neighbors and residents are imprisoned in their homes at night behind burglar bars on their windows and alarms. And yes, many of them are armed citizens who understand that the ability to defend themselves with deadly force is necessary when confronted with violent armed criminals.

CASE STUDY

Robert was a career military man who had recently retired. Although he admitted to owning a shotgun for home defense, he was against concealed carry, calling me and other armed citizens "Jack Bauer" wannabes, in several online discussions. Robert retired from military service and returned to the States with his wife and family. One night he and his wife were walking the family dog on a pleasant evening. Robert spied two men across the street and his gut told him that they were up to no good. The men approached Robert and his wife. Robert is a big strapping and powerful man and told his wife to walk away back the way they had come as he covered her withdrawal. The men got within striking distance. As one approached from the front, the other flanked Robert and "sucker punched" him.

Robert fled and soon realized he was bleeding from the side of the head. He had not been punched but rather stabbed in the side of the head. Fortunately he did not lose his eye or his life.

Far too many people are like Robert. They want to believe that people are fundamentally good and that violent crime is something you only read about in the papers or watch on the news. It is no surprise that Robert chose to retire to the State of California where concealed carry, at this time, is reserved strictly for politicians, celebrities, the wealthy and the politically connected. Let us hope that those laws, based on recent court rulings, soon change.

The threat we are talking about is very real. Although we maintain alertness and awareness and hope we never have to resort to force to defend ourselves, we accept that evil men and violence exists. We legally arm ourselves with the capability to defend our life with deadly force through firearms. We have less-lethal alternatives available as well, such as pepper spray, a Taser or impact weapon, understanding that we are more likely to need these than deadly force.

Working as a Deputy Sheriff assigned to corrections early in my police career, I learned that although many inmates could be cordial, polite and want to be your "buddy" (even Class A seriously violent offenders), they were all doing it to get something from you, such as preferential treatment or the smallest thing such as turning a TV on early or off later. I was always polite and professional with them but I never forgot the threat they represented.

CASE STUDY

Gary was 17 years old at the time of his arrest for rape and multiple other charges. A serial burglar, he had raped an elderly woman and was on the run for some time before his arrest. He was cunning and devious and would walk over anyone to get what he wanted. He was segregated from the mainstream population until he was convicted. One evening he and I were talking as he was inside the "tank" (a separate section of the floor where Gary was housed which had a shower and phone). There was a small door or lockable port in the door into the office I was manning. Gary was waiting to use the phone and he had his head, right arm and right shoulder through the port. As we were talking, another Deputy asked Gary if he thought he could get through the port in the door and into the office. Gary said, "Yep. If I can get my shoulders through, I can get my body through (his stint as a serial burglar providing him the experience). It was clear to me that Gary would try to escape if given the opportunity.

Some months later, Gary and another inmate successfully escaped from the jail. Gary was the mastermind. In the weight room at the jail, which was monitored by civilian employees, Gary and the other inmate beat the civilian into unconsciousness, put on his clothing and then used a bar from the weight equipment to break through the locks (with other inmates slamming weights to cover the noise) and into the catwalk area. They broke through the metal screens covering the exterior windows and broke through the glass. At this time a deputy happened to look into the weight room and put out an alarm. Jumping from the window, they looked like two joggers running through the streets and into an alleyway. Unfortunately their getaway driver had parked his car too far away and a member of my police department apprehended the men at gunpoint.

Gary was 17 at the time of his arrest. He was intelligent, cunning and an extremely violent man with absolutely no remorse. There is no doubt in my mind that Gary would have killed a police officer to escape or evade arrest. There is also no doubt that Gary would have killed an innocent citizen to commit a burglary or other crime. At the time of this writing, Gary is still incarcerated serving the remainder of his 87-year sentence on the 18 felonies, including four First Degree violations. The parole board will determine if he is eligible for earlier release.

TYPES OF ATTACK

We will examine two different types of attack and how you can be alerted to developing violence. In the first, an attacker perceives that you, a family member or companion, car, home or property, are open to attack, theft or other criminal act. They may commit a crime in the spur of the moment based on this perceived opportunity. An example of this would be a subject on the prowl who sees a target of opportunity, such as a mugger or robber. We will refer to this type of incident or attack as spontaneous. Little warning is given in a spontaneous attack. Your biggest tool in the fight against a surprise, spontaneous attack is awareness and alertness. You observe the potential attacker and situation developing prior to commencement of the attack.

In the second, the attacker specifically targets you, others in your company, your home, car or property. An example would be a burglar who has checked out your house or a car thief who has seen your car and sets out to steal it. We will call these types of crimes or attacks non-spontaneous.

NON-SPONTANEOUS ATTACKS

In non-spontaneous attacks, you may have more time and warning. If you are an employer who has fired a problem employee, for instance, you may have prior warning from his articulated threats to "get you," or "you're gonna regret this!" Certainly any previous incidents of violence from the subject, or other indicators such as excessive alcohol use, drug abuse, previous arrests, etc., must serve as fair warning of the potential for attack.

It is certainly not true a "barking dog doesn't bite." As indicated by research done by Darrell Ross, PhD., relating to resistance to law enforcement officers, there seems to be a "flow" or continuum of resistance demonstrated by suspects.

- In 36% of the incidents studied, there was verbal resistance followed by pulling or pushing.
- In 27% of the cases, there was verbal resistance, then pulling/pushing and finally punching or kicking.
- And in 24% of the cases reviewed, the suspect resisted by pulling/pushing prior to punching or kicking the officer.

As an analogy, if you are a business owner dealing with an irate customer, you will see a progression of verbal then physical loss of control, which may lead to attack or assault.

John D. Byrnes writes about this progression or continuum of violence in his book Before Conflict: Preventing Aggressive Behavior (Scarecrow Press, 2002). This "thermometer of violence" starts with a Trigger Phase, if unabated raises to the Escalation Phase. In this phase we start to see the results of a sympathetic nervous system (SNS) response.

The SNS is commonly known as fight or flight and is started as a hormonal secretion in the brain in response to threat. (More on this in a later chapter as it pertains to you and your response.) What you need to know about the SNS as it pertains to a potentially threatening individual is that anger (preparation for the fight) results in physical and physiological responses that can be seen. For instance, in an SNS response the subject is not thinking with the upper reason processing parts of the brain. The mid-brain takes over control. Perceptual changes affect the way the person sees and hears, with peripheral vision reduced and auditory exclusion possibly reducing what the subject can hear as he continues to ebb into fight or flight. The body prepares for the fight by closing down the capillaries to fuel the major organs for battle. This may cause the person to pump their hands subconsciously as their fingers feel numb. As adrenalin and noradrenalin course through their system the subject may begin to pace around. Shallow chest breathing takes over and is visible as they become more agitated. This non-verbal leakage must be read by you as the subject's body prepares for battle:

- Aggressor's head tilts back
- Facial color turns pale
- Breathing progresses from fast/shallow to fast/deep
- Aggressor's hands begin pumping
- Veins in arms, neck and facial area are bulging
- Target glancing

Interpersonal communication skills deteriorate with the person stumbling over words or becoming less articulate, possible cursing more and becoming louder.

"Behavior is our first glimpse into the emergence of aggression in others."
~Dr. John D. Byrnes

If things deteriorate or the subject continues to lose control, we enter into the Crisis Phase.

According to Calibre Press, a leading law enforcement training company, here are some early warning signs that aggressors may exhibit prior to physical attack:

- Conspicuous ignoring – Ignoring you or your attempts to stop their actions
- Excessive emotional tension – Emotional tension that is over the top for the circumstances
- Exaggerated movement – Pacing or excessive movement, often a result of an SNS response
- Ceasing all movement – The calm before the storm. They have physically readied themselves
- Repetitious questioning – The brain is in fight or flight and they cannot think well
- Physical crowding – Testing the waters and trying to physically intimidate you
- Looking around – Looking around for police, witnesses, cohorts
- Assuming a pre-attack posture – Readying themselves for assault

Pre-attack postures can include:

- Boxer stance – Strong foot is moved rearward
- Hand set – Hands come above the waist
- Shoulder shift – Shoulders like feet ready for strong side power punch
- Target glance – Glancing at the target they into to assault
- 1,000-yard stare – Out there were the buses don't run
- Clothing rearrangement – Ball caps hunkered down on the head, trousers hiked up

Once again, if some type of weapon assault is planned or commencing, the aggressor will oftentimes touch or shift the pistol in his belt or the knife in his pocket. Most times they will have their

Changes in foot position into a "fighter's stance" can indicate a looming attack.

As agitation increases, the hands raise above the waist, indicating a pending punch.

Pointing, along with changes in facial expression, voice tone and voice level, can indicate impending attack.

hands on the weapon, since they likely do not actively practice their draw-stroke or presentation of the weapon from their belt or pocket.

Remember that criminals prefer a surprise attack, the armed or unarmed version of a sucker punch. They intend to display, threaten or use their weapon first so that their victim is never given a fighting chance. Think back to "Karlos." He stabbed his victim John before he even knew Karlos had a shiv.

Similarly the rapist will punch or strike his victim to disorient them so that the victim offers less or no resistance.

In the non-spontaneous attack, you hear breaking glass or the attacker attempting to kick in the front door. You have more time to access weapons, alert family members, move to cover, etc.

You hear breaking glass in your home, investigate and find this armed threat. Did you take the time to arm yourself?

CASE STUDY

17 April 2014: According to WDIV, Channel 4 in Detroit, the homeowner and family members of a residence in that city were in the basement playing video games when they heard a crash as the front door was kicked, and footsteps after two suspects entered the location through a side window. Shots were fired in the home by the homeowner with the suspects then fleeing. After one suspect exited, the suspect turned and fired at the homeowner. The homeowner returned fire, killing the getaway driver. Two suspects then fled the scene and have not been apprehended at this time.

SPONTANEOUS ATTACKS

Spontaneous attacks are you and the attacker, in a violent encounter, now. Time is at a premium. Weapons must be on your person or within close reach. Shouts of warning such as "Get Down!" may be given to family members, but there is no time to formulate strategy and certainly no time to "get ready."

CASE STUDY

According to the Buffalo News (14 April 2014), a pizza delivery man was attacked by a gang of robbers in the front hallway of a house as he delivered a pizza. A masked attacker hit the pizza driver in the head with a hammer and then displayed what looked like a gun. The deliveryman drew his own handgun and fired a shot, hitting the suspect. The other members of the gang then scattered. The pizza deliveryman was treated and released. The suspect is hospitalized in police custody.

Spontaneous attacks are dealt with by tactics and training already conducted or rehearsed.

CASE STUDY

Dave, a uniformed patrolman, responded to a domestic violence call. The suspect was the son of the residents of the home. He had been assaulting his parents with the prosthetic hooks he used for hands. His hands had been blown off eight years prior when his homemade hand grenade exploded in a confrontation with state police in a neighboring state. After his release from prison, he headed to his parent's home. As Dave exited his patrol vehicle after arriving on scene, he was shot by the suspect through the abdomen with a .308 deer rifle, which he had taught himself to hold and fire with his hooks. The gunshot ripped through Dave's abdomen at belt level, tearing a fist-sized hole out of his back and blowing his duty belt apart. Dave never stopped and never dropped. He and his partner got their handguns out, moved to cover and successfully delivered accurate fire on the suspect, killing him.

I received a call from a coworker of Dave who told me the officer wanted me to know that he heard my words in his ears, "Stay in the fight! Get your gun out! Get rounds on target! Get to cover!"

Dave is a testament to a solid officer doing things right despite the intense violence involved. It is also a testimony to the impact of an instructor's words and training.

Dave recovered from his wounds but was forced to retire from his injuries. God Bless him! and well done!

The specific tactics, techniques and training you can use to win out in a violent encounter are covered in other chapters.

To conclude this chapter, I'll relate the following story.

CASE STUDY

As a young deputy I was assigned to work corrections at the county jail. One day I was sitting in the office of Range 3, which housed Class A offenders – rapists and murderers.

Dean, a law professor and the "jail monitor" appointed by the Federal Court after a lawsuit filed by inmates' attorneys on overcrowding and other issues, walked into the office.

As we were talking about crime and punishment, I looked out over the inmates sitting on tables and milling around the jail range. I said, "Dean, people don't believe there's such a thing as monsters such as werewolves and vampires. But look around, these people, if given the opportunity, these people would walk right over you. They come out at night and prey on the elderly or those less able to defend themselves and tear them to pieces."

Dean said, "You're right. I try to never forget that."

Day or night, monsters really do exist. Are you trained and ready? Have you been paying attention?

CHAPTER THREE:

THE RESEARCH

According to Dr. Robert Sapolsky in his book Why Zebras Don't Get Ulcers (Owl Books, 2004), as part of our nervous system we have the voluntary and the autonomic nervous system. The voluntary system allows to us walk on our own and do any variety of voluntary movements. The autonomic nervous system (think automatic) controls such things as sweating of which we have limited to no control.

The parasympathetic nervous system, or PNS, controls low levels of automatic responses and works in conjunction with the sympathetic nervous system.

The sympathetic nervous system, or SNS, controls high-level arousal such as the Four Fs: fight, flight, fear and reproduction.

The SNS is triggered in response to fear or stress. According to Dr. Sapolsky, "When something stressful happens or you think a stressful thought, the hypothalamus secretes an array of releasing hormones into the hypothalamic-pituitary circulatory system that gets the ball rolling. The principal such releaser is called CRH (corticotropin releasing hormone)…" There is then a cascading effect of other hormones released including epinephrine (a.k.a. adrenalin) and norepinephrine.

The SNS changes the way we see, hear and think, and impacts our eye-hand coordination.

Optimum performance is an SNS response. In other words, fight or flight helps prepare us for battle, and if we are not overwhelmed with the SNS response, our performance improves.

Another fall-out of the SNS is how it impacts performance under stress. Why does a big, strong police officer well-versed in his suspect control skills grab and pull an offender to his center and "power him" or "wrestle him" to the ground instead of employing a more sophisticated technique? Why does an officer who is a very accomplished marksman on the range fire an entire magazine at an offender and not hit him once in an actual street encounter?

Seldom does an officer "rise to the occasion" in a serious use of non-deadly force encounter. It is even more rare in an officer-involved shooting. They may perform as they have trained but, because of reduced cognitive abilities and skill degradation under stress, will oftentimes be unable to engage in sophisticated thinking and movement. As an example of what this may look like, let's take a look at how shooting and thinking deteriorates in the stress of law enforcement agency firearms qualification. As a firearms instructor I frequently see officers on the range who react under this small amount of stress. Their hands shake. They get tunnel vision, focusing just on the target directly in front. They fumble an otherwise simple pistol reload. They are so focused on their shooting they don't hear the range commands, and more.

The fact is that decision-making under stress slows overall response time (reaction time plus movement time). The other part of the SNS response (fight or flight) not often talked about is "freezing," known scientifically as "hyper-vigilance." When subjects are so overwhelmed with life-threatening stimuli, they can lock down and do nothing (sensory overload). Ever have another motorist pull in front of the car you're driving? All you could do was slam on the brakes.

Even at the firearms range under mild stress, performance can deteriorate.

Relatively simple actions can be fumbled under SNS.

Sophisticated movements like pumping the brakes didn't happen. The wrists, elbows and shoulders locked down on the steering wheel as your foot tried to put the brake pedal through the floor. This is why ABS (Anti-Lock Braking Systems) brakes on vehicles work. The computer within the system automatically pulses the brakes so they don't lock up, traction is increased and you have the ability to steer during the process.

The human equivalent of ABS is training. The more realistic the training program, the more control of the SNS response a subject may have. Of course even the best of us can be blindsided, caught off guard, sucker punched, ambushed or otherwise attacked by an unseen or unknown opponent. We teach and encourage armed citizens to maintain mental awareness and constantly survey their environment for threats, but experience (and non-activity) has a way of lulling even the best of us into a false sense of security or non-awareness.

As Bruce Siddle from Human Factors Research has pointed out (PPCT Violent Passenger Management Training, 2001), an SNS response may be triggered by:

- Objective "threat" perceptions
- Objective "fear" perceptions
- ATP depletion (exhaustion)
- Deadly force startle response
  Objective threat perceptions include:
- The threat is within close proximity

We must endeavor to train as realistically as possible. Here a student practices extreme close quarters shooting using Airsoft on an armed partner.

- The time needed to control the threat is minimal
- The subject is not confident in his/her abilities
- The threat is a new experience

Objective fear perceptions include:
- Fear of death
- Fear of injury
- Fear of killing
- Fear of making an incorrect decision
- Fear of failure
- Fear of fear

Physical exhaustion: ATP/PC (adenosine triphosphate/creatine phosphate) is the first energy system the body uses, but it only lasts around 10 to 15 seconds. Once the ATP/PC system is exhausted, performance drops 45% within 30 seconds. Next up is the lactic acid system, which is active from 10 seconds to two minutes. The final energy system is the aerobic system, which is dependent on conditioning.

When I was first exposed to this science it explained why I felt I felt a sudden drop in energy levels about 10 to 15 seconds into a use-of-force or resisting arrest encounter. It also explained why I experienced a corresponding drop in performance (45% according to the research). Most violent encounter incidents are anaerobic affairs lasting less than two minutes. They are more like a sprint than a marathon, with armed citizens dropping in their performance 70% within 90 seconds.

In a deadly force startle response:
- Threat is spontaneous
- Threat is unexpected
- Threat is within close proximity
- Unexpected loud noise (such as gunfire)
- Unexpected impact or touch (such as a sucker-punch)

Energy stores are quickly depleted in a fight. Here a law enforcement officer student practices controlling a violent resistor wearing a padded FIST suit. Lesson: Be effective right from the start, don't engage in long drawn out battles.

SYMPATHETIC NERVOUS SYSTEM RESPONSES

We know that the SNS response changes the way we think, move, see, hear and remember. In an instant, heart rate and blood pressure increase, the SNS changes the blood flow in the body, wicking away the blood from the extremities, fueling the major organs for fight or flight. The body dumps powerful chemicals (epinephrine, norepinephrine, Glucocorticoids, glucagon, endorphins and enkephalins) into the system for pain tolerance and continued energy output.

Additional effects of the Sympathetic Nervous System on
Performance SNS Effects on Vision

- Binocular dominant – both eyes wide open
- Loss of night vision – reduced ability to see in low or
    subdued lighting
- Loss of depth perception
- Loss of peripheral vision – visual field shrinking to tunnel
    vision
- Loss of near vision – inability to see pistol sights
- Involuntary tracking of threat – the eyes tend to focus on the
    threat

SNS Effects on Cognitive Processing
- Increased reaction time – increased time to mentally
    process
- Loss of cortex accessing – higher cognitive thinking not
    accessible
- Auditory Exclusion – tunnel hearing
- Hypervigilance – overwhelming sensory input; the "freezing"
    part of the SNS

SNS Physiological Effects
- Increased adrenal activity – preparing the body for the fight
- Immediate increase in heart rate – increasing above 120 to
    150 bpm
- Immediate increase in respiration – chest breathing
- Vascular flow redirects away from extremities – powering
    internal organs and large muscle masses
- Pupil dilation
- Contour of the eye lens changes

~Bruce Siddle,
Violent Passenger Management Training, 2001

In his book On Combat (PPCT Research Publications, 2004), author Col. Dave Grossman writes, "…then suddenly someone tries to kill you. Your body's response is total SNS arousal. PNS (Parasympathetic Nervous System) processes like digestion shut down: We don't need no stinking digestion. You guys blow the ballast and get down to the legs where I need you," which explains incidents of soldiers and lawman in high-stress situations voiding their bladders and bowels during combat.

The SNS response does a lot to explain why subjects get stuck in "performance loops" wherein they repeat the same, often ineffective, technique over and over. Higher cognitive processing is required to shoot and then "stop and assess" before proceeding. This is one of the flaws of the outdated method of the "double-tap" when shooting. The thought was that we should fire two rounds, stop and assess before continuing to shoot, possibly even transitioning to the head for follow-up shots. What we find now is that this level of performance under stress is virtually unheard of, with most subjects shooting after they perceive a deadly threat and then continuing to shoot until they perceive there is no longer a threat (the suspect is down, dropped his gun, etc.). During this period of response time to start and response time to stop, a fairly large number of shots can be fired. Dr. Bill Lewinski has done significant research with his Force Science Institute (www.ForceScience.org) in this area.

Although we hope and pray for high performance based on realistic and relevant training, we understand that suboptimal physical performance as well as poor decision-making can occur under an SNS response.

ACTION, REACTION AND RESPONSE

It is simply not possible for you to wait until an armed attacker raises his pistol to fire before you draw your handgun and fire. It is also not possible for you to wait until an attacker, armed with a knife or club and within ten feet, lunges toward you in attack before you raise and fire your handgun from low ready. Human response times prevent this from being a worthwhile proposition. To do so means that at the very best, you achieve a tie, or what Filipino Martial Artists (primarily a blade based art) call a "mutual slay." Let's examine this process from scientific study and current research.

We will quote here from Motor Learning & Performance (1991, Richard A. Schmidt, Human Kinetics Books). What we normally think of as reaction time is actually response time.

According to Schmidt, "Reaction Time (RT) is the interval of time from a suddenly presented, unanticipated stimulus unto the beginning of the response."

We want to avoid the "mutual slay" – attacker and intended victim both killed.

Here a role player is holding a plastic training rifle. But if the lights were lowered or you were under an SNS response, could you tell?

Research has shown us how fast a subject can fire and raise a fire. Armed subjects are deadly threats.

If this subject fired and then turned away, our rounds would probably impact him in the back.

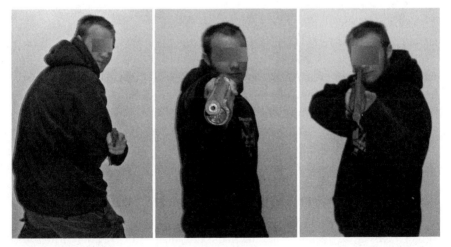

Seldom does range training and firearms targets prepare you for this.

Research has shown how perceptual distortions under SNS can cause tunnel vision.

It might later turn out to be an Airsoft rifle, but in low or subdued lighting while experiencing fight or flight, can you afford to wait to be absolutely sure?

In other words, reaction time is a mental process. MT or Movement Time is defined as the time between the beginning and end of the movement, such as the time you start to draw your pistol until the first shot is fired. Response time is the combination of the two.

Let's give an example on how reaction, movement and the total response time work.

It is zero-dark-thirty and you are walking to your car in the parking deck after a late-night shift at work. As you approach your car, out of the shadows you see a subject in a dark hooded sweatshirt move toward you. The male subject increases his gait in a line to intercept you before you make it to the safety of your car. You shift your direction so that a parked car is in between you and him as you set your briefcase on the pavement, place your hand on your holstered pistol and give a verbal warning, "Stop! Don't come any closer!" The attacker doesn't utter a word as he produces a knife, blade glinting in the light, twenty feet away on the other side of the parked car. Seeing the blade in his hand, you draw your pistol out and up on target and order him again, "Stop! Drop the knife! Don't come any closer or I'll shoot!" The attacker now sees your pistol aimed at his chest, drops his blade and runs away into the darkness. You take a couple of deep breaths; scan the area for any additional attackers and possible witnesses. Finding none, you reholster your pistol and with shaking hands call 911 to report the encounter to the police and give a suspect description, then wait for officers to report the crime.

In this case, there are two response times involved. The first is based on the attacker brandishing his knife. This is the period of time from the perception of a threat (stimulus of the attacker presenting his knife), the mental reaction time from that threat stimulus until you start your draw, and then the movement time from the beginning of the draw-stroke until you are up on target.

The second response time involves the perception that the threat no longer exists and the attacker has dropped his knife, the mental reaction to the immediate threat no longer being immediate, and the physical movement of lowering the pistol.

There are some important elements here to consider. Optimum response time (performance) is based on the following: immediate perception and recognition of the threat, clear mental decision making, a well-trained motor program (draw-stroke in this case, what layman refer to as "muscle memory") and control of the sympathetic nervous system.

Imagine, if you will, a brand new skier competing in an Olympic downhill race. Poised at the gates, he is waiting for the start signal but is mentally distracted by thoughts of something else and is totally overwhelmed with the adrenaline coursing through his bloodstream. His visual field is narrowed, his hands shake and he feels the need to urinate. As the buzzer sounds and the light flashes, he is brought back to reality but trying now to play catch-up.

He pushes off and attempts to accelerate but he struggles with the basic motions and movements to gain speed and ski. He has never skied in these conditions and under this pressure before, only learning on beginner hills with all the time in the world and under the direct tutelage of his instructor.

The outlook for our neophyte racer is not good. We can only hope that he is not seriously hurt in the process. And this is not even with bullets flying and his life on the line.

But with time and training our skier could have done better. In a deadly force encounter, we need not be an Olympian to win. But if we based our preparation and training on the science of skill development and include dynamic confrontation simulation we can improve our responses to deadly threats.

Put simply, repetition of motor skills develops training competence, competence = confidence, and confidence helps control the SNS.

STIMULUS AND RESPONSE

In order to reduce our reaction and subsequent response time, we must match our motor skill response to a stimulus (perceived threat). Too often in defensive firearms training we practice our draw-stroke, presentation from low or high ready, and firing of the gun to an audio or visual signal, i.e. "when the whistle blows, draw from the holster and fire two shots."

Fortunately modern advances allow us to do this today. Training tools such as the SIRT (Shot Indicating Resetting Trigger) pistol, which is a non-firing replica with dual indicating laser beams, and Airsoft pistols that use propane to

A police student learns while using airsoft to respond to a deadly threat by moving, while drawing his pistol, then placing accurate fire on target.

fire plastic 0.2 gram BBs can be used. These relatively low-cost training devices ($100 to $200 per pistol) with proper safety gear (the biggest safety gear is eye protection but a relatively inexpensive paintball mask is encouraged for Airsoft training) can help you match your response (draw-stroke and firing) to a real-istic threat perception (role-player drawing or attempting to draw a handgun or knife).

We cover these specific training modalities in the chapter on training.

What we are attempting to do with stimulus/response training is to improve overall response time and match the motor program to a specific threat or sus-pect action.

CASE STUDY

Over my 32+ year law enforcement career there have been many times when I responded to a perceived threat without conscious thought. In other words, I subconsciously perceived some type of threat and drew my pistol without any conscious thought to the action. This response was based on many different factors: nature of the call I was on, i.e. armed robbery, narcotics dealer, man with a gun; perception of threat – a suspect found in a home on a burglary, a suspect with "hidden hands;" the body language of the suspect or verbal threats. It was if "magic" happened – here I was, perception of threat and Tada! pistol is in my hand pointed.

To get there, and have control over the SNS response with gun in hand, that's what we train and strive for.

As a historical footnote, wax and cotton bullet projectiles powered only by a primer have been used for years in this type of training. During training of Office of Strategic Services (precursor of today's C.I.A.) operatives, Colonel Rex Apple-gate used wax bullets to help train spies and agents prior to and during WWII. The late Bill Jordan, famed Border Patrol patrolman and amazing quick draw artist, used wax bullets to train with as well. With wax or paraffin bullets a pistol casing is loaded with a primer and the casing is pushed through a sheet of paraffin. The resulted projectile can be fired fairly accurately for a short distance.

During my early law enforcement training, circa 1982, we used cotton bullets to train in confrontation simulation scenarios. Once again a large pistol primer was loaded into an empty casing. A cotton ball was then stuffed into the casing. The resultant cotton projectile is good for short range.

Both can cause injury and, as the recipient of cotton bullets as a bad guy role-player, you can experience powder burns at close proximity and serious eye in-jury can occur if safety glasses are not worn. Please don't attempt wax or cotton ball training except under the direction of a qualified instructor.

PROXEMICS AND DISTANCING

Distance equals time, and in a confrontation you cannot afford to give the attacker too much time to act, formulate a strategy, respond or the time to assault.

Joe Ferrera is an accomplished law enforcement trainer and a friend. Several years ago Ferrera did research on the ability of officers to defend themselves at certain distances. In law enforcement this distance is referred to as the "reactionary gap." What Joe found was that if an officer allowed a suspect to get within touching distance, the suspect could assault the officer before the officer could react and respond.

Joe Ferrara's research showed:

◆ Average time to assault an officer at touching distance = .319 Seconds
◆ Average time to assault officer at 6 Feet = 1.042 Seconds

What Ferrera found was that if officers increased distance from suspects to the edge of the "reactionary gap" at six feet, they increased the time available to react and respond by a factor of more than three. Also, by having your hands up in some version of a high guard (hands above the waist, palms out, forearms outstretched, elbows in), a defender was better able to protect their head and body from attack by a punch, than having your arms down at the side. You are essentially reducing movement time and putting something between their fists and your face.

This is an important part of maximizing physical response to attack: your platform or stance (we hesitate to use the term stance as it equates to a fixed position, and in armed confrontations standing still is not a good thing when projectiles are coming in your direction).

In law enforcement we refer to officers who confront suspects with feet positioned close together and their weight on their heels as standing in a "bowling pin" stance. In other words, they are getting ready to get knocked on their a**.

Now it is imperative that you understand that distraction or inattentiveness

increases response time dramatically as do multiple response options. Just a relaxed state of alertness, as Colonel Jeff Cooper recommended, improves response time tremendously.

Author presses forward toward student. Author is armed with the ShockKnife which emits a shock to skin. Student has to block, evade and respond.

In the March 1983 issue of SWAT magazine, author/police officer Dennis Tueller wrote, "How Close is Too Close?" Tueller had been asked by one of his students at which distance a suspect armed with an impact weapon (knife or club) was a deadly threat. Tueller went to the range and found that "an average healthy adult male can cover the traditional seven yard distance in a time of... about one and one-half seconds." Tueller had come to the conclusion that at one and one half seconds was the average time for a trained and prepared shooter to draw and fire two shots.

Trained and alert is a central theme of Tueller's article and often forgotten. He wrote, "First, develop and maintain a healthy level of tactical alertness. If you spot the danger signs early enough, you can probably avoid the confrontation altogether. A tactical withdrawal (I hesitate to use the word "retreat") may be your best bet..." Here we are reminded once again of the importance of awareness and alertness.

Keep in mind that Tueller was talking about "Those of us who have learned and practiced proper pistolcraft techniques..." A new or fairly inexperienced armed citizen may take more time.

Dennis Tueller and his associates used stop watches to conduct their research. In 1996 Ray Rheingans and the late Tom Hontz from the Scottsdale Arizona Police Department conducted more scientific studies using high-speed video cameras as they had officers from their agency complete various "suspect" actions.

Published in Police Quarterly, Vol. 2, No. 4, December 1999, "Justifying The Deadly Force Response," Tom Hontz reported:

Average time for attackers to complete various movements (in seconds):

Run 15 feet. 1.28
Run 20 feet. 1.57
Run 25 feet. 1.79
Run 30 feet. 2.06

Hontz then wrote about the realities of one shot not reliably stopping an attacker. More shooting requires more time and allows the attacker to travel further or complete other assaultive behavior.

AGGRESSOR'S ACTIONS, MOVEMENTS AND ATTACK

A man with a gun in his hand is a serious threat because he will always be able to raise and fire before you can react and respond. Hontz and Rheingans also video recorded officers from their agency performing various "suspect" shooting actions, including raising a handgun from a position beside the leg, drawing from the rear inside the pants with hand on the handgun to start, and draw and fire with pistol inside the pants at the front belly position hands at the side. The time concluded at the end of one fired shot from the pistol. Using the tape with time generator only "movement time" (time from the beginning to the end of the movement) was recorded.

An attacker can run the distance of thirty feet in about two seconds.

Fifteen feet away, an attacker can reach you in less than a second and a half.

You do not have to wait until he is within arm's reach.

Average times as recorded in seconds:
Front draw 1.09
Rear draw 0.78
Raise and fire 0.59

In addition, average times were recorded for officers to respond – the process of reacting and moving (firing) in response to a visual cue (light signal) above range target(s):

One Large Target 1.15
Two Large Targets 1.11
One Small Target 1.56
Two Small Targets 1.58
One Large Target, Draw From Holster 1.90

Based on this research of suspect movement and draw times for officers Hontz wrote, "The results of this study show that 21 feet is too conservative a distance. This means if an officer has her weapon out at the ready position and aims for body mass (large target), the officer should be able to get one round off before the suspect can cover 15 feet. However, if the officer attempts a precise shot (small target) the suspect will be able to cover 20 feet. If the officer's gun is in the holster and she draws and fired to body mass, the suspect will be able to cover almost 30 feet. Again, it is important to emphasize that these are probably best-case times by the officers. If the weapon is not apparent, the officer is unclear in her mind if the suspect is really a threat, or if the officer is surprised by the attack, the response times will probably be longer."

CASE STUDY

At the 2014 International Law Enforcement Educators and Trainers Association conference in Lombard, Illinois, Joe Ferrera presented a special program titled "Gunman in the Lobby," which was a debriefing of a shooting that took place at his police station in 2012. In November of that year a 64-year-old suspect entered the Southfield (MI) Police Department lobby, approached the desk area and pointed a handgun at the officer who was sitting behind bullet resistant glass working the desk. The officer responded by ducking down below the counter area of the desk and hitting the panic alarm as well as announcing, "Man with a gun!" Two sergeants working in the back part of the building circled around, entered the lobby and confronted the man with their pistols drawn. Loud verbal orders to "Put the gun down!" are met by a slight movement by the suspect as he appeared to be lowering the gun to the floor. With a quick movement of his wrist, the gunman pivoted the pistol toward one of the sergeants and fired, hitting the officer in the shoulder. Both uniformed supervisors returned fire with multiple rounds, incapacitating the suspect. The suspect died from his wounds. The sergeant recovered from his injuries.

As Hontz and Rheingans proved and with later research by Dr. Bill Lewinski of Force Science confirming, attackers can raise guns and fire, pivot while standing or seated, even move from a prone position and fire the gun in their hand before officers can react and fire in response.

This has serious implications when confronted by armed attackers and will drive our tactics in response.

CHAPTER FOUR:

THE REASONABLE PERSON

What can you legally do to protect yourself? The answer is, "what a reasonable person would do in like or similar circumstances."

The Reasonable Person Doctrine: The standard against which your use of deadly force in self defense will be measured is called the standard of the reasonable person. This criterion asks, "Would a reasonable person under the same circumstances, knowing what you knew at the time, likely have used deadly force in self defense?" If you can convince the jury that they would have done the same thing, then you will walk free. On the other hand, if the members of the jury say to themselves, "No, I wouldn't have pulled the trigger under those circumstances," then the verdict will probably not be in your favor.

~Marty Hayes, J.D.
What Every Gun Owner Needs to Know About Self-Defense Law
Armed Citizen's Educational Foundation, 2014

Reasonable Person: A hypothetical person used as a legal standard, esp. to determine whether someone acted with negligence; specif., a person who exercises the degree of attention, knowledge, intelligence, and judgment that society requires of its members for the protection of their own and of others' interests. The reasonable person acts sensibly, does things without serious delay, and takes proper but not excessive precautions. Also termed reasonable man; prudent person; ordinarily prudent person; reasonably prudent person; highly prudent person.

~Black's Law Dictionary (8th ed. 2004) as quoted by Mitch Vilos,
Esq. and Evan Vilos in *Self-Defense Laws Of All 50 States*
(2nd Edition; Guns West Publishing, Inc.; 2013)

"Under traditional self-defense doctrine, also known as perfect self-defense, a defendant is justified in using a reasonable amount of force against another person if she honestly and reasonably believes that (1) she is in imminent or immediate danger of unlawful bodily harm from her aggressor, and (2) the use of such force is necessary to avoid the danger. Traditional self-defense doctrine requires necessity, imminence, and proportionality. Additionally, the threatened attack must be unlawful and the defendant must not have been the aggressor."

~Cynthia Lee *Murder and the Reasonable Man*
(New York University Press; 2003)

CASE STUDY

Wayne was a law-abiding citizen. Working security for the United States government, he carried a handgun in his job. Wayne also carried concealed off duty. At that time, the state Wayne resided in did not have a concealed carry law in place. The law did allow for citizens to carry concealed when "reasonable men" would do so. As such, it was an affirmative defense, meaning that if you were arrested you could use as your defense the assertion that a reasonable man in your position would have done the same thing. This commonly pertained to merchants making bank deposits or transporting cash after hours or so. Wayne carried routinely on a daily basis. On the day in question, Wayne was confronted by a person whom he believed to be a deadly threat. He shot and wounded the man. But instead of staying on scene and articulating who he was, what he did for a living and more importantly, why he feared for his life and fired, he got scared and left the scene. Wayne was charged with felonious assault and sentenced to state prison.

As eminent trainer Mas Ayoob has said, and it certainly was true in this case, "flight equals guilt." If Wayne had stayed on scene and his reasons for firing were legit, he may not have been charged with any crime. We will never know, and a good man went to prison.

It pays to know the law. Imagine as a concealed carry permit holder you elect to carry onto a premises which has a "No Guns" placard, such as a mall. In the event that you decide to carry into this location and get involved in a shooting and then leave the scene, your "flight" will definitely appear as "guilt" and "may" erase the lawful nature of your use of deadly force, even if you saved lives. Better to stay, articulate your actions with your attorney, and face whatever consequences come your way. In my state, carrying in a "no guns" area would be a misdemeanor (unless it's a school safety zone) and possible revocation of your permit. It is true in most jurisdictions that fleeing the scene of a shooting, however righteous, would certainly equate to felony charges against you. Note, I am not suggesting that you carry onto premises with placards. Better to go elsewhere and deny these establishments your business. Always follow the law.

As we see with Wayne's case and we think of George Zimmerman and his use of deadly force to save his life against Trayvon Martin, there are legal and political consequences to defending yourself and your loved ones.

It is certainly true, in police and citizen use of force cases, that there is a tremendous amount of work, clarification, explanation and active defense that must be done on the back end of even a completely lawful armed encounter. The law oftentimes refers to the "reasonable person" in self-defense situations without providing clear guidance as to what a reasonable person can and can't do. The law may not be crystal clear as it pertains to your situation, think of the George Zimmerman defense case. Even incidents that are clearly proper uses of deadly force can develop political momentum, some examples of this are cross racial shootings, shooting a female or the shooting of a young offender. These incidents may be prosecuted for political reasons, i.e. to satisfy special interest groups who may be ignorant of the facts and circumstances but who clamor for prosecution. We need look no further than police uses of deadly force cases that have been prosecuted despite the facts of the case.

USE OF DEADLY FORCE: THE SCALE OF DEADLINESS

Some justifiable homicides or shootings in self-defense are more easily investigated and cleared than others by police and prosecutors.

Stranger firing at armed citizen, family member or another

Scenario: You are walking your dog in your neighborhood on a pleasant evening. As you walk down the sidewalk, a car slows down as it drives past you. The car pulls to the curb, and passenger, who you don't know, exits the car, yells racial epithets at you, produces a handgun from behind his leg, and begins to fire at you. You draw your pistol and return fire, striking the attacker who falls to the ground. The vehicle takes off away from you. You take cover as you continue to cover the downed male attacker and scan the area in case the vehicle returns or other threats present themselves. You call 911 and await the police.

In this situation, you as an armed citizen are in public lawfully carrying concealed and are fired upon by a complete stranger. In other words, you are an innocent citizen who has been attacked with deadly force by someone unknown to you. It could be a mentally ill subject off his meds, a random act of senseless violence, a terrorist – whomever the attacker is, he has open fired on you and you are armed at the time or able to access a firearm and return fire, wounding or killing the attacker.

The threat posed by the assailant was obvious and deadly. Failure to use deadly force by you may have resulted in death to you or other innocent victims.

In these types of situations or armed encounters, witnesses may or may not be present who corroborate your story. In today's day and age, do not expect to be hailed as a hero and certainly expect a full police investigation, as well as intense scrutiny into your background by the media. Names may or may not be released to the press. You should also have built a strategy for a civil suit for wrongful death or injuries sustained by the assailant. Unfortunately we live in a litigious society. We talk more about legal strategy later in the "Investigation" chapter.

Stranger attempting to stab, slash or cut with knife or edged weapon

Scenario: You and your family are walking through a downtown area headed back to the parking deck where you've parked your car. As your party comes adjacent to an alleyway, a deranged man with manic eyes, disheveled hair, tangled beard and wearing an oversized coat steps from the alleyway screaming, "I'll kill you! I'll kill you all!" You see the large military knife in his hand as he slashes the air and advances toward your family. You step in front of them, yell "Stop!" You draw your handgun as the maniac is now closing in and fire multiple shots into his torso as he stumbles, then falls to the pavement against a building.

Once again, this is a stranger attack at close range necessitating the deadly force (gunfire) by the armed citizen to save your life or the life of another. Amazingly, to some people a knife does not represent a deadly weapon, or at least the knife-armed man does not, in their view, warrant a deadly force response. Recently the Albuquerque Police Department came under scrutiny for a shooting involving a violent and long-term mentally ill subject armed with two knives. Citizen outcry such as, "Why did the police shoot the man, couldn't they have just talked to him or let him go? Why did they shoot the man in the back? They should have tried over less-lethal means of force to control him." Even though the police had tried several hours of negotiation and orders for the suspect to disarm, deployed flash-bangs as a distraction, attempted to control with Taser projectiles and then deployed a police K9, when the suspect moved toward the police officer/dog handler and was within several feet, he was shot several times and killed. The police had literally exhausted all their options: verbal persuasion, crisis intervention, officer presence, non-deadly attempts at control, the suspect refused to comply or disarm after several hours and made the voluntary action of threatening with two knives and moving toward an officer.

To an informed person, it is readily apparent that the suspect in the preceding scenario presented a deadly threat. Certainly turning and running or trying some martial arts move learned in a dojo years ago may result in being stabbed in the back or being seriously wounded or killed.

However, as we scale downward in threat levels it is important to note that armed encounters may require more articulation and explanation, as the threat may appear less immediate or the circumstances less threatening.

A diagram that I have used over the last few years was developed by Tom Aveni of The Police Policy Studies Council. This triangle, the strongest of all geometric shapes, refers to a reasonable amount of force based on reasonable perceptions and the totality of the circumstances.

In the two cases cited, we can easily see that firing in defense of one's life or the life of another is a reasonable force response based on reasonable perceptions and the totality of the circumstances.

Stranger armed and threatening the use of deadly force against the armed citizen, family member or another

In this case the aggressor has produced a handgun and threatened the victim (armed citizen) or a member of his family, friends or another innocent citizen with death or in the commission of a crime of violence such as felonious assault, rape, robbery, burglary, carjacking, etc. Rounds are not being fired by the aggressor, nor is he not actively attempting to stab you. He is using his firearm, edged or impact weapon as a tool to commit a violent crime.

---

*Not every case in which you could
legally shoot means that you must shoot.*

Although he is not actively attacking, he is a deadly threat. Whether you use deadly force in this or similar cases is a tactical question, not a legal one. The aggressor, by way of his actions, has placed you or another in reasonable fear of death based on the totality of the circumstances. Shooting the aggressor would be a reasonable use of force, but your ability to successfully draw your firearm without being shot and deliver accurate fire on target without endangering others must also be considered.

Scenario: You are in your vehicle alone driving home from work. Stopped in traffic at a red light, you look to your left to see a person armed with a handgun run up to the driver's side door of your car. He attempts to open the door. Pointing his handgun at you, he yells, "Get out of the car or I'll blow your f'ing brains out!" With no room to drive away to the front or rear of your car, the attacker has the drop on you. You put the car in Park, take off your seat belt with your left hand as you draw your handgun with your right, as you open the car door, you shoot the suspect multiple times stopping him.

In this case, the armed attacker threatened you with death or serious bodily harm and had the apparent means to follow through with his action. It is certainly a reasonable response to use deadly force to stop the violent actions based on the totality of the circumstances. In this case, it was simply waiting for an opportune moment to be able to access and deploy your self-defense handgun.

An armed subject threatening
you is a deadly threat.

Scenario: You are at the counter of your bank making a deposit. At the next teller's window a person in dark hat, wearing dark sunglasses, produces a handgun and tells the teller, "This is a robbery! Don't touch the alarm! Put all the cash in this bag!" as he hands the teller a grocery sack. This person is obviously a deadly threat to the teller, you and anyone else in bank, coming into the bank or in the parking area after he leaves.

Do you attempt to draw your handgun and possibly get shot before you can do so? Do you engage in a shoot-out in the bank's crowded lobby? Or do you attempt to be the best witness you can be and only plan on using deadly force as a last resort if the gunman attempts to harm someone or move the customers and staff into the back of the bank?

These are tough tactical questions that you must think about now, prior to becoming involved in such a scenario. Not every case in which you could legally shoot means that you must shoot.

Stranger brandishing a firearm, edged weapon, bludgeon or other weapon

In this case, the armed citizen is confronted with a person who has a firearm, edged weapon or bludgeon in their hand. No threats are articulated by the subject but the weapon is out.

Scenario: You are walking through the parking lot of the mall when you see a male subject walking towards you. As you look at his hands, he has a black pistol in his right hand partially concealed by his jacket. He continues to move toward you. You draw your handgun order him to stop but he continues to move toward you.

Scenario: You are in traffic when the motorist behind you begins to tailgate you, flashing his lights and beeping his horn. You pull over to the side of the road to allow the motorist to pass. He pulls in behind you. You exit your vehicle and say, "What's the problem buddy!" The motorist gets out of his car with a baseball bat and begins to move aggressively toward you.

A subject threatening you at close range with an impact weapon, such as a crowbar or baseball bat, is a deadly threat.

In both cases, fearing for your life based on your reasonable perceptions of the totality of what is going on, the use of deadly force could be a reasonable response.

Life-threatening weaponless assault

Scenario: You are returning to your apartment building at night. As you enter the foyer and unlock your mailbox on the wall to get your mail, an unseen attacker steps in behind you and punches you in the face. Stunned and dazed, you fall to the floor. As you look up a large man with a hood over his face stands over you with balled fists and says, "Give me your f'ing money or I'll f*ck you up!" As you turn to the left to reach into your left front pants pocket to grab your wallet, you reach to your right hip and draw your pistol. Turning you shove your pistol out and fire into your attacker's torso.

Even though the attacker had no deadly weapon with which to attack, his weaponless attack was capable of killing you or causing you serious bodily injury. Your position on the floor with him looming and threatening above you

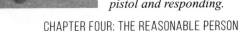

Being beaten to death is not an appealing option. Here a student learns to fight off an unarmed by extremely violent assailant while accessing his pistol and responding.

was certainly a very dangerous and life threatening position and circumstance to be in. It could be that you were larger or stronger, but the element of surprise was against you and a serious attack already commenced.

It's not required that the aggressor attack you. If in a similar circumstance above in that apartment foyer, a person larger or stronger slams you up against the wall, verbalizes a threat and criminal intent and, based on these reasonable perceptions, you believe that your life or the life of another is threatened, then deadly force may be a reasonable response.

Deadly force would not be a reasonable response to an aggressive panhandler who approached you, asking for money. Depending on the totality of the circumstances (low or subdued lighting, being alone) a reasonable response may be drawing your pepper spray or Taser, or even putting your hand on your holstered pistol, possibly even drawing to low ready if you feel threatened, but absent more aggressive/life threatening circumstances, deadly force is generally not called for when a stranger approaches.

Aggravated burglary and burglary

Seldom does the law in any state permit the use of deadly force to stop a property crime. That said, when can a homeowner fire on a burglar? The obvious answer is the same as when the armed citizen is outside of the home – when the citizen reasonably believes based on the totality of the circumstances that the subject poses a threat of death or serious bodily harm. But do you have a "duty to retreat" or a duty to attempt to avoid confrontation?

Attorney Andrew Branca writes, "Today the majority of jurisdictions – thirty-three – do not have an explicit duty to retreat, but a sizable minority – seventeen – are "Duty to Retreat" states that require that you take advantage of any safe avenue before using force in self defense. In "Duty to Retreat" jurisdictions the failure to retreat when it is safe is fatal to your self-defense claim.

Every state with a duty to retreat has exceptions to that duty. These exceptions make up the "Castle Doctrine" and include, at minimum, that you don't need to retreat in your own home. This means even though you could go up your stairs into your bathroom, or out your back door, you do not have to do so.

Every state defines what makes up your "castle" a little differently.

Stand Your Ground – Today a large majority of states, thirty-three, don't require you to retreat when it's safe. Instead they allow innocent people who are in a place they are allowed to be to defend themselves, subject only to the other four principles *(Author's note: Branca's principles are: Innocence, Imminence, Proportionality and Avoidance). States that have held this "no retreat" rule for many decades call them "True Man" laws, while those that adopted them more recently call them "Stand Your Ground" laws.

Importantly, Stand Your Ground only applies to legitimate self-defense. If you fail on another principle – for example, if you used disproportionate force

What does the law say about dealing with threats such as this?

– Stand Your Ground is irrelevant, as you were not, under the conditions set by law, acting in self-defense at all.

The greatest value of Stand Your Ground from my perspective is that it limits the power of overreaching prosecutors.

Be careful here, though. In some Stand Your Ground states, even though retreat isn't required, not doing so can still fail the principle of reasonableness. In those states, a prosecutor can't argue that you had a duty to retreat, but they can still argue that "retreat was so apparent that not doing so was unreasonable." (Andrew Branca, *The Law of Self-Defense: Second Edition* (2013; Law of Self Defense publishers))

CASE STUDY

Barry, an off-duty county sheriff's sergeant, was in his house at night when he heard commotion from the back patio area. Arming himself with his handgun, he asked his wife to call the police and then went to investigate. As Barry approached the patio door he looked out to see and hear a person growling and tearing the molding out from around the patio window. Barry gave verbal warnings to the male subject who continued to growl and rip at the window

A violent and incoherent subject is actively breaking into your home despite your warnings. What can you do?

edging/molding. Fearing for his and his wife's life if the subject burst through the window, Barry fired his handgun at the subject, killing him. The subject was unarmed at the time of the shooting. Barry and his police union maintained that at the moment Barry fired he was acting as a law enforcement officer attempting to apprehend a violent felony suspect. The county maintained that Barry was acting as a private citizen in his own home. After some fighting, the county finally was forced to represent Barry (they paid his attorney's fees). The shooting was ruled a justifiable homicide by a law enforcement officer.

Multiple individuals attacking or threatening physical harm

Years ago, Rorion Gracie from the famous Gracie Jiu-Jitsu® was asked about his family's ground fighting system and how, according to critics, it left practitioners open to attacks from multiple individuals. Mr. Gracie explained that attacks from two or more individuals were almost always a deadly force encounter. Rorion Gracie explained, "On your best day, could you beat two of you?" In other words, could you defeat two unarmed but attacking assailants your same size and weight? In an interview with James Williams and Stanley Pranin at Aikidojournal.com, Rorion Gracie states, "Basically, I don't believe one person can fight two people effectively. Of course, I don't want to grapple with one guy and let the second guy kick me in the head." Mr. Gracie further goes on, "This is why even though I've been doing Jiu-Jitsu some forty years, I also have a gun."

---

*Multiple individuals violently attacking you
is almost always a deadly force situation.*

CASE STUDY

Fred is an off-duty police officer. He has a confrontation with a drunken and aggressive individual and is dealing with him while another assailant blindsides Fred, punching him in the head and dropping him to the ground where he is further attacked.

The sucker punch or a blind-side attack is a preferred method of attack by street criminals. Regardless of ones' prowess in unarmed combatives, it is always possible that while dealing with one subject to your front, you can be hit from the side or rear.

Therefore, two or more attackers of decent size and weight, who are actively and aggressively threatening or attacking you with such force causing you to reasonably believe they are capable of causing your death or serious physical harm, are a deadly threat.

CASE STUDY

In 1992, 36-year-old construction truck driver Reginald Denny was driving near the Los Angeles intersection of Florence and Normandie. In the wake of acquittals of police officers charged with excessive force on Rodney King, riots spread through some areas of Los Angeles. Denny was driving a dump truck when he came upon rioters blocking the intersection. Several of the rioters pulled Mr. Denny from the cab of his truck; four of them beat and kicked him. As he was down on the ground incapacitated, Damian "Football" Williams, a 19-year-old member of the Crips street gang, threw a brick into the head of Reginald Denny from close range. Mr. Denny suffered permanent injuries and almost died from the attack.

Damian Williams was sentenced to 10 years in prison. He was released from prison in 1997 but was subsequently convicted and sentenced to life in prison for the 2000 murder of a dope dealer.

TOTALITY OF THE CIRCUMSTANCES

In law enforcement, the Supreme Court of the United States (SCOTUS) has applied the 4th Amendment of the Constitution to use of deadly and non-deadly force by police:

The right of the people to be secure in their persons, houses, papers, and effects, against unreasonable searches and seizures, shall not be violated, and no warrants shall issue, but upon probably cause, supported by oath or affirmation, and particularly describing the place to be searched, and the persons or things to be seized. ~Amendment IV, U.S. Constitution

Part of the Bill of Rights of the first ten amendments to the Constitution, the 4th Amendment and the other amendments in the Bill of Rights guarantee personal freedoms and limit the government's power.

The standard for the 4th Amendment is Objective Reasonableness. In the SCOTUS case Graham v. Connor, the Supreme Court noted: "the test of reasonableness under the Fourth Amendment is not capable of precise definition or mechanical application," its proper application requires careful attention to the facts and circumstances of each particular case, including the severity of the crime at issue, whether the suspect poses an immediate threat to the safety of the officers or others, and whether he is actively resisting arrest or attempting to evade arrest by flight."

Further the SCOTUS noted: "The calculus of reasonableness must embody allowance for the fact that police officers are often forced to make split-second judgments – in circumstances that are tense, uncertain, and rapidly evolving – about the amount of force that is necessary in a particular situation."

Although law enforcement officers are empowered by state or federal law to enforce laws and use force to arrest, detain, and involuntarily commit subjects, as well as squelch riots and other official acts, the guidelines of use of force by law enforcement can be used to help describe, articulate and defend an armed citizen who threatens or uses force in self-defense.

In law enforcement, these components – severity of the crime, whether the suspect poses an immediate threat to the safety of the officers or others, and using force in circumstances which are tense, uncertain and rapidly evolving – help comprise the totality of the circumstances in use-of-force situations. They are not the only elements to be considered in the totality of the circumstances. Certainly an armed suspect firing at a police officer comprises the highest risk of threat an officer can face, same too with an armed private citizen being shot at.

Other issues and components that comprise the totality of the circumstances and may have an impact on the decision of an armed citizen to use deadly force include:

◆ Sympathetic Nervous System / "Fight or Flight" – The brain prepares the body for the fight, or to flee, in an instant. Although optimum performance is a branch of the SNS, it helps prepare us for combat, cognitive changes, perceptual distortions such as tunnel vision, and physiological changes impact our performance. We rarely think and perform at our highest level during fight or flight. The SNS explains why.

◆ Distance – As stated earlier, distance equals time. Almost everything at close range is perceived as an emergency. The brain perceives there is not enough time to respond. Further, distance drives tactics and technique. Those stances, tactics and firearms techniques that may work from 21 feet may not work at close range. It is entirely possible that the close quarters or extreme close quarters armed encounter may look more like a "fight with guns" than a traditional "gun fight." Additionally, close range encounters may cause the armed citizen to slip into a Sympathetic Nervous System reaction more so than one where more distance (time) is available.

◆ Time – As just mentioned, time or the perception of little time to respond impacts performance. Imagine opening a stairway door in a parking deck and encountering what you believe is an armed man with gun in hand. The brain perceives the immediate threat and responds in SNS versus a more prolonged (longer) encounter where fight or flight may not impact as much. The more time available, the more options such as retreat or escape may be available.

◆ Lighting – Can you properly identify what is in a person's hand? Is it a gun, knife, or an innocuous item such as a cell phone, wallet or keys? In very high profile police shootings, officers have misidentified the item in a subject's or suspect's hand(s). We have talked about SNS and the effects on performance, but night vision is also adversely impacted by fight or flight. Much in this realm has to do with context (how the item is wielded or held). In several shootings with LE personnel the officer did not have the item or the ability based on the suspect's actions (holding the item with two hands like a handgun and pointing it at the officers) to withhold their fire.

In low or subdued lighting, a flashlight or weapon light is vital to properly identify a threat and prevent a tragedy.

◆ Injury – If you are injured in an initial attack or wounded by an assailant's physical or armed attack, this will certainly have an impact on your ability to defend yourself or others, as well as to move, perform physical actions, etc. Injury, depending on scope and severity, can allow the armed citizen to escalate the use of force.

◆ Physical limitation or debilitation – A man confined to a wheelchair, using crutches, suffering from disease or recovering from surgery or an accident may lack the physical attributes of an uninjured or healthy person. This may severely affect self-defense options.

◆ Size – Relative size is a factor in confrontations and threats of confrontations. A 90 lb. armed citizen facing a 200+ pound man threatening physical harm may escalate sooner than a healthy person of the same size, considering the reasonable fear of the innocent citizen. Does this mean that a 200+ pound man cannot be in reasonable fear of a 120 lb. assailant? No, it is only one factor out of many to be considered.

◆ Gender – On average, a female citizen can use more force to defend herself against a male attacker than can a male citizen. Relative size and strength must be considered, but the norm is that most 16-year-old boys have more upper body strength and size than the average adult female.

◆ Skill level – If you knew that the assailant was a very skilled armed or unarmed fighter, it would impact how you approach or deal with him.

◆ Criminal history – In law enforcement we deal with "frequent flyers," or suspects who have a lot of experience as suspects in criminal cases. If you know that the attacker has a violent criminal history, you

Age can be a factor in the use of deadly force.

can factor that in your response and it may be introduced in your defense in court subsequently.

- ◆ Mental state – Rage, anger, suicidal thoughts, hallucinations, delusions, derangement – all of these and other mental states can affect your defense and can be indicated by a subject's words and actions. All can potentially be perceived as a threat to cause harm to you or others, and possibly support the assertion that communication or a rational, non-violent confrontation was not an option.
- ◆ Presence of weapons – Prior knowledge of an attacker's propensity to carry, have or use weapons, or perception at the time of an attack based on your observations, may be factored in to your decision to use force. In many cases, the mere presence of a weapon cannot be used as the sole justification for using deadly force. Absent other elements, such as threats or threatening or criminal behavior, it is entirely possible that the subject has every legal right to possess the firearm.
- ◆ Exhaustion – According to research by Bruce Siddle from Human Factor Research Group, most violent confrontations take place in less than two minutes. They can be properly classified as anaerobic activities. The primary fuel source used by the body in such confrontations is ATP/PC but it only lasts for around 15 seconds, once the ATP/PC system is exhausted, performance drops 45% within 30 seconds. Exhaustion in an armed confrontation can happen quickly and seriously impact cognitive and physical performance.
- ◆ Availability of other options – We strongly advise the armed citizen to have other lesser-force options available. You will probably have more need of non-deadly force tools such as pepper spray or the Taser than you

The author is a big advocate of less-lethal options such as this OC spray or the Taser C2.

will deadly force. Even if the tools could not possibly have affected or prevented an armed encounter, you can state that you had them available, if only the person had not presented a deadly threat.

◆ Environment – Many environments we find ourselves in during emergency situations are not conducive to self-protection. If the environment provides physical perils to the armed citizen – such as from third parties, vehicle traffic, hostile crowds, cluttered rooms preventing movement or possibly causing a trip or stumble, stairs or other risks of falling, rain, snow or other hostile weather – then this must factor in to the totality of the circumstances. An armed encounter at the side of the road on a busy highway presents physical risks not present on a closed, flat, safe firearms training range.

Each of these and many more factors come into play when considering the totality of the circumstances. Remember, it is the totality of: who you are, who the attacker is, what type of threat is present, what's been said and done by all parties, other assailants and innocent citizens present, how close or far, and the physical / environmental issues such as lighting, layout and threat.

*If you are interested in further reading on police use of force and the subsequent investigations involved, I would recommend a copy of my book, *Use of Force Investigations: A Manual for Law Enforcement*; (Responder Media; 2012).

Issues and elements that may complicate the investigation by authorities or muddy the waters are:

◆ He said / He said – Absent clear evidence that you are the innocent victim, it is entirely possible and very probable that the assailant will claim innocence and insist that you were the aggressive party and he was the victim. Absent clear evidence or witnesses of what actually occurred, uniformed police will frequently arrest both parties and let the investigators or courts figure it out. This is a problem when both parties know each other. As an example, on a domestic violence call, if both sides have equal injuries and conflicting stories, both may be arrested.

◆ Previous violent contact – This is not to say that you cannot use deadly force to stop a homicidal attack against you from a person you know. However, if you and victim had previous unreported violent contact (a dust-up, threats or physical altercation and the police were not called) then it can muddy the waters. The working hypothesis may become that this was a long-standing feud that finally erupted into gunfire and you are an equal part, not an innocent victim. If you've been threatened or assaulted by someone and are an innocent victim, report it to the police. You are building a defense in case that person presents a non-deadly or deadly threat to you in the future and you have to use force. If you engaged in mutual voluntary combat, i.e. a fistfight, and lost, that does not give you the right to resort to deadly force.

◆ Alcohol – You don't lose the right to self-defense based on voluntary intoxication but police will examine the case more closely and question legitimate self-defense more vociferously. Police officers, especially in urban or busy jurisdictions, handle a large number of violent encounter calls – shootings, stabbings, etc. Many, if not most, are alcohol related. Intoxication brings up questions about your judgment and often equates to recklessness, i.e. "the subject while voluntarily intoxicated did recklessly fire his handgun at Mr. Doe…"

◆ Flight – As I pointed out with the story of Wayne in the beginning of this chapter, "flight equals guilt." Even if you made a mistake. Even if you are innocent but scared, don't leave the scene unless it is physically dangerous for you to stay. Even then, get on the phone as quick as possible and give police your situation and location.

◆ Incriminating spontaneous statements – "I didn't mean to shoot him!" "It was an accident!" "The gun just went off!" These statements can be damning and seriously impact the subsequent investigation. I believe these statements are reactions to the shock of what just transpired. What you meant, based on never having to go through something as emotional and as traumatic as a shooting, is to say, "I didn't want to shoot him but I had no choice," or similar. Innocent victims have gone to trial in homicide cases and have even been convicted based on damning statements post incident. Take a deep breath, think before you speak. We cover the police response and investigation in other chapters.

◆ Manipulation of the crime scene and evidence – Any attempts to "clean-up" or somehow move or manipulate evidence can hurt you. Cleaning up can look like you're a cold and calloused suspect more interested in saving your living room carpet than rendering aid to a man you just shot. Tampering with evidence is a crime, oftentimes a felony, and impacts your perceived motive and mindset.

◆ Profanity – The "language of the street" or profanity is oftentimes equated with loss of control and anger. Police have long understood that suspects don't react to verbal orders such as "Get down on the ground!" or, "Show me your hands!" and use what have become known as "command intensifiers" which include profanity. Having pointed guns at hundreds of people during my SWAT career, I can say that oftentimes, "Get down on the f'ing ground!" was more effective. That said, articulated threats such as, "Don't move or I'll blow your f'ing head off!" tend to show the person was not in control of his/her emotions.

◆ Verbal parting shots – Police officers oftentimes hurt themselves with spontaneous statements after a use of force. It is usually emotions of the stressful encounter boiling over. In other words the officer is simply running off at the mouth. But imagine how the jury might react to a statement such as, "I hope you f'ing die!" post shooting? Or how about, "You deserved it you piece of sh*t!"

Once again these types of elements don't turn a good shooting into a bad one, but they make it harder for you to prove your innocence.

SEGMENTATION AND THE DECISION POINT APPROACH

The court noted in Graham v. Connor that "The "reasonableness of a particular use of force must be judged from the perspective of a reasonable officer on the scene, rather than with the 20/20 vision of hindsight." This 20/20 hindsight is disastrous to officers, since their force is to be judged "at the moment" it is used.

The United States Department of Justice has recently begun using "segmentation" or what they refer to as the decision point approach, to examine police use of force. They then examine the incident as to the decision points an officer had along the way prior to the use of force and whether the officer through bad decision making or tactics, created the jeopardy that led to the shooting. This hindsight and Monday morning quarterbacking is contrary to the Graham case and poses a serious threat to law enforcement officers.

I believe that the armed private citizen should be very concerned with the decision point approach as it relates to armed encounters. Since the armed citizen, unlike police, is not to be judged "at the moment" the trigger is pulled, it is entirely possible that prosecutors will examine the timeframe and decisions that led up to the shooting.

Did the armed citizen have the time or ability to retreat, move to cover, call the police, veritable panoply of tactical options to avoid an armed encounter? Did the armed citizen create the jeopardy that led to the shooting?

This all leads to the obvious tactics of avoidance if at all possible and retreat from a potential threat if tactically feasible.

The legal and financial liabilities involved in using deadly force, here again, even if completely in the right, can expose you and your family to extreme financial hardships including possible depletion of savings and bankruptcy.

To those citizens who state, "It's better to be tried by twelve than carried by six." This is a simplistic notion that ignores the risks and perils involved in armed self-defense.

IAOJ FORMULA

In an effort to instruct and explain the use of deadly force, some trainers use the following formula. In this formula for proper use of deadly force, all of the elements must be present.

◆ Intent
◆ Ability
◆ Opportunity
◆ Jeopardy

Intent – Does the individual have the intent to cause you or another death or serious bodily harm?

Ability – Does the individual have the means by way of a firearm, other weapon or life threatening weaponless assault to kill or seriously hurt you or another?

Opportunity – Can the means of their attack get to you? Firearms have the ability to reach out at a line of sight distance and kill. But what of a knife, impact weapon such as a tire tool or crowbar, and a physical assault?

Jeopardy – Does the individual's attack or actions place you or another in reasonable fear of death or serious bodily injury?

The IAOJ or AOJ standard is not required by law and can be confusing in an actual encounter.

My problem with this formula is that in many circumstances most of these elements cannot be absolutely proven, defined or ascertained. Let's break these down a little.

It is not possible to ascertain or determine intent. We are not mind readers. Oftentimes, we cannot fathom why a subject would legally have a gun in hand or want to point or threaten us with it. It matters not, since absent a law enforcement operation or maybe a mistaken identity situation where the subject believes you are someone else who has threatened them, what matters is that they have pointed a gun at you and presented a threat of death or serious bodily harm. We can only base our decision on threat or manifest intent. In other words, based on our senses we believe, the subject's actions are a threat to us or others. It is reasonable to believe that a man, unless he is a law officer in performance of his duty, who points or threatens us with a firearm or other weapon capable of causing death or serious bodily harm, has displayed deadly intent. We understand, based on action versus response time that we are under extreme threat by a man with gun in hand.

Because of the problems with determining another person's intent, this part of the formula has been removed by some trainers and just AOJ is used.

Next up is ability. Do they have the means by which to kill or seriously hurt us or others? In most cases, however, what we are really quickly assessing is their perceived ability of deadly violence. Take for instance the bank robber who uses a BB gun or other non-firearm as a tool to commit robbery, or places his hand in his pocket and holds it out threatening a teller, as he announces a "stick-up." In all actuality he does not have the ability to cause death, but under the totality of the circumstances and time frames it cannot be safely and correctly ascertained. When the crack addict attempted to rob me years ago armed only with a cigarette lighter, which looked like a small pistol, as I recounted at the beginning of this book, I could have lawfully used deadly force to stop him. It was a conscious decision to not shoot him, but lawfully it would have been a "good shoot" had I done so.

In the dynamics of real life encounters, opportunity is based on a victim's perceptions as well. Does it reasonably appear that the individual can deliver his attack or threats? If a man has a gun, then it is certainly possible that at most confrontation ranges he can kill you.

CASE STUDY

A couple of years ago my wife and I were in the house on a fall evening. Gunfire in our suburban neighborhood is not unusual. We have become use to hearing the sounds of citizens target shooting. On this night, however, we heard a shot close-by toward the western edge of our property line approximately 100 yards away, then the sound of shotgun pellets whizzing through the trees above our house. I walked downstairs from my office and heard another shot and the pellets once again fly through the trees. I grabbed an Armalite M15 carbine from my bedroom safe and turned off all lights on the first floor. As I scanned the outside perimeter of our property, I could not see anyone. I called the local police department and continued scanning for threats. I grabbed a pistol and spare magazine and put them on my belt. As the police officer arrived, I went outside and met him in the drive and identified myself. He asked if I had walked back to check for suspects. I clapped him on the back and told him with a smile, I was off-duty and that it was his job. I did tell him that if he got in trouble to give me a call.

The young officer walked back and checked. Minutes later he informed me that the caretaker for the property owner next door had been shooting at squirrels. Since the man cannot discharge a firearm within 300 feet of another home, he was in violation of the law (and more importantly of common sense). That said, I did not ask that he be arrested, just warned.

If I had come downstairs and observed a man shooting into our house from off our property, could I have used deadly force to stop the threat? Absolutely, even though my wife and I could have taken cover and just called the police (hoping to not get shot). I could have used deadly force to stop what, based on reasonable perceptions and the totality of the circumstances, was clearly a deadly threat.

But what of the man with a knife or club who begins running at you from 30 feet away? Do you have to wait until he gets closer before you can use deadly force to stop him? No, as stated earlier, the average time for a subject to run 30 feet is 2.06 seconds. You only have one and one-half seconds before he can stab or strike you from 20 feet away.

The last element is jeopardy and refers to the "reasonable fear" you have for your or another's life or debilitating injury. Once again, it is a reasonable fear that anyone armed with a gun and firing or pointing at you is a threat. But what of other weapons or situations you may encounter?

Good use-of-force decisions
are based on solid training.

Scenario: You are in your home at night and hear a large commotion outside – shouting, profanity, tires screeching and screaming. You arm yourself with your pistol, turn on the front porch light and step outside onto the porch to see what's going on as you tell your significant other to call the police. You see several assailants in the street with ball bats beating a man who is motionless on the ground. You yell out, "Hey! Stop that! The police are on their way!" The multiple assailants turn their attention to you, threaten you with profane acts of violence, and start running toward your house. You yell, "Stop or I'll shoot?" Can you fire even though the distance is around 40 feet?

Based on the reasonable fear of multiple individuals who are not only armed and have threatened you, but considering the totality of the circumstances (you have seen these individuals viciously attack another person), I would say deadly force is lawful.

The IAOJ or AOJ formula seeks to give guidance as to the deployment of deadly force. In my opinion it may complicate the issue to use deadly force and burden the armed citizen's decision making and is not required, since the standard is that you have a reasonable fear of death or serious bodily harm based on the totality of the circumstances. Post-shooting or in court you may be able to prove that the individual had all the elements of the formula, but out on the street, or in your own home in the middle of the night when you're facing an immediate perceived threat, you don't have to be perfect, you only have to be reasonable.

A COUPLE OF CONCERNING CASES

In research conducted for this manual, I looked at two cases, one in 1992 and one recent, in which home owners used deadly force on two young unarmed subjects.

CASE STUDY

In 1992, Yoshihiro "Yoshi" Hattori, a Japanese exchange student, was shot and killed in Baton Rouge, Louisiana, by home owner Rodney Peairs. Yoshi and the 16-year-old son of his American host family, Webb Haymaker, were headed out to a Halloween party at an address of 10131 on the street. Instead the two boys juxtaposed the numbers and seeing Halloween decorations at 10311, five doors down, stopped and approached the wrong house. Rodney Peairs, his wife Bonnie and her son from a previous marriage were in the home. Bonnie Peairs responded to the doorbell ringing at her front door by going to the side door, turning on the porch light and opening the side door. Bonnie first encountered Webb Haymaker who was dressed as an accident victim with a bandage on his head and wearing a neck brace from an actual medical issue. But Bonnie Peairs' fears were raised when Yoshi, wearing a white Tux coat came quickly around the corner toward her. According to Bonnie Peairs' statements she "instinctively" felt fear that something wasn't right. She slammed the door and called out to her husband to, "Get the gun!" Rodney Peairs heard the terror in his wife's voice and responded by grabbing his .44 magnum 8" barreled revolver with a hunting scope attached.

Rodney went to the side door and armed with his handgun looked out through the blinds. Seeing no one, he opened the door. The two boys were in the driveway, now walking away. Upon hearing the door behind them, Yoshi turned around and began walking quickly to toward the door and Peairs. As he entered the garage near the parked cars, Yoshi was smiling and laughing. Peairs stated he was terrified. Yoshi had a camera in his hand. Peairs ordered the teen to, "Freeze!" but Yoshi continued moving toward the homeowner getting as close as five feet from Rodney Peairs. Peairs stated that, "The adrenalin was so high in my system. It was just fear. I couldn't see any alternative but to fire to stop this person." Peairs fired one round from his revolver, which hit the young man in the chest. Yoshi Hattori died enroot to the hospital.

Rodney Peairs was indicted and tried but acquitted for the death of Yoshihiro Hattori. A deciding factor, according to a juror interviewed, was that Yoshi kept moving toward the homeowner, "He made no attempt to stop and he kept advancing."

~Justice Files, TV Show, 12/23/95

Subsequently the Hattori family sued Rodney Peairs in civil court and won. According to reports the Hattori family won a judgment of $650,000 in damages and funeral expenses.

Certainly this was a tragedy. An unarmed youth who was a visitor to our country, lost on his way to a party, was shot and killed. There are no winners in this event that was the culmination of many different issues and circumstances.

Just because "you can shoot" does not mean "you must shoot." Oftentimes, if the apparent threat is not imminent and time, distance and cover allow some protection, then waiting for the police is a better response.

CASE STUDY

As I write this, another man, homeowner and gun owner is on trial for the shooting death of an unarmed 19-year-old young woman. Theodore Wafer of Dearborn Heights, a suburb of Detroit, was asleep in a living-room recliner before 5:00 a.m. when Renisha McBride, disoriented and intoxicated from vodka and marijuana, began banging on his door after crashing her car into several parked vehicles six blocks from the homeowner's residence. Wafer has testified that he fumbled to find his cell phone in the dark but could not. According to Mr. Wafer, he crawled on the floor from the living room to the kitchen and then bathroom looking for his cell phone but could not locate it. Mr. Wafer stated that, "I was upset. I had a lot of emotions. I was scared. I had fear. I was panicking." Grabbing his 12 gauge the homeowner went to the front door and opened the steel inside door, firing through the screen door at a figure on the front porch. The shot hit the young woman in the face, killing her.

~Julie Bosman, New York Times, Man on Trial Over Killing on his Porch Speaks of Night Filled With Fear (Aug. 5, 2014)

Theodore Wafer is charged with 2nd Degree Murder, Manslaughter and related weapon charges. According to Michigan law:

780.951, Sect. 1, (1): "…an individual who uses deadly force or force other than deadly force under section 2 of the self-defense act has an honest and reasonable belief that imminent death of, sexual assault of, or great bodily harm to himself or herself or another individual will occur if both of the following apply:

(a) The individual against whom deadly force or force other than deadly force is used is in the process of breaking and entering a dwelling or business premises or committing a home invasion or has broken and entered a dwelling or business premises or committed home invasion and is still present in the dwelling or business premises, or is unlawfully attempting to remove another individual from a dwelling, business premises, or occupied vehicle against his or her will.

(b) The individual using deadly force or force other than deadly force honestly and reasonably believes that the individual is engaging in conduct described in subdivision (a).

On August 7, 2014, Theodore was found guilty of all charges.

Once again, like the Peairs case, we see a tragedy based on a confluence of circumstances. Could both of these cases have been prevented? My opinion is yes, based on knowledge of the law, proper training leading to competence and control of the SNS response, both of these young people might still be alive. Yes, Rodney Peairs was acquitted, but his family went through hell in the interim. Peairs may still believe it was the right thing to do "at that moment" but one wonders if he had it to do over again, would he?

SUMMATION

"Because the necessity, imminence, and proportionality requirements turn on the reasonableness of the defendant's perceptions, the reasonableness or unreasonableness of the defendant's beliefs and actions becomes the key to whether or not the defendant is acquitted. Reasonableness, however, is a standard capable of different meanings."

"Requiring the defendant to be right or correct about the existence of justifying circumstances is extremely problematic. First, in most cases it is impossible to know, after the fact, whether the victim was going to attack the defendant. One can only know the facts and circumstances that led the defendant to believe, reasonably or unreasonably, that he was being threatened with an imminent attack. Second, as a practical matter, requiring the defendant to be right would just about eviscerate self-defense as we know it. The defense would only be available to those defendants lucky enough to kill or assault individuals who were actually going to kill or attack them. However, requiring a reasonable act does not have to mean that the defendant is right about the existence of justifying circumstances."

~Cynthia Lee Murder and the Reasonable Man
(New York University Press; 2003)

Just because you can does not mean you must! There may be times when you could shoot and instead you make the tactical decision not to. As long as that decision is a conscious thought and does not recklessly place you or your loved ones at risk, cool deal.

Sadly, in my opinion, too many police agencies are burdening officers with policies and restrictions on use of force which leaves them feeling reluctant to use force period, even to use deadly force to stop an armed and deadly suspect.

Police training history has numerous examples of when officers could have but did not shoot, and lost their life or were seriously wounded as a result.

Several years ago, police trainer Pat Martin presented a program at the 2006 American Society of Law Enforcement Trainers annual conference. The program was titled "Shut Up and Shoot." The central theme of Pat's program was that officers are indecisive about deploying deadly force and unnecessarily expose themselves and others to death or serious bodily harm by verbalizing too much to a suspect who presents a deadly threat.

As part of Mr. Martin's program he broke down the statistics of officers killed in the line of duty. I'll do the same thing but update the stats using the ten-year stats of officers killed between 2003 and 2012 (the last ten year sampling available at this time).

According to the Federal Bureau of Investigations Officers Killed Summary, between 2003 – 2012:

- 535 officers were killed
- 115 officers were ambushed/killed

This means that 420 Officers were feloniously killed (in non-ambush altercations).

- 252 officers did not use or attempt to use their firearm

That means that 60% of Officers killed in non-ambush confrontations in that ten-year period did not use or attempt to use their own firearm!

Despite being confronted with men with gun in hand and similar armed encounters, these officers chose not to shoot, were uncertain if they could shoot, ignored the danger signs of an armed man or situation, were surprised or were completely caught off guard by the events.

How does this impact us? We must, to the greatest extent possible, educate ourselves on the legalities of using force – both deadly and non-deadly. We must train so that our skills do not require conscious thought, i.e. trying to draw from a holster we haven't practiced with. And we must train in a style and method that teaches us how to control our SNS (fight or flight) response. This dynamic training gives us safe experience in stressful situations and confrontations so that we are not overcome by events and are able to function and operate efficiently.

To the greatest extent possible, we avoid and retreat whenever able and safe to do so. You want to protect yourself and your family but you want to show that shooting was a decision made based on the threat and actions from the assailant. That the assailant's actions offered you no alternative and that a reasonable person when put in like or similar circumstances would have done as you did. Based on the Totality of the Circumstances and your Reasonable Perceptions as to the threat and actions of the individual(s), deadly force was a Reasonable Use of Force.

It is not as easy as simply carrying a gun. It is not as easy as going to a basic CCW permit course. The armed citizen to efficiently and legally operate, must continually train, study and educate him/herself to the vagaries and complexities of the law.

SELF-DEFENSE GUIDELINES

As an example of state law as it pertains to the use of deadly force when defending your life or the life of another, I submit the following from the Attorney

General's Office of the State of Ohio. This information was obtained from the online pamphlet Ohio's Concealed Carry Laws and License Application (State of Ohio Attorney General; 2014) available at www.ohioattorneygeneral.gov.

In Ohio, deadly force can be used only to prevent serious bodily harm or death. Deadly force can never be used to protect property only. Depending on the specific facts and circumstances of the situation, use of deadly force may lead to criminal charges and/or civil liability.

Self-defense

Depending on the specific facts of the situation, an accused person may claim that use of deadly force was justified to excuse his actions, which would otherwise be a crime. Self-defense or the defense of another is an affirmative defense that an accused may assert against a criminal charge for an assault or homicide offense.

The term "affirmative defense" means the accused, not the prosecutor, must prove by a preponderance of the evidence that he acted in self-defense or in defense of another. In other words, the defendant must prove that it is more probable than not that his use of deadly force was necessary due to the circumstances of the situation.

Whether this affirmative defense applies to the situation or whether it will likely succeed against criminal charges depends heavily on the specific facts and circumstances of each situation. The Ohio Supreme Court has explained that a defendant must prove three conditions to establish that he acted in defense of himself or another.

Condition 1: Defendant is not at fault

First, the defendant must prove that he was not at fault for creating the situation. The defendant cannot be the first aggressor or initiator.

However, in proving the victim's fault, a defendant cannot point to other unrelated situations in which the victim was the aggressor. Remember, the focus is on the specific facts of the situation at hand.

If you escalate a confrontation by throwing the first punch, attacking, or drawing your handgun, you are the aggressor. Most likely in this situation, you cannot legitimately claim self-defense nor would you likely succeed in proving your affirmative defense.

Condition 2: Reasonable and honest belief of danger

Second, the defendant must prove that, at the time, he had a real belief that he was in immediate danger of death or great bodily harm and that his use of deadly force was the only way to escape that danger. Bear in mind that deadly force may only be used to protect against serious bodily harm or death. The key word is "serious."

In deciding whether the bodily harm was serious, the judge or jury can consider how the victim attacked the defendant, any weapon the victim had, and how he used it against the defendant. Minor bruises or bumps from a scuffle probably do not meet the legal definition of "serious." In court cases, rape has been determined to be serious bodily harm, as has being attacked with scissors. Serious bodily harm also may result from being struck with an object that can cause damage, such as a baseball bat or a wooden club.

The defendant's belief that he is in immediate serious danger is important. The defendant's belief must be reasonable, not purely speculative. In deciding if the belief was reasonable and honest, the judge or jury will envision themselves standing in the defendant's shoes and consider his physical characteristics, emotional state, mental status, and knowledge; the victim's actions and words; and all other facts regarding the encounter. The victim must have acted in a threatening manner. Words alone, regardless of how abusive or provoking, or threats of future harm ("I'm going to kill you tomorrow") do not justify the use of deadly force.

Condition 3: Duty to retreat

A defendant must show that he did not have a duty to retreat or avoid the danger. A person must retreat or avoid danger by leaving or voicing his intention to leave and ending his participation in the confrontation. If one person retreats and the other continues to fight, the person who left the confrontation may later be justified in using deadly force when he can prove all three conditions of self-defense existed. You should always try to retreat from a confrontation before using deadly force if retreating does not endanger yourself or others.

If the person can escape danger by means such as leaving or using less than deadly force, he must use those means. If you have no means to escape the other person's attack and you reasonably, honestly believe that you are about to be killed or receive serious bodily harm, you may be able to use deadly force if that is the only way for you to escape that danger."

'Castle Doctrine'

"Castle Doctrine" generally encompasses the idea that a person does not have a duty to retreat from the residence he lawfully occupies before using force in self-defense or defense of another. Additionally, there is no duty to retreat if a person is lawfully in his vehicle or is lawfully an occupant in a vehicle owned by an immediate family member of that person.

However, being a lawful occupant of a residence or vehicle is not a license to use deadly force against an attacker. The person who is attacked, without fault of his own, may use deadly force only if he reasonably and honestly believed that deadly force was necessary to prevent serious bodily harm or death. If the person does not have this belief, he should not use deadly force. Again, if it does not put your life or the life of others in danger, you should withdraw from the confrontation if it is safe for you to do so.

The law presumes you to have acted in self-defense or defense of another when using deadly force if the victim had unlawfully and without privilege entered or was in the process of entering the residence or vehicle you occupy. The presumption does not apply if the defendant was unlawfully in that residence or vehicle. The presumption does not apply if the victim had a right to be in, or was a lawful resident of, the residence or vehicle.

The presumption of self-defense is a rebuttable presumption. The term "rebuttable presumption" means the prosecutor, and not the defendant, carries the burden of producing evidence contrary to the facts that the law presumes. However, a rebuttable presumption does not relieve the defendant of the burden of proof. If the prosecutor provides sufficient evidence to prove that the defendant created the confrontation or that the use of deadly force was not reasonably necessary to prevent death or great bodily harm, then the presumption of self-defense no longer exists.

Statutory Reference(s): ORC 2901.05 sets forth the rebuttable presumption.

ORC 2901.09(B) establishes that there is no duty to retreat before using force if a person is a lawful occupant of his vehicle or a lawful occupant in a vehicle owned by an immediate family member.

Defense of others

A person may defend another only if the protected person would have had the right to use deadly force in self-defense himself. Under Ohio law, a person may defend family members, friends, or strangers. However, just as if he were protecting himself, a person cannot use any more force than is reasonable and necessary to prevent the harm threatened.

A defendant who claims he used deadly force to protect another has to prove that he reasonably and honestly believed that the person he protected was in immediate danger of serious bodily harm or death and that deadly force was the only way to protect the person from that danger. Furthermore, the defendant also must show that the protected person was not at fault for creating the situation and did not have a duty to leave or avoid the situation.

WARNING: The law specifically discourages citizens from taking matters into their own hands and acting as law enforcement. This is true even if you think you are performing a good deed by protecting someone or helping law enforcement. The Ohio Supreme Court has ruled that a person risks criminal charges if he interferes in a struggle and protects the person who was at fault, even if he mistakenly believed that person did not create the situation.

In other words, if you misinterpret a situation and interfere, you may face criminal charges because your use of deadly force is not justified. If you do not know all the facts and interfere, you will not be justified to use force. It does not matter that you mistakenly believed another was in danger and not at fault.

Of greater concern than risking criminal charges is the fact that you may be putting yourself and others in danger. If you use your handgun to interfere in a situation and an officer arrives on the scene, the officer will not be able to tell if you are the criminal or if you are the Good Samaritan.

Ohio law does not encourage vigilantism. A license to carry a concealed handgun does not deputize you as a law enforcement agent. Officers are trained to protect members of the community, handle all types of situations, and enforce the law. Do not allow the license to carry a concealed handgun to give you a false sense of security or empowerment. Let law enforcement officers do their job. If you want to be a Good Samaritan, call the police.

Conclusion: Self-defense issues

If the defendant fails to prove any one of the three conditions for self-defense or defense of another, he fails to justify his use of deadly force. If the presumptions of deadly force in the home or vehicle are removed and the defendant is unable to prove that he did not create the situation or that the use of deadly force was reasonably necessary, he fails to justify his use of deadly force. Under either condition, if convicted, an individual will be sentenced accordingly.

Defense of property

There must be immediate threat of serious bodily harm or death in order to use deadly force. Protecting property alone does not allow for the use of deadly force. A property owner may use reasonable, but never deadly, force when he honestly believes that the force will protect his property from harm.

If a person's property is being attacked or threatened, he may not use deadly force unless he reasonably believes it was the only way to protect himself or another from being killed or receiving serious bodily harm. Deadly force can never be used solely to protect property no matter where the threat to the property occurs.

Conclusion

A license to carry a concealed handgun does not bring with it the automatic right to use deadly force. The appropriateness of using any force depends on the specific facts of each and every situation.

The author would like to thank Marie D'Amico, Esquire, for her assistance with this chapter.

CHAPTER FIVE:

TACTICS

1. To be a fair stand-up boxing match in a 24-foot ring, or as near that size as practicable.

2. No wrestling or hugging allowed.

3. The rounds to be of three minutes' duration, and one minute's time between rounds.

4. If either man falls through weakness or otherwise, he must get up unassisted, 10 seconds to be allowed him to do so, the other man meanwhile to return to his corner, and when the fallen man is on his legs the round is to be resumed and continued until the three minutes have expired. If one man fails to come to the scratch in the 10 seconds allowed, it shall be in the power of the referee to give his award in favour of the other man.

5. A man hanging on the ropes in a helpless state, with his toes off the ground, shall be considered down.

6. No seconds or any other person to be allowed in the ring during the rounds.

7. Should the contest be stopped by any unavoidable interference, the referee to name the time and place as soon as possible for finishing the contest; so that the match must be won and lost, unless the backers of both men agree to draw the stakes.

8. The gloves to be fair-sized boxing gloves of the best quality and new.

9. Should a glove burst, or come off, it must be replaced to the referee's satisfaction.

10. A man on one knee is considered down and if struck is entitled to the stakes.

11. That no shoes or boots with spikes or sprigs be allowed.

12. The contest in all other respects to be governed by revised London Prize Ring Rules.

~*"the Queensbury rules for the sport of boxing"*

~*John Graham Chambers (1865)*

~**Later to be known as the Marquess of Queensbury Rules*

Sportsmanship and fair play are worthy goals in sport, whether in the "sweet science" of boxing, the Ultimate Fighting Championship® or your child's soccer match.

There are no rules in a street fight. As Karlos proved to John, a standing fair "fist-fight" is an anathema. What may start as an empty-hand mano-a-mano "straighten-up," as the Brits refer to them, can change in an instant to a savage mass attack by multiple individuals, a knife assault or a felonious assault against you with a gun. Get the concept out of your head – there is no such thing as a fair fight.

CASE STUDY

While working security at an outdoor concert facility in the Midwest we responded to a fight call. The "fight" between two combatants had quickly turned into an assault when one grabbed a broken beer bottle and slashed the throat of the other. The victim was extremely lucky that day since the assailant just missed severing the victim's carotid arteries and the jugular veins in his neck. You could literally see these exposed blood vessels through the slashed open flesh.

We want to avoid the altercation if at all possible. We can help accomplish this by practicing awareness and preparedness.

THE RIGHT MIND

"All things are ready, if our minds be so."

~*William Shakespeare; Henry V, Act 4, Scene 3*

Awareness is the early warning radar of self-defense and the armed citizen. As we've already stated, being caught off guard or the victim of a surprise attack, necessitates us trying to play catch-up in the action/reaction (response) game. Oftentimes, surprised citizens or law enforcement officers are victimized before they can even formulate, let alone field, some type of response.

As related to the science of body language and victimization discussed earlier in this manual, criminals frequently seek out the seemingly least aware and prepared among us. Walking through a mall, parking lot or on a sidewalk, do not be distracted by the bane of the modern citizen, the smart phone. Talking or texting, even having ear buds in as you walk along, denies you the ability to see, attend to, acknowledge or respond to situations, attacks, encounters or pending threats to you or your companions.

You want to walk with your head up and scanning your environment. No, it does not require that you hop around in a paranoid state like John Belushi did as the character Bluto in the movie Animal House. It does mean that you are looking at, paying attention to and preparing responses to developments in your environment.

It is probably true that most victims are not aware that they are in the process of being victimized since they have missed the developing indicators. For instance, the subject has selected you based on his observation or surveillance. As trainer Payton Quinn said, you are being "interviewed" as a potential victim at this time and this is an interview you want to fail.

THE NATURE OF MOST ATTACKS: AMBUSH

Over the last couple of years we have seen ambush as the leading cause of death for law enforcement officers due to gunfire.

CASE STUDY

Four officers from the Lakewood, Washington, Police Department are inside a coffee shop at the beginning of their tour of duty. The opportunity to get some caffeine, work on some reports on their laptops and ease into the day is a routine that is repeated by law enforcement officers throughout this country (and probably throughout the world). As the officers are either sitting at a table or ordering their coffee, suspect Maurice Clemmons enters with two guns on his person and murder in his heart. As Officer Tina Griswold is sitting at the table with her back to Clemmons, he walks up behind her and shoots her in the back of the head, killing her. He then turns the semi-auto on Sgt. Mark Renninger and shoots and kills him, then his pistol jams. Officer Ronald Owens charges the suspect, who draws a back-up revolver and shoots and kills Officer Owens. Officer Gregory Richards attacks Clemmons; he draws his Glock .40 and is able to fire a shot, which strikes the cop killer in the abdomen. An intense close range gun battle commences and, despite being wounded, Clemmons is able to disarm the fourth officer and kills him with a shot to the head. Clemmons then runs away. Clemmons' cop killing will be stopped 42 hours later when he is shot and killed by a Seattle police officer.

This tragedy reminds law enforcement officers that there is never a time when you can lower your guard and you must always be ready. But I believe that most attacks against citizens are ambushes as well. There is no such thing as a fair fight, and most attacks – robberies, rapes and other criminal assaults – are some version of ambush.

That said, I ask my law enforcement students the following and I'll ask the same of you: How would you do it?

Say, for instance, you are a police officer assigned to go after a dangerous suspect. Rather than attempt the arrest in the environment where he is most dangerous, has superior knowledge of the terrain and has possible access to his weapons, you elect to "set him up" or ambush him elsewhere. Items to consider in your plan:

◆ Gather as much info as you can. Know your target.
◆ Learn his routine. Use it against him.
◆ Isolate him. Get him by himself and away from his stronghold and vehicle if possible.
◆ Take the offensive, don't be reactive.
◆ Attack at a chokepoint where his options are limited to surrender or become the recipient of overwhelming force.
◆ Maneuver him into your "kill zone" (for lack of a better term).
◆ Have the high ground advantage.
◆ Use cover.
◆ Use distraction.
◆ Use coordinated overwhelming force.
◆ Knock him on his heels (stun or disorient him).

How would tactical officers ambush this hostage taker as he was moving his hostage to a vehicle for getaway? With overwhelming force based on solid training and planning.

That said, we can see that criminals are using these same tactics against armed citizens and police officers. They are watching us and, based on their perceptions of our perceived awareness and ability to defend ourselves, they make a decision to assault or attack. How then can we reduce the likelihood of an ambush?

COUNTER-AMBUSH TACTICS

Knowing how you would "ambush" a violent suspect, counter-ambush tactics need to limit a criminal's use of these same methods against you. Avoid routine i.e. parking your car in the same place, the same time every day, locking up your business the same time and in the same way, etc. Limit "choke-points" – locations where you are isolated and have little room to move or maneuver. Deny opportunity by being a hard target. Scan your environment and what comes into it as to the potential threat it presents, and listen to your "gut instincts" about the potential for violence. All are solid counter-ambush tactics.

Once the trap is initiated, assaulting into the ambush is a standard military doctrine. To be effective in your response requires that your skills be second nature, i.e. stimulus (perception of the attack) leads to response (movement while drawing your pistol and getting accurate fire on target). Have you trained the presentation of your pistol (draw) from its holster to the point you can do it without conscious thought? An effective response to ambush requires it.

CASE STUDY

A female citizen has entered the vestibule of her apartment when she is attacked by a man who threatens to kill her if she does not comply. The female victim is forced out of the foyer and into her car where she drives the assailant to an ATM to withdraw money. The man then forces the victim to call a friend and bring more money before she is finally released.

To say this could have ended tragically is an understatement. To say that this lady was put through a terrible ordeal, one in which she feared for her life for several hours, is also an understatement.

Many victims do not understand when they are being lined up or interviewed by a potential attacker.

Whether the assailant has ambushed based on more extensive planning and surveillance or a hasty ambush based on target isolation and opportunity is irrelevant. The chances of becoming a victim of either can be reduced by proper awareness and scanning your environment for threats. You must understand the locations and environments when you are more isolated and more easily at-

Have you learned how to respond with deadly force while in a vehicle? An ambush may push your training to the limits for you to survive.

tacked. Passive security measures, such as closed circuit video cameras at an apartment building, businesses or other locations, may help identify an attack after the event, but they do little to prevent the assault or crime.

Many victims do not understand when they are being lined up or interviewed by a potential attacker.

CASE STUDY

A female clerk who is pregnant is working at a convenience store/gas station when a male enters, engages in mindless chatter about the weather, then closes the gap and punches her in the face from across the counter. He then rounds the counter area and forces the woman to open the cash register. Fortunately she is not seriously hurt.

Oftentimes this chit-chat is an "interview" by the criminal and you may not even know it. During this time he is ascertaining your awareness level, his ability to close the distance to get within close proximity to you and your ability to defend yourself. Many times we subconsciously perceive this interview and dismiss it as paranoia.

CASE STUDY

In Gavin DeBecker's excellent book The Gift of Fear (Dell; 1999), the author tells the story of an airline pilot who was troubled by an incident. The pilot had stopped off at a local convenience store to purchase a few magazines. The pilot got out of his car, opened the front door and something in his gut told him not to go inside. The pilot would later here of the armed robber inside who shot and killed a uniformed police officer as the officer walked into the store. The pilot was at a loss as to why he was spared and the officer lost his life. The pilot was able to recall seeing a vehicle in the lot with two subjects inside and the engine running, he remembers seeing the unease in the eye of the clerk as he began to open the door and seeing the suspect, who did not look at him and had an overly long/warm coat for the weather. DeBecker makes the point that the police officer possibly saw these same things when he walked into the store but ignored them. These "gut feelings" or survival signals are possibly subconscious perceptions we have not mentally processed and we ignore them at our peril. Survival signals are as much a part of our survival as any tactic or conscious thought. In law enforcement we call these "sixth sense" or "street sense." Unfortunately, since violent incidents don't happen that much, this police officer's experience may have led him to ignore these same signals.

Like the pilot in Gavin DeBecker's book, how many times do you go to this type of quick mart? Are you "tuned in" and listening to your "survival signals" when you do?

BEHIND THE WHEEL

When in your car on the way to work, home or any destination, look ahead in traffic scanning for hazards or developing risks ahead. You don't want to drive 65 mph only looking at the bumper of the vehicle directly ahead with only one car's length between your car and theirs. You want to check your rearview mirror for traffic behind or the side mirror when changing lanes. You limit distractions while driving, understanding that cell phone conversations expose you and whoever is in the car with you to risk. You don't text and drive because doing so reduces your response time worse than operating a vehicle under the influence of alcohol. If you don't practice these types of "tactics" while driving the result could be disastrous. If you are distracted or unaware, and wait until the car in front slams on their brakes before you brake, it means that you've not given enough distance (time) to respond and stop your forward momentum.

Even Mario Andretti could have caused an accident if he drove in the city without paying attention.

And yet, despite training and experience, many people violate these driving rules every day, causing accidents and injuries. Familiarity breeds contempt, as they say. But it also breeds inattentiveness and unawareness because – usually nothing much happens, does it?

CASE STUDY

Birmingham, Alabama – Just this weekend a five-year veteran of Birmingham PD was killed off-duty as he was behind the wheel of his personal vehicle in the parking area of a carry-out. Apparently as the officer exited the store the rider of a motorcycle accused him of hitting his motorcycle with his car door. Information is sketchy at this point, but the officer stated he had not hit the motorcycle, then entered his car whereupon he was shot and killed. The officer, a father of three, had just celebrated the birth of his first son two weeks prior.

MANIFESTED AWARENESS

You want to manifest your awareness of your environment and who comes into it. You don't necessarily want to appear challenging to subjects with your scrutiny, which may result in an aggressive, "What are you looking at?" But you do want to acknowledge their presence. This non-hostile type of manifested awareness has prevented an untold number of violent encounters for citizens and law enforcement alike. Simply stated, it is a non-verbal "I see you" and "You're not going to surprise me or victimize me."

Awareness is comprised of several different factors or elements:

◆ Acknowledgement of the threat – The first step towards self-protection and self-defense is an acknowledgement and acceptance that the threat actually exists.

◆ Refusal to be a victim ¬– The next step is that you make the decision to not be a victim and that if you attend to your environment the threat can be reduced, stopped outright or mitigated.

◆ Target hardening – You then set about making yourself, your family or significant others, your car and your home a hard target.

◆ Opportunity denial – Awareness denies easy opportunities for the individual to ambush, surprise attack or otherwise target you.

◆ Resolute – Being resolved means constantly attentive to your environment and determined to keep yourself and your loved ones safe.

◆ Determination – Determination manifests itself in the way you constantly scan and observe your environment, non-verbal communication in how you stand, move and carry yourself, as well as how you respond to negative changes to your environment.

◆ Vigilance – Thomas Jefferson said, "Eternal vigilance is the price of liberty." The modern self-defense equivalent is, "The cost of safety is eternal vigilance." You simply must be forever vigilant in attending to the safety of your environment.

◆ Habituation – Maintaining your awareness and preparing to defend yourself and your family/friends is a habit. We have good habits and bad ones. What you chose to develop is up to you.

◆ Observation – In order to react to a pending or active threat against you, you must first have observed it. This is not a casual glance but an educated view anticipating a threat. It is not paranoia, but mental preparation.

◆ Threat perception – Based on your observation you now perceive a threat. The circumstances have gone from a casual attention or observation to a specific person or set of circumstances.

◆ Threat identification – Observant to your environment and what is moving within it you are able to I.D. a specific person, vehicle or circumstances that pose danger or are threatening.

◆ Threat pattern analysis – The pattern or totality of the circumstances is quickly analyzed and assessed as to severity and threat level.

CASE STUDY

A young lady from the capitol city of my home state was recently on the news. One night she was stabbed by a robber in the parking area of the gym where she works out. After she recovered from her injuries, she and friends from the gym set about hardening their self-defense armor much as they had strengthening their muscles and fitness levels. They attended training programs in the Israeli martial art of Krav Maga and then went to a local firearms range where they went through a CCW course.

They are only part of the way to their goal, however. So much of self-defense and being effective as an armed citizen involves mental awareness and preparation. It's one thing to have the skills, it's quite another to be "dialed in" as military and police "operators" refer to the mental aspects of preparation.

CASE STUDY

You see a police officer whose equipment is in a sorry state and who is seemingly oblivious to the goings-on around him. Within seconds, you've made a mental assessment of the man and his ability to perform his job. On the street, suspects survey this officer based on a quick glance and come to the conclusion that he is no real threat to them. He is "tried and tested" on the street more than other officers because of his apparent lack of mental and physical preparation.

PROJECTED PREPAREDNESS

Along with awareness, the armed citizen can project a state of readiness or preparedness. This is not just the aura of a man or woman who is armed, but one who can take control of his environment and put forth an effective response to any type of attack.

- Competence – Competence is based on the ability to perform a task or function. When it comes to self-defense, competence radiates like an aura around you. Criminals, at least sober or non-impaired, mentally sound criminals, will pick up on a citizen who appears to be competently prepared. Quite simply, competence means that criminals attacking you are in more danger from you than you are from them.

- Confidence – Competence leads to confidence, a confident but not cocky air that you have the abilities to prevent or stop violence against you and yours. Confidence helps control the Sympathetic Nervous System, allowing you to operate more effectively.

- Composure – The ability to maintain your composure in emergencies can be developed through training and is an indicator of the prepared armed citizen.

- Readiness – An important part of readiness pertaining to the preparation of the armed citizen is the physical act of being armed. You are not "ready" to defend yourself by way of deadly force in a lethal assault against you if you are not armed or within one to two motions of arming. A Maserati in the driveway is no good if the gas tank is empty.

- Decisiveness – You must know self-defense law first and foremost and you must have preplanned, practiced and trained response. Knowledge, competence and confidence lead to decisiveness and the prevention of the tendency to dither in a confrontation or crisis.

- Intention – Inclination is fine; intention puts meaning and energy into your actions. A committed and intent man is a dangerous man and hard to stop.

- Dangerousness – Loosely defined as the ability to be violent or use violence. We desire and strive to be peaceful, but we are prepared to do violence against those who would hurt or kill us.

- Capacity – Indicates the ability to perform. In the armed citizen, capacity relates to physical ability and readiness but also to the mental capacity to perform acts of lawful violence in defense of oneself or others.

- Capability – As it relates to the armed citizen, means that you are capable and able.

Certainly there are overlaps in these elements, qualities and attributes, and this list is certainly not exhaustive.

What is most important is that all of the foregoing elements and qualities of awareness and projected preparedness can be developed. The primary method

The price of safety is training, preparedness and awareness.

to learn, perfect and develop these attributes is through research, study and training. Not one class or course, but a lifetime of study. Such is the price of personal safety.

CASE STUDY

A female police officer in the Midwest is confronting a hyper-violent individual in an armed encounter. Rather than shoot the suspect, she voluntarily disarms herself to show him she means him no harm. He shoots and seriously wounds her. She was lucky to have survived, but is forced to retire from the police agency based on her injuries.

CASE STUDY

From 1989 to 1992, a watch dealer in Los Angeles arms himself with a .38 revolver after several merchants in the area are robbed. Soon after, two armed robbers enter his store. "In an instant, I decided not to be a victim." He shoots and wounds one of the robbers with a shot to the face. "I was scared to death!" Lance Thomas went to the range and began improving his odds by practicing at the pistol range as well as working out at the gym. Lance obtained several more handguns and strategically placed them in his shop and also worked out tactics in his head as to what he would do if he was robbed again. Less than four months later he was robbed again. Two armed robbers come through the door with guns out. Thomas came out firing, and in the ensuing gun battle killed the robbers while he got on the phone and called 911 for help. Lance Thomas was wounded in the gunfight but stated, "I'm faced with an armed intruder. Now, I have to make a mental decision to be a victim of his mercy or exercise the right of self-defense and fight back. In fighting back, part of that is the willingness to die and to kill. Hard choice!" In two years after this shooting, Lance improved the security in his store, hired a part-time security guard, trained at the range and increased his weaponry. Then his store was robbed again by a pistol wielding robber. Lance Thomas grabbed a pistol and fired killing the robber. Thomas was again wounded and survived. When asked by a reporter "Why do anything? If you hadn't reached for your gun, maybe you wouldn't have gotten shot?" Lance Thomas responded, "Would have been up to him wouldn't it? He had his finger on the trigger, and he intended to negotiate. There's no negotiation. My life is too precious for that."

Lance Thomas then installed a double security door in his shop. Robbers came in anyway. Two robbers affiliated with one of L.A.'s most violent street gangs came into the store. While in the store acting as customers they went to leave then pivoted, raised their weapons, said, "You're dead!" and open fired. Lance Thomas was quicker though and shot and killed both robbers.

A police investigator assigned to the shootings stated that every robber had an extensive violent criminal history and that Thomas was completely justified in everything he did.

Lance Thomas survived four different shootings at his watch shop until he closed up and moved to a private on-call style of doing business.

~Justice Files TV Show; Don Kladstrup, reporting

Two different and distinct mind-sets and mental preparations – one, a law enforcement officer employed, armed and charged by society to protect and serve, as she enforces the law, the other a citizen forced by increasing crime and violent criminals to arm to protect himself and conduct his lawful business.

The officer was empowered by her city as a law enforcer, yet unwilling and/or unable to employ deadly force to stop a threat against her, the other an armed citizen who refused to be a victim.

The similarity here is that both were armed or had firearms readily available and had trained in their use. The analogy stops there however. The differences are so stark, obvious and so tragic that they exemplify the proper mental preparation versus submission and subsequent victimization.

The late firearms trainer, Jeff Cooper (known as the Father of the Modern Technique), compared men who owned guns with musicians, stating, "Owning a handgun doesn't make you armed any more than owning a guitar makes you a musician."

The good thing is that you don't have to be a "steely-eyed-killer" to be an armed citizen and effectively defend your life or the life of your family or

As Colonel Jeff Cooper stated, "owning" a firearm doesn't mean you're prepared. That takes diligent study, practice and intent.

friends. You can develop these mental attributes, which have proven to work over the years for law enforcement officers, military personnel, security professionals and armed citizens at home, on the street or at work.

In September 2012, the F.B.I. published Killed in the Line of Duty: A Study of Selected Felonious Killings of Law Enforcement Officers (1992: Uniform Crime Reports Section; Federal Bureau of Investigation: United States Department of Justice). From that report:

Offenders' perspectives

The offenders were asked what, in their opinion, the victim officers could have done, if anything, to prevent their deaths. Because of lack of eyewitness or surviving officers, the exact facts surrounding the initial confrontation between the offenders and the officers are quite difficult to verify independently. 8% of the offenders felt that if the officers had been more "professional," these officers may not have lost their lives.

Some offenders responded to this phase of the study by indicating that they felt that they had the tactical edge on the officers even before the officers were aware of the imminent threat. In these cases, the killers did not shift the blame to the officers by stating that the officers could have taken an alternate course of action to prevent their deaths.

Here we see the failure of a combination of different elements in officer survival.

First is that officers who win armed or violent confrontations have a different mental approach, they believe that, A) "It" does in fact happen, B) That "it" can indeed happen to them, C) That they must train and prepare, and D) That their tactics and training will save their life.

They believe in the following concepts:
- Acceptance of the existence of dangerous men and women
- That a winning mindset is vital – that despite what they are confronted

with, they can win the day

◆ Winning is dependent on training and preparation
◆ Regularly conducted skill building and skill maintenance practice is necessary
◆ That they must have a conscious awareness of their environment and subjects within their environment
◆ That they must have mental and physical options trained to a competent level and thought out
◆ That they will experience fear, but can control the Sympathetic Nervous System with their training and autogenic breathing

Many times armed self-defense can turn into a hardware conversation or a focus on guns and gear when it should be mostly about "software" or the mental aspects of winning. Hundreds, no, thousands of people have saved their lives with .22 caliber firearms or what some would consider antiquated pistols, shotguns and rifles. Indeed, the old quote; "Beware the man with one gun, because he probably knows how to use it…" comes to mind. An intent man or woman focused on stopping a threat against them, their children or family member can be a hard thing to stop.

CASE STUDY

Several years ago my wife took time off from work to help take care of her elderly mother who was in home hospice care. My mother-in-law was mostly confined to a hospital bed in the home of another daughter. On the day in question, I was actually teaching new law enforcement firearms instructors for the state academy. My subject before an hourly break had been the Sympathetic Nervous System and fear control. My wife called on the break. She had been sitting in the front living room of the house when she heard a noise and looked up to see a strange man standing inside the side door

It's not about hardware, it's about software – will, drive, intent, among other mental attributes.

of the house. Challenging him with a "What are you doing here?" He responded with a weird comment of, "Well…what are you doing?" She immediately ran to a bedroom and grabbed her sister's .38 special revolver. Coming back to the living room she got into a two handed isosceles stance, pointed the handgun at the subject and ordered him to "Get out!" in a loud voice. The subject stammered but went out the door.

After the subject departed, her knees started knocking and the inevitable "parasympathetic backlash" occurred, which is your body regulating itself after a stressful incident. During the backlash, your hands may shake, you may become exhausted, feel light-headed or even become nauseous as your body deals with the residual stress chemicals such as adrenalin and noradrenalin.

My wife received a call from a family member who reported that the man was a friend who had been hired to perform repairs at the house and to whom my wife's sister had given a house key.

All of this could have been avoided with communication and advisement from the sister that the man was coming. Further, he should have knocked on the door rather than just entering the home. Additionally he should have said, "Excuse me…" and alerted my wife to his presence and his reason for being there. Because my wife had been trained to understand the body and mind's response to stress as well as shooting and tactics, it ended well. Without that training and just possessing a gun, it could have been a catastrophe.

Put simply, in addition to having the equipment, you must know how to competently use your deadly and non-deadly force options, observe pending danger, strategically avoid if possible, be prepared to repel or stop the threat efficiently while handling the stress of the encounter – to shoot (if necessary), move and communicate.

WHEN/THEN THINKING

"Victims focus on their vulnerabilities, survivors focus on their ability to respond." ~Ultimate Survivors video, Calibre Press, 1991

When I first started in law enforcement, the concept of "If/Then" thinking was introduced. The notion was that by visualizing a "Plan A" if things went south when dealing with a violent subject, you would lower your response time and be more efficient in your reaction.

Law enforcement trainer and retired lawman (Coach) Bob Lindsey (ILEETA law enforcement trainer of the year, 2013) rephrased the concept to "When/ Then" thinking. It is not the idea that "if" it happens but rather "when" it does. This mental paradigm shift more fully prepares you for a response to violence. By constantly asking yourself, "When this happens…then I will respond by doing this…" you have preloaded your response. All you await is the stimulus of an attack or threat.

When/then thinking is all about developing tactical options.

CASE STUDY

At the graduation banquet of a police academy class held at a local hotel banquet room, a young officer who was a former Marine and combat veteran of Fallujah came up to my wife and me as we were leaving. "Officer Davis," he said as he shook my hand, "There are five entrances and exits to this room." What the cadet was referring to is my intonation during his training that you should be aware of the physical layout of the room you are in and scout for escape routes, cover opportunities and where threats might emerge. Further, that you should always scan as people enter/exit the room and approach your position. While we talked, I had my right hand in my pocket. In that pocket I had an Uncle Mike's nylon pocket holster holding a Glock 26, 9mm semi-auto pistol. There is preparation and then there is "real preparation."

This same When/Then thinking has been played out for me for years and years and served me well. When I walked my eldest daughter down the aisle, looking quite dapper in my tuxedo, I had that same Glock 26 in an Uncle Mike's ankle holster (tuxedo trousers look good but usually lack belt loops which allow you to carry a belt holster, and the jackets oftentimes prevent quick access to the belt carried handgun as well).

When/then thinking is based on tactical options.

Pocket holster similar to the one the author carried on that day and his current second gun method of carry.

Many of the detectives at that time carried S&W Chief's Special revolvers but placed them in their desks or in the glove boxes of their DB cars versus carrying the issue S&W 5906. Thankfully things have changed.

THE TACTICAL OPTIONS CONTINUUM

"If all you have is a hammer, everything looks like a nail."
~Bernard Baruch

The armed citizen has as his final option deadly force, but that is not the only option.

Years ago I was assigned to research and report on the equipment, training and tactical response capability of my agency's detective personnel. What I found was shocking. Many detectives at the time (mid to late 90s) did not even carry firearms on duty. They would lock their handguns in the glove boxes of their plain clothes cars parked in the basement or would take off their sidearm and place it in their desk drawers. Most did not carry handcuffs during their duty day either.

Those who carried a handgun would frequently carry a five shot revolver in .38 special with no reloads on their person. Now, keep in mind that this was a time when our agency had recently shifted to carrying a 15-shot 9mm pistol as a duty sidearm and allowed a smaller capacity semi-auto to be carried in plain-clothes or off-duty. Yet, these detectives chose, based on the faulty assumption that their risk was minimal, to carry a handgun with only five rounds available. If they were involved in a shooting, and exhausted those five rounds, they had a very poor club to use.

Further, the detectives force options were limited to empty hand control (punching or striking a suspect) and shooting them. These are the only options they had available, but not the most effective or lawful. Just because you don't have any non-deadly force options available, does not mean you can shoot some-one who poses a non-deadly threat.

The Tactical Options Continuum includes:
- ◆ escape or avoidance
- ◆ police assistance and intervention
- ◆ verbal de-escalation techniques

- ◆ empty hand control
- ◆ non-deadly force options (pepper spray, taser, etc.)
- ◆ deadly force

This is not to say that you must exhaust other options prior to using deadly force if you are attacked by a man armed with a knife or gun. It simply means that, to be truly ready and prepared for defense of self, family, friends and home, you must have equipped and trained in other options. These options can also be used in your defense after a shooting incident as well.

Let's examine a hypothetical interview with a police detective after you've shot and killed an armed robber *with the presence of your attorney during the interview:

Detective: Mr. Smith couldn't you have just run away?

You: Detective the man had a gun and I was in fear of my life. If I had tried to run away I might have gotten shot in the back.

Detective: Did you see him approach? Couldn't you have avoided contact?

You: I attempted to move away from the man when I first saw him but he continued do move toward me. I warned him to stay away but he kept coming toward me and boxed me in. I didn't see his gun in his hand until he was too close. I had my pepper spray out as I was walking but it was not an option.

Detective: Why was pepper spray not an option?

You: If he had no gun and just threatened me or was going to attempt to rob me by force, I could have tried to pepper spray him, but he showed me his gun and I had no choice.

Let's say the individual never presented a deadly threat and just menaced you instead. In this case, avoidance and verbal warnings may have worked but when it did not, you had the option to use pepper spray. With more options available, you give yourself the ability to control a non-deadly threat with other means rather than resorting to deadly force. The reason law enforcement officers use pepper spray and electronic control weapons, like the Taser, is that they are remote controls that can be applied from a distance (there are always risks in close range or hand to hand confrontations), are effective, are less injurious to the officer and cause less injuries to the suspect. These factors can all benefit the armed citizen as well.

TACTICAL BASICS: FIREARM SELECTION

There have been books and thousands of articles written on firearm selection for self-defense. Indeed, I've written my fair share. I'll refer the reader to these books for more detailed coverage, especially the works of Massad Ayoob, such as The Gun Digest Book of Concealed Carry and The Gun Digest Book of Combat Handgunnery, among Mas's many other titles.

I'll just break the subject matter down into the basics: the firearm must be well made and reliable, be accurate, have decent sights and trigger, with sufficient power to stop an assailant, contain enough bullets or shells, and be relatively easy to shoot under stress.

That said, thousands if not tens of thousands of citizens have defended themselves over the millennia with single barrel shotguns, rifles and all manner of handgun – from the rusty old six-shooter to two-shot derringers.

What we strive for and are most aided by is an efficient and reliable tool (firearm) to help us accomplish our task, which is to save our life or that of a family or loved one.

This is best accomplished by a modern, reliable firearm. It need not be the most expensive handgun or long-gun on the market or some custom design (indeed these can be finicky and not the most reliable). It just has to effectively do its job.

In the cop world, law enforcement officers in the late 80s early 90s began switching to modern semi-auto pistol designs. Smith & Wesson, Glock, Sig Sauer pistols began showing up in the holsters of modern lawmen. Indeed, all of the aforementioned makers, as well as Colt, Remington, Taurus, Ruger, Beretta and many others, make quality and reliable firearms in calibers of sufficient size (9mm, .45 and .40) to stop criminal suspects.

In most cases five or six shot revolvers and smaller caliber (.38 special and .380) handguns have been relegated to off-duty or back-up role in law enforcement. As well, higher capacity handguns now dominate law enforcement with the average uniform officer carrying more than 46 rounds of ammo on his person – with three magazines of at least 15 rounds of 9mm (which is the most popular caliber) and one round in the chamber of the holstered pistol.

This is not to say that you are not served by carrying a single-stack .45 or .40 Glock with less than 15 rounds onboard.

Over the years we have found that semi-auto pistols are easier to shoot and normally contain more rounds than a revolver. The ease of shooting has to do with the trigger manipulation, which can be substantially easier than a revolver

(15 pounds over a longer trigger arc of movement in a revolver fired in double action, versus a five pound press of a standard Glock or S&W M&P

Excellent concealed holster the Phantom by Raven Concealment Systems and a dual spare magazine carrier by BladeTech.

S.A.F.E. Act compliant carry for New York state. DoubleStar 1911 with Wilson magazines loaded with seven rounds of Liberty Ammunition .45 ammo. Unfortunately the Wilson mags must be downloaded from eight to seven to be within the law.

pistol). That higher capacity handgun doesn't mean that you have to shoot 15 rounds or more at an assailant, it just means you are capable of firing 16 rounds before a reload is necessary.

Unfortunately, a few states – New York and Colorado as example – have passed laws that limit magazine capacity and rounds that can be carried on-board. The New York state S.A.F.E. Act which accomplished the exact opposite, limits handguns carried in that state to magazines which can hold ten or less but can only be loaded with seven rounds. Even as a traveling lawman, unless on official business such as a prisoner extradition or investigation, I have to carry my Glock 26 (ten-round magazines) loaded with only seven rounds in each. What is amazing in New York is that I can carry 20 magazines on my person but they are limited to seven rounds in each. In Colorado, Governor Hickenlooper signed into law a bill passed by the state legislature that limits magazines purchased after the date signed to 15 rounds. Even lawmen that carried Glock 17s or S&W M&P pistols while on-duty, when they retire, cannot purchase new magazines that can hold more than 15 rounds.

Note – This is not to say that retired lawmen should be exempt. Indeed some police unions and groups such as the International Association of Chiefs of Police are short-sighted in this regard, advocate for gun control and against citizen concealed carry. They don't understand that, once retired, law enforcement officers are bound by these draconian gun laws as well. Of course, the IACP are made up of increasingly political chiefs of police, oftentimes more interested in staying in office. It should be noted that a survey completed by PoliceOne. com of 15,000 law enforcement officers was pro Second Amendment and pro concealed carry for citizens.

*At this time it is unclear if the magazine limit is in effect. The NYSAFE website still indicates that magazines must be limited to ten round capacity with only seven rounds loaded. CCW permit holders must know the law. If you are traveling and have reciprocity in that state, you must comply with state law.

Your ammunition must be a reliable performer and expander. Here Remington representatives conduct ballistic testing on their excellent handgun ammunition.

More rounds on board mean that you can deal with a worst case scenario – multiple bad guys, longer gun fight – than you can with a semi-auto holding eight rounds or a revolver stuffed with six shots.

CALIBER AND AMMUNITION

We carry handguns concealed because of their ease of carry and the ability to hide them from view, not because it is the best choice in defending our lives. If and when we have time, long guns – shotguns, carbines and rifles – are ballistically more effective. Handguns in the calibers of 9mm, .38 special, .357 magnum, .40 S&W, .45 GAP and .45 ACP are all capable of stopping an assailant, with the right ammunition. If we were talking about full-metal jacketed rounds, the largest bullet, .45 ACP at an average of 230 grains, makes the most sense. Bigger bullet, bigger hole with non-expanding bullets, this is why many special operations units that are restricted by the Hague Convention from carrying expanding ammo

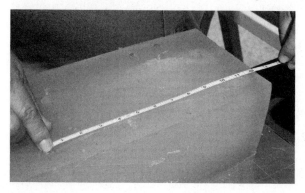

We want adequate penetration without over-penetration. Remington Golden Saber Bonded fills the bill.

carry Government Model 1911 semi-auto-pistols such as the excellent Colt Close Quarters Battle Pistol for Marine MARSOC – Marine Corps Forces Special Operations Command operators.

By and large I would not recommend calibers smaller than .380 or .38 special for self-defense. Yes, .22s and .25s can and have been used successfully by armed citizens to stop deadly threats, but they do not have a high probability for doing so. If they did, LEOs and the military would carry them. If physical limitations such as arthritis or other limitation makes it impossible for you to shoot or fire a larger caliber, then these sub-calibers can be used. Seek out the best ammunition available in .22 or .25 to improve your performance, and practice to achieve the best accuracy possible.

When we talk about law enforcement and private citizens' ammunition however, we see that the 9mm is the most widely issued caliber carried by domestic law enforcement officers. Many large agencies carried .40 caliber pistols but even the Federal Bureau of Investigation is reported to be changing to the 9mm based on improved hit performance on target and reduced recoil. My own experience is that, despite being a larger officer, I do not enjoy the "snappy" recoil of the .40. My agency has had several shootings with our 9mm pistols and they have fared well. As an instructor, I have seen ladies who have been forced to shoot .40 caliber pistols because their husbands were enamored with the caliber, only to develop a flinch and fail or struggle with qualification courses.

Fellow Ohio lawman, trainer and blogger Greg Ellifritz at ActiveResponseTraining.net has completed and published a caliber study based on actual shootings. His articles An Alternate Look at Handgun Stopping Power and Handgun Stopping Power: Science vs. 40 years of Experience are interesting reading. Ellifritz reports, after studying 1,800 shootings, that the average number of rounds to stop a person is:

Here a Remington Golden Saber Bonded 124 grain bullet is removed from ballistic gelatin.

According to studies by Greg Ellifritz there is little difference in performance between 9mm, .40 and .45 such as these excellent Black Hills rounds.

- .45 = 2.08
- .40 = 2.36
- 9mm = 2.45

Ellifritz covers stopping power with every caliber from .25ACP to .44 Magnums, shotguns and rifles, and his articles are worth your time.

CASE STUDY

As a law enforcement officer my own perspective is that shot placement is the key. You must accurately deliver fire into a suspect's mediastinum (upper chest area – where the heart and major blood vessels lie), the brainstem or the lateral pelvis. I once rolled onto a homicide in which the deceased, a bad-guy, was deader than a doornail from one shot from a .25ACP pistol. The .25 FMJ round had penetrated his heart and stopped him immediately with death only a few steps away. Other than headshots on victims I've responded to on the street, this is one of the few "one shot stops" I've witnessed.

Hit placement is the key. For more in this regard, I would recommend our friend Dr. James Williams' Tactical Anatomy book and course. Dr. Williams is an E.R. doc, shooter, hunter and police trainer who lectures law enforcement and qualified citizens on the subject. Try Dr. Williams site at TacticalAnatomy.com for his training schedule and book.

THE MYTH OF THE ONE-SHOT STOP

The purpose of modern expanding ammunition is to improve performance on target while not over-penetrating. According to ballistic and forensic experts, we want a decent amount of penetration while not passing completely through the human body, which often happens when using full-metal jacket or round nose bullets.

CASE STUDY

In 1986, members of the FBI in Florida were hunting for serial armed robbers who had hit several banks and an armored car in the Miami area leaving two guards wounded. It was later found that the two robbers – Michael Platt and William Matix had previously killed a citizen and stolen his car. They would shoot and wound another citizen and steal his car as well. An FBI task force encountered the suspects in the stolen car and, fearing more lives lost if they did not act, rammed the car. In the ensuing gun battle, Platt, armed with a .223 carbine, killed two FBI agents and wounded five others before being shot to death by FBI Agent Edmundo Mireles. Amazingly, Platt was able to shoot and kill two

The FBI began looking into the stopping power of handgun rounds in an attempt to improve agents effectiveness in shootings. In 1989, Special Agent Urey Patrick wrote Handgun Wounding Factors and Effectiveness.

From S.A. Patrick's report we read, "Realistic and regular law enforcement training must counterbalance and mentally and emotionally override the fallacy of the one-shot drop still promoted by some media. Short of disrupting the brain or severing the upper spinal column, immediate incapacitation does not occur."

"Physiologically, a determined adversary can be stopped reliably and immediately only by a shot that disrupts the brain or upper spinal cord. Failing to hit the center nervous system, massive bleeding from holes in the heart, or major blood vessels of the torso causing circulatory collapse is the only way to force incapacitation upon an adversary, and this takes time. For example, there is sufficient oxygen within the brain to support full, voluntary action for 10 to 15 seconds after the heart has been destroyed."

"A review of law enforcement shootings clearly suggests that regardless of the number of rounds fired in a shooting, most of the time only one or two solid torso hits on the adversary can be expected."

This FBI panel led to the Bureau adopting the 10mm as its caliber. This transition was never successful, however, with agents complaining of recoil and other factors. The FBI then adopted the .40 S&W as its caliber and used that for many years. It has already been noted that, at this point, information I have received is that the agency is moving back to 9mm as its caliber of choice.

There has been the myth of the one-shot stop over the years with witty sayings such as, "They all fall to hardball!" implying that the 230 grain .45 round is the most reliable stopper.

CASE STUDY

I met a former law enforcement officer who now works for a major firearms manufacturer. He related a shooting he was involved in where, undercover posing as a stolen goods "fence," he was encountered by a large man armed with a knife attempting to rob him as he sat behind his desk in his "office." The detective shot the man in center torso with one round of .45ACP, 230 grain hardball. The round traveled through the suspect and skittered along the ground as the suspect stayed upright and in the fight. The lawman prevailed, but he related that it was not because of the infamous 230 grain FMJ he fired into the suspect and it was certainly not a "one-shot stop."

Don't get me wrong, I have a couple of .45 semi-auto pistols that I am very fond of. I trust my life in my DoubleStar 1911. However, all my .45s use expanding hollow-point ammunition.

Once again, many books and article have been written on ammunition. Trainers like Mas Ayoob have attended autopsies and examined hundreds if not thousands of shooting reports. I would refer the reader to Mas's writings and to work done by eminent ballistician Dr. Martin Fackler, M.D. for more.

Liberty Ammunition's Civil Defense loads use a solid copper projectile, which is devastating in soft tissue but penetrates sufficiently as well.

There is a lot of great ammunition available to the armed citizen. Remember that the goal is to have adequate penetration to hit the "good stuff" within a target's body and not over-penetrate. Understand that the one-shot stop is a myth and that, even when individuals are hit with devastating rounds in the mediastinum, they can have enough oxygenated blood in their system to stay upright and dangerous for quite some time.

As medical professionals who study deaths in military combat have stated, most battlefield deaths are due to exsanguination or blood loss. This takes time. While this is good for you, meaning that if you are wounded, most injuries are survivable, it also means that you should continue shooting until the threat is stopped and this may take multiple rounds. This is another reason why higher capacity pistols are recommended.

Master competition shooter and instructor Ron Avery puts stopping power this way, "Air in, blood out." The more rounds you put effectively on target, the better chance the individual will stop.

READY POSITIONS

Based on perception of the threat, there are a variety of different positions that allow you to confront threats, search, move around people and to fire more effectively.

Hand on the holstered pistol

Placing your hand on a holstered pistol is certainly the first step in a successful draw stroke or presentation of the pistol from the holster. It is not a panacea however. Too many officers are shot and killed when confronting a threat by just placing their hand on the pistol instead of drawing it. Placing your hand on a gun is not a serious deterrent to a street criminal. Further, it does not raise a "force

Getting your hand on your pistol, if the situation dictates, is faster than a standard draw.

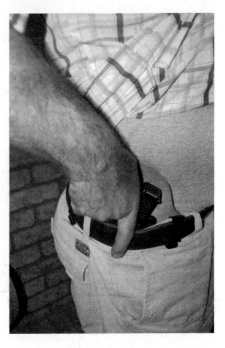

field" around you to protect you from incoming bullets. In many street thugs' world, even pointing a gun at them poses little threat. I've pointed all manner of firearms at suspects. It was the tactically sound thing to do at the time, and more than a few simply turned and fled.

Placing your hand on your pistol can be used when there is not a defined threat but only the possibility of a threat, e.g. a suspicious individual who approaches you late at night while you've pumping gas and does not heed your warnings to, "Stay back!" It could be just an aggressive panhandler or a robber, the idea is that without perceiving a deadly threat you want to add emphasis to your verbal warnings. It should be noted that this is a preparatory tactic when you feel real fear based on the totality of the circumstances.

In most states, your Concealed Carry Permit is in jeopardy for reckless display or unreasonable threatening with the gun.

There is an old and stupid saying that, "The only time my handgun comes out of its holster is when it's smoking." Consider that having a gun in hand speeds response time. Even the fastest draw stroke cannot beat an already drawn pistol. With that said, we must understand that we should not draw a pistol without provocation. In most states, your Concealed Carry Permit is in jeopardy for reckless display or unreasonable threatening with the gun. Depending on the circumstances, this may even equate to criminal charges against you for menacing or assault. So, drawing a gun must be a conscious act in response to a threat that you can articulate based on the totality of the circumstances.

The question then is, what ready position do you assume? The answer is that all of the following, as well as having your firearm in hand, are options.

Hidden or low profile ready

Some may argue with this, but street cops have long drawn their handguns and held them behind their legs, hidden from view, in traffic stops and other suspicious person encounters. Held behind the same side leg, the handgun can be elevated onto target in short order to stop a deadly threat. If you live in a high-crime area and there is a loud knock on your front door at night and the sound of a drunken individual, it might behoove you to draw your pistol or get it from your quick access safe and hold it in your hand behind the evening paper. Taking a look through your door's peephole, you can warn the person away. If you must open the door to speak with the subject, hopefully you have a well-installed security chain that prevents the door from opening all the way and can withstand a kick from the potential intruder.

The problem with having gun in hand is that you cannot shoot simply because you have your firearm out, so reholstering is necessary if you are wrong in your assessment of danger or that non-deadly force is necessary.

Low ready

Standard low ready is with the muzzle depressed at about a 45-degree angle downward. Many systems only teach this ready position, but consider that if you were to rotate around a 360-degree circle with your handgun or long-gun at low ready you would inevitably sweep the muzzle across others from their hips to their feet depending on the distance they are from you. This sweeping could include innocents, family members or whoever is within distance.

Further, low ready may mean that you are not pointing the handgun at a specific threat and are completely off target with your muzzle. If you are challenging a threat at gunpoint or are holding a man until the police arrive, and he suddenly goes for a gun, your muzzle is not on target. Low ready then is useful when you have no specific threat and when you want the muzzle pointed downward.

High ready

If you have a potential threat and are holding them at gunpoint or have not been threatened with death and cannot yet fire, then holding on the hips of the individual accomplishes a couple of good things. First, if the person suddenly presents a threat such as attempting

Standard low ready is at approximately a 45 degree outward angle.

to draw his own gun, then you can fire immediately. Second, by lowering your muzzle to a point on his hips you can more easily see his hands and what is in them. Additionally, holding at low ready or high ready on the hips is less fatiguing than holding at point shoulder position.

Chest ready or air marshal ready

Pulling the pistol into the chest, which would be position three of a four-count draw stroke, the top and back of the slide is held about one hand spread from the chin. Your forearms are held against the ribs with the muzzle pointed toward the threat. In this ready position the handgun is pulled closer to your center and not at arm's reach so that you have more control over the handgun and your profile is reduced. Chest ready is appropriate when entering a small room to

Chest or FAM ready has the pistol within arm's reach of the chin with the forearms resting on the ribs.

search, such as a bathroom or within a doorway or tight confines where a more extended position is not possible. This ready position is taught to Federal Air Marshals to use in the close confines of the passenger compartment of an aircraft.

There is a variation in which the muzzle is canted downward. The thought is to have the support of the forearms on the ribs while having the muzzle pointed at the deck. I'm partial to the muzzle being parallel with the floor.

CASE STUDY

I once responded to a burglary call with other officers. I encountered the suspect coming out a second story window. I held the suspect at gunpoint as I had him hang halfway out the open bedroom window, with my flashlight held in what is known as the Chapman Flashlight Technique, until the key holder arrived and other officers entered the home and took him. This took some time, around 15 minutes, and holding close in at high ready, I did not fatigue while covering him with my 9mm pistol.

Chest tuck or CQB position

This would be count two of our four-count drawstroke. The pistol is held in one hand at the side pectoral area. As an index, the shooting thumb is held against the side of the pec. The pistol should be canted slightly outboard to allow the slide to reciprocate in firing. The shooting elbow is pointed to the rear.

This ready position offers more control and is even tighter to the body than

Position 2 of the 4 count draw-stroke is the pistol indexed at the outside of the pectoral area and canted slightly outboard.

Here the author demonstrates shooting extreme close quarters using the chest tuck technique.

chest ready. If you are moving forward to open a door or need your support hand to do something, then you can pull the handgun back into this tuck position to maintain control, prevent an attempted gun takeaway and shoot if necessary. Since accuracy in shooting from chest tuck is affected by the angle of the wrist, this position is not accurate past five feet or so.

Position Sul is a transition position versus a ready position and not to be used when confronted by a threat.

Position Sul

Firearms trainer and former Marine Max Joseph is credited with developing Position Sul. Sul is Portuguese for South and was developed when Joseph was training forces in Brazil. It should be noted that Position Sul is not a "ready position," but a transition position when other more affective positions cannot be assumed and should never be used if a deadly threat is encountered. In Sul, the handgun is held against the chest with muzzle pointed downward between the feet. Position Sul can be used when you are in close confines to others and can have the handgun protected by the off-hand. Sul can also be used to transition from one position to the next. Imagine you are facing forward with your handgun at low ready and want to turn around to encounter a perceived threat. Rather than turn with muzzle at a 45-degree angle and "flag" or "laser" others with your muzzle, you pull back to your center chest, point the muzzle at the floor and pivot, then extend the handgun at low ready or point shoulder position.

Critics of position Sul state that it is a weak wrist angle to hold a handgun, and that is certainly true; but when used for its intended purpose it averts the muzzle from covering friendlies.

Indoor ready is for a long-gun when moving inside a structure or within close confines. Here author works from indoor ready with 12 gauge pump shotgun.

Indoor ready

Indoor ready position is used for long-guns and allows a tighter profile than low ready. In the Indoor Ready position, the muzzle is pointed down and outboard toward the floor. Exercise care to not point the muzzle at the support side foot. Imagine you are in the center of a Hula Hoop®. The muzzle would be inside this hoop or what some call your "safety circle."

If a door needs to be opened or a threshold crossed while using a long-gun, indoor ready allows this to be done.

One-handed ready positions

All of the foregoing ready positions can be accomplished with one hand and indeed may have to be. Remember it is a handgun, not a handsgun. Our off-hand may need to be freed up to open doors, push back offenders, hold flashlights, maneuver our loved ones out of the way, etc.

Point shoulder or up on target

If there is a defined threat at more than muzzle extension distance, then the handgun and long-gun should be up at eye level. The target area on the threat, which usually equates to "center of mass" on the individual, the front sight and the rear sight are all in a line. This is true whether we are focusing on the sights or not. This is the default position we aspire to – both hands on the handgun held

Remember it is a "handgun" not a "handsgun" and oftentimes you may have to use your off-hand for something else, such as holding or fending.

Shooting great Todd Jarrett demonstrates the two-hand point shoulder position using a modern isosceles stance.

at extension, sights in view. We always shoot better from this position, which is count four of the four-count draw stroke.

ALL positions should be assumed with finger off the trigger and outside the trigger guard unless you are taking a shot at a threat. Scientific studies have indicated the presence of what has been called a sympathetic press or interlimb effect (Involuntary Muscle Contractions and Unintentional Discharge of a Firearm; Roger M. Enoka, PhD; 2003). Dr. Enoka's study has been supported by further research reported by Force Science (Dr. Bill Lewinski; Force Science Institute; Force Science News #3; Can You Really Prevent Unintentional Discharges) with data conducted from research my German PhD candidate Christopher Heim:

"A large number of different groups of muscles in different parts of the body work together." These "involuntary muscle actions" can play a role in unintentional discharges by affecting the grip and trigger finger. Besides a sudden loss of balance and the use of other limbs (during a rapid tactical building entry or a struggle with an attacker, as examples), Heim believes that a "startle reaction" can also stimulate a dangerous involuntary muscle reaction."

Let's examine how these ready and shooting positions work in a scenario: You are awakened late at night by a loud crash downstairs from your living room area. You roll out of bed and obtain your handgun with its integral white light from its quick access safe mounted near the bed. With finger off the trigger and outside the trigger-guard, you move toward the hallway door at low ready. As you near the doorway you pull the handgun back to chest ready, then to cqb tuck as you step into the doorway. Using the frame of the doorway as cover you roll out and extend the pistol up to point shoulder as your off-hand touches the white light switch illuminating the hallway. Seeing nothing you move at low ready position toward the steps downstairs to the first floor. Retracting the pistol to chest ready, you grab the stairway rail with your off-hand to support yourself and you step down the stairs. As you near the bottom of the stairs you roll out from cover and extend your pistol on target, touching the momentary switch on your weapon light, pistol up at point shoulder. Moving down the first floor hallway to the living room at low ready, you pull back the pistol to chest ready, as you approach the corner of the wall, and then to cqb tuck with your off-hand up to fend off any attacker. As you "slice the pie" or angle out from the corner of the wall, the pistol moves from low ready up to point shoulder, low ready up to point shoulder until the room is cleared.

These ready and transition positions allow you to flow, more safely and efficiently moving with a gun in hand.

USE OF COVER

Cover is a lifesaver. Cover, as defined here, is something that will slow or stop bullet penetration. Of course, cover is relative to the firearm and ammunition being shot in your direction. What suffices for cover against an assailant armed with a .22 may not work against someone armed with an AK-47 stoked with steel core ammo.

Cover is different than concealment. Concealment may be offered by darkness, foliage or common household walls made of sheetrock. Can you have cover and not concealment? Yes, the common bullet resistant polymer Lexan comes to

Proper use of cover minimizes the shooter's exposure.

Survey your world and identify the cover available should shooting erupt. Here, concrete cover is available.

mind. A note here on structures that have "bulletproof glass." The proper terminology is bullet resistant and, once again, its ability to withstand penetration is based on design, rating and the firearm/ammunition being shot against it.

Ideally you want both, cover and concealment, when bullets are coming in your direction. Regardless, getting your derriere behind something, time permitting, before bullets start to fly, is an excellent idea.

Examine the cover opportunities available throughout your living or work space. They may be comprised of sheetrock, wooden studs, brick, rock, block, steel, aluminum, insulation, plywood and/or various combinations of these materials.

A standard sheetrock wall offers more resistance to bullet penetration at the corners than at flat section of wall due to the wooden studs or aluminum framing. The problem with using corners of structures for cover is that they do not provide a lot of room to maneuver. This issue may be compounded if furniture is up against the wall at the doorway or corner where you are taking cover. A bedroom chest of drawers against a wall next to the doorway may not allow you an angle to cover the hallway where an intruder will move through to attack you. This may necessitate that you withdraw into the room further, hopefully behind another point of cover, and focus attention on the doorway as you await police response.

Points of cover within a room may actually offer more bullet resistance than the walls. Hardwood furniture, refrigerators or other major appliances, sofas, chairs, entertainment centers, washers & dryers, full bookshelves, even a gun safe – all offer more resistance than a standard sheetrock wall.

The physical lay-out of your home, business or whatever structure, outside area or parking lot in which you find yourself offers varying degrees of cover and concealment.

It is best to stay away from cover and not "hug" it if at all possible. When bullets strike a hard surface, such as cinder block, asphalt or concrete, they tend to parallel the surface, i.e. they skim the surface at about eight inches off. Therefore if rounds are fired onto the hard cover surface in front of a target, they may "skip" off and into the target if it is close by. Rounds fired into hard cover like concrete block may create secondary missiles that can cause injury. By "hugging" cover or being up too close you expose yourself to impact from the bouncing projective as well as secondary missiles or fragments. You should stay off the cover at least one arm's length if possible.

Standing use of cover

"Roll out" from cover to minimize exposure. You want to have your handgun, carbine or shotgun up and already on the sights, and roll out from the waist up. When you step out from cover, you first expose your lower leg betraying your position. So too, by using a standard rifleman's technique of strong-side elbow up, you expose about one foot of forearm before your carbine or shotgun sights clear the side of cover.

Rolling out can be accomplished by placing whatever foot is to the outside of the cover forward and bending that knee. In this way, you roll or bend forward and out from the waist and not step out. I've found this knee bend technique to be the fastest and most secure technique when shooting from a standing position. Shooting in this way you expose only your firearm and less than half of your head.

"Rolling out" from cover means that the firearm is up and ready to shoot and you roll out from the hips, thereby minimizing exposure.

CASE STUDY

Several years ago my agency was conducting a tactical use of cover training exercise that I developed. The officer/trainee was in a warehouse area with multiple pieces of cover available – large wooded pillars, washing machine, and other simulated cover positions – armed with a training pistol capable of firing Simunitions® marking cartridges. I was the "bad guy" role-player who was at the far end of the warehouse behind covered positions as well as panels of Plexiglas. I was armed with a paintball rifle. The trainee's job was to roll out, find my position and fire accurate rounds on target. I would fire into their covered position but if they rolled out correctly, minimizing their exposure, and shot accurately (using their sights), they controlled the encounter. They could then move to another position forward and we would repeat the exercise until an "End Ex!" (end exercise) was called by me. Having paint balls thwack into a piece of plywood or into the washing machine you were hiding behind was a unnerving experience for many. On one particular training day, "Bob" a burglary detective was the trainee. Bob stepped out from cover much like the fictional TV character "Sabrina" from Charlie's Angels. He gave me half of his body as target. I started shooting at his feet and despite the warnings of my training-instructor partner yelling at Bob to get behind cover, he continued to step out exposing himself. I began raising my point of aim with my paintball rifle until finally I hit him in the chest. Even with body armor on, Bob said "Ow!" My partner said, "Well get your ass behind cover!"

It is interesting to note that in this same training drill, which I learned at the Federal Law Enforcement Training Center, several more "timid" officers and detectives would hug their cover, extend the pistol over the top or side and fire blindly. Many of these marking cartridge rounds would impact into the ceiling above, which was around 20 feet high.

It is more advantageous to shoot around cover than over it. The reason is that if the cover position allows you to shoot around the side, you expose less of yourself than you do when shooting over. Because our eyes are about 1/3 of the way down from the top of our head, we expose our brain bucket when shooting over cover. If your cover is a low wall or vehicle, however, you must be able to use it effectively without endangering yourself by unnecessary exposure.

When shooting around the weak-side of cover, the left side if you are a right handed shooter, you expose less of yourself if you switch hands going from gun-hand to support-hand. The problem with this is that we tend to not shoot as well with our support hands and it is virtually unheard of in an actual gun battle. You can switch to your support-side with long-guns as well but this may be somewhat cumbersome depending on what sling, if any, you have.

In order to shoot effectively from the support-side of cover, you should roll the support elbow under. Even then, you are exposing more of your head until the strong-side eye and sights are on target.

As my friend and fellow LE trainer Andrew Blubaugh (Apex Shooting and Tactics) states, using cover correctly is much like the game "whack-a-mole" played at county fairs. In the game you stand with a padded "hammer," when the fictional "moles" pop-up from their holes, you are supposed to whack them with the hammer. If the mole keeps popping up from the same hole it's easy to target. When using cover and rolling out or popping up from the same position again and again, you set a pattern and it is easy to "whack" you.

Based on reaction and response time of the opponent, your thought should be, "I'm up, he sees me, I'm shooting, or I'm back down" as a timing exercise. You have to be able to get rounds on target before your assailant sees you and can fire upon you. Constantly changing position or elevation behind cover helps you accomplish this. You effectively fire on target while minimizing your exposure and you don't set a discernable pattern.

Kneeling use of cover

There are a variety of kneeling positions: kneeling supported; kneeling unsupported; double kneeling; Surefire or Strategos modified prone.

The standard supported kneeling position is when the gun-side knee is down, the support side knee is up and the support elbow is braced on the support knee or thigh. The rule here for increasing accuracy and decreasing wobble is to place

Firearms trainer Andrew Blubaugh set up this cover exercise. Don't be the mole in the "whack-a-mole" game, "I'm up, he sees me, I'm either shooting or I'm down," constantly changing your position.

the support elbow on the thigh muscles or the support triceps on the kneecap. Never place bone to bone, i.e. elbow to kneecap. This is a braced position that can be gotten into and out of fairly quickly. Used in the open to lessen your exposure profile or to take a more braced and accurate position to fire at distance, the supported kneeling is good as it is when varying your position from standing behind a wall or tall covered position. The problem is that the position cannot be used to shoot over most cars for instance, because it does not elevate your pistol high enough to accomplish this.

Unsupported kneeling is actually faster to get into, offers the advantages of being able to change your elevation behind cover quickly and it allows you to shoot over vehicles and similar height pieces of cover such as low walls. Firing unsupported, you can achieve decent accuracy with a handgun out to medium distance using this technique.

Shooting from behind low cover while rolling out to take the shot.

Double kneeling is a little slower to assume and to get out of but allows you to roll-out from both sides of short cover (think mailbox or maybe a washing machine) as well as sit back on your heels and get a little lower. If you have a piece of cover with an intermediate height, in between the hood of a vehicle and underneath the car, double kneeling gives you an option.

Shooters shoot over low cover with braced or supported kneeling position.

Once again, when using any kneeling position, stay back from cover, have the pistol or longgun up, and "roll-out" versus exposing your position to gunfire.

Urban prone allows a shooter to shoot under a vehicle.

Modified prone is a position I first saw demonstrated by former Navy SEAL Ken Good who once instructed at the Surefire Academy, who now has his own company Strategos International. This kneeling position can be used behind a vehicle or other low cover. The shooter is away from his cover, kneeling on the strong-side knee with the support-leg outstretched toward cover. By bending forward at the waist, you can conceal your upper body behind cover. The eyes are on the sights of the handgun or long-gun. In order to fire, you pivot as you bend back up, find your target and fire or bend back down again. Even with bad knees, I'm able to use this technique.

Modified prone where shooter can dip down behind cover or roll up to engage.

Squatting and using cover

The squat or "rice paddy prone" is a technique used to quickly drop behind cover and be able to fire. The squat means exactly that, you drop your butt to the deck while both feet are flat on the ground. More flexible shooters may be able to brace the triceps on the kneecaps for added stability and accuracy.

Seated using cover

A seated position can be very effective shooting over low cover or at an assailant a distance away. To assume the position, sit down on your butt. Flexible people can cross their ankles and sit without removing their support hand from their firearm. Most people have to go to a kneeling position, place their support hand back and then sit. You can cross your ankle and place the elbows on the inner

Squatting allows a quick use of low cover use as when shooting over the hood of a car.

thighs for more support or keep the legs opened depending on preference and flexibility. The seated position is slower to get into than prone in many cases and is slow to get out of as well.

Remember to keep the muzzle pointed toward the threat when assuming and getting out of the seated position.

Prone using cover

To effectively use cover from a prone position you must modify your technique to a "roll-over prone" position wherein you can shoot from around the side of cover without exposing your body. If you were to use traditional sniper prone position your body would be directly behind the rifle in an upside

Here author uses modified prone to shoot around the edge of cover without exposing his body.

down "Y" configuration. This would allow an adversary to see, and fire, at half of your body. By using the roll-over prone, your body is angled back toward the cover position. To assume roll-over prone, angle your feet slightly outward from your cover position, drop down to a kneeling position, then extend the pistol outward toward the threat. You lie on your strong side with shooting arm or carbine extended, by bending the support-side knee upward to relieve pressure off the diaphragm making a more comfortable position.

You can roll into and out of roll-over prone by using the legs as counterweights and rolling. You can roll out to shoot then roll back behind cover.

Supine shooting using cover

If you have a low piece of cover, i.e. a curb, you can effectively shoot over it, minimizing your exposure to gunfire, by shooting from a face up position or supine.

In order to get into the supine position a right-handed shooter should be facing the right with muzzle pointed toward the threat. Using the support hand to steady yourself, sit down and then lay back with pistol or long-gun across your chest toward the threat. You use the leg to drive or roll over onto the support-side, take the shot(s) and then roll back flat.

Supine can be used to shoot over low cover, like over a street curb.

Urban prone using cover

Urban prone allows the shooter to shoot under very low cover such as a vehicle. Urban prone can be assumed by a right or left handed shooter by facing to the strong side. Assume a kneeling position then laying down on the strong side with the shooter's elbow tucked under. The handgun or long-gun is held sideways. The handgun can be held outstretched in both hands. With the long-gun such as a carbine, the stock is still indexed in the pectoral area but the support

Urban prone allows a shooter to shoot under a vehicle.

hand lies underneath the forearm supporting it. Shooting under a car using this method, only a very small amount of elevation is possible and only ten inches of the target can be fired upon (depending on the height of the vehicle).

In order to make effective use of the tire, wheel and axle area of a car and to minimize your exposure, you can place your feet against the wheel and shoot from the side of the tire.

If size or flexibility prevents you from getting down on the ground low enough to use the urban prone, a version known by the pop-culture reference of "Brokeback Mountain" prone can be assumed. In this version you are kneeling with your head down and rump in the air. It can still be done effectively and is the position of choice by SWAT team members whose helmets prevent them from getting on their sides to see their sights.

A note here on mechanical offset with carbines, the barrel of an M-4 or M-16 lies about two to two and a half inches below the line of sight. Quite simply you can see over a piece of cover but unless the muzzle clears it, you'll shoot into it.

In this case the officer can use the tire, wheel, axle as cover while engaging the targets from under the vehicle.

This can be an embarrassment to the shooter at the range, but can cause injury on the street in an actual shooting. More than a few police officers have shot into pieces of cover when not taking mechanical offset into consideration.

CASE STUDY

In a famous bank robbery, hostage taking incident in the western part of our country, a SWAT sniper took up a position away from a chest high wall to his front as he shot using a tree as support. Through his scope he could clearly see the hostage taker holding a handgun to a female hostage's head. His first shot impacted into the wall causing the bad guy to look around. The second shot went into the same wall at which point the sniper realized his mistake, elevated the muzzle and ended the hostage incident by placing a round squarely into the suspect's head.

Even solid marksmen can make this error. If using a long-gun, make sure you visually clear the cover with the muzzle.

COVER CONSIDERATIONS

Understand that what may constitute cover on the same height, for instance ground level, may be a completely exposed position if a threat is on the second or third floor. So, too, cover like a vehicle that exposes your feet and legs to fire can be detrimental.

Remember that you should not expose any portion of your body from behind cover. A foot, elbow, knee or the top of your head can be shot without you knowing it is exposed. While attending the Federal Law Enforcement Training Center

– Multiple Weapons Instructor Course years ago, I was put through a use of cover exercise. Because I had my head down, I thought I was concealed behind my cover. Turns out that the top of my head was exposed and the role-playing instructor shot my head with a paintball. The protective helmet that I wore saved me from a more serious reminder of my tactical faux pas but I have remembered the lesson since and have passed it on to my students. This is just one of the values of force-on-force training.

All of this knowledge of cover can be used by you against an assailant as well. More than one suspect has been stopped by officers who shot under a vehicle or skipped rounds off a wall and into the suspect's head or torso.

CASE STUDY

During the infamous North Hollywood bank shootout between heavily armed robbers Larry Phillips and Emil Matasareanu in 1997,members of the L.A.P.D. S.W.A.T. engaged Matasareanu on the street after he attempted to carjack a pick-up truck. Retreating behind his getaway car, the suspect and the SWAT officers exchanged heavy gunfire. The SWAT team members shot under the vehicles, impacting Matasareanu in the legs after which he surrendered. Matasareanu would die from his wounds.

Taking cover is dependent on time available. Mediocre cover one step away that can be taken now is better than cover yards away. Certainly getting the best cover position you can as fast as you can is important. If the threat is not imminent, move to the best covered position available.

Using an "L" maneuver one can place cover more quickly between you and the threat. In other words, a lateral movement may place cover in front of you while still several feet away. Imagine a large tree thirty feet in front of you but one you can place in the shooter's line of fire with a quick movement. You are not safely behind the cover but you are still protected by the tree. To improve your covered position you may then move closer to the object.

BE COVER CONSCIOUS

As you go about your daily routine, be cover conscious. Outside, walking your dog or working on your car in the driveway of your home, cover opportunities may be provided by trees,

While parking decks and lots can be dangerous, isolated locations, they offer great cover opportunities.

wooden utility poles, parked vehicles, brick walls or other objects or structures.

In a parking deck, concrete walls may be available that provide solid cover. Vehicles, including your own, offer some protection from small arms fire.

In my working environment I have concrete block walls and steel door frames in most of the building. Recent modifications are sheetrock and aluminum that offer less protection but are certainly better than nothing and may offer opportunities to evade detection from view (concealment opportunities).

Going to a mall (less likely for me by choice) or a store such as a book or hardware store, cover opportunities exist such as display racks, counters, kiosks in the open areas, or corners of brick and marble.

In the downtown area where my office was situation up until last year, there were concrete trash bin holders and vehicle barricades as well as brick building corners, mailboxes and vehicles.

Standard glass windows offer points of observation but are easily shot through and present secondary missile dangers from glass spalling (shards or fragments).

PROS AND CONS OF VARIOUS POINTS OF COVER

Trees and wooden utility poles

Medium to large diameter trees are bullet sponges; treated wooden utility poles actually offer more resistance to bullets than trees of similar diameter. Even smaller diameter trees may offer protection for your center of mass. Negative issues are that many housing allotments nowadays have very few trees or at least trees of a size suitable as cover. Because of their lack of depth, cover such as a utility pole can be easily flanked by a moving antagonist. There is also the tendency to "hunker down" behind a solid piece of cover and "hide" versus moving and putting more distance between you and an attacker, even when movement may be a better tactic.

CASE STUDY

Several years ago in Van Nuys, California an incident occurred captured by Court TV. A suspect armed with a revolver attacked an attorney outside a courthouse. The attorney took cover behind a medium size tree and with the suspect shooting at him from within arm's reach moved side to side placing the tree in between the suspect's gun and himself. Though wounded, the attorney lived through the close range attack.

Cinder block or brick walls

Concrete block is fairly resistant to gunfire from side arms. If there is an angle involved rather than 90 degrees perpendicular, there may be less penetration and more deflection. In an excellent video you can watch on YouTube, "military shooting test 1/3, 2/3, 3/3" researchers from the Naval Surface Warfare

*Poured concrete and concrete
block can offer great cover.*

Center under direction from the
Marine Corps Warfighting Lab
conducted penetration tests on
many of the military's standard
small arms on standard ½-inch
sheetrock and 2X4 constructed
interior rooms with ½-inch exterior plywood walls as well as a section of cinder
block and brick outside wall.

Rounds were fired from about 19 meters (60 feet) at angles of 90 and 45 degrees. *Note – the distance used (60 feet) is reported as the average distance for
"military" urban fighting. Mannequin targets placed inside the rooms were situated behind standard commercial grade office furniture (desks and file cabinets).

Small Arms Tested Included:
- ◆ Beretta M9 9mm Pistol (Military Ball Ammo)
- ◆ 12 Gauge Shotgun
- ◆ AK-47 (Military Ball Ammo)
- ◆ M-16 (Military Ball Ammo)

Sheetrock-only walls were easily penetrated by all rounds but notice the protection offered by block or brick to even the 5.56mm round fired from a full-size
M-16A2 with 16 inch barrel.

AK-47 Rifle

Target	Firing Angle 0° / 45°
Sheet Rock	Yes / Yes
Plywood	Yes / Yes
Block	Yes / Yes
Brick	Yes / Yes

M-16 Rifle

Target	Firing Angle 0° / 45°
Sheet Rock	Yes / Yes
Plywood	Yes / Yes
Block	No / No
Brick	Yes / No

*Remember the issues of secondary missiles such as fragments coming off the
wall toward you as well as the issue of bouncing or skipping rounds or buckshot.

Interior walls in homes and businesses

The Bureau of Alcohol Tobacco and Firearms (ATF) conducted a ballistics and penetration test of 9mm carbines, shotguns with slugs and 5.56 carbines (Data Analysis of .223 Caliber Ammunition). The ATF presentation relied on data gleaned from: FBI's "Weapons Selection Test," San Diego County Sheriff's Department's, "Structural Penetration Testing," and the DEA's "Construction Material Test":

From the ATF presentation:

How far will a projectile travel before it falls to the Earth? Based on the weapon system firing 60 inches above ground level:

◆ 870 Shotgun – 12 Gauge Slug . . . . .200 Yards
◆ H&K MP5 Subgun – 9mm . . . . .200 Yards
◆ M4 Carbine – 5.56mm . . . . .500 Yards

The ATF study also refers to a "San Diego Penetration Test" with four walls approximately five yards apart. The walls were constructed of: ½" Wood Siding; Stucco material; Insulation; ½-inch Gypsum; Cinder Block.

The average penetration listed:

◆ 9mm 147 grain Hydra Shock . . . . 3 Walls
◆ .40 cal. 165 grain Hydra Shock . . . . 3.6 Walls
◆ .223 55 grain Federal Tactical . . . . 3 Walls

> ### CASE STUDY
>
> Several years ago, as reported to me by a federal agent, members of his agency had been involved in a shooting inside a mobile home. Both .40 caliber standard issue handguns were fired as well as 5.56mm rounds from M-4s. Rounds from inside the trailer penetrated the exterior wall of the suspect's prefab home, through both walls of another mobile home, through an exterior wall of a third trailer, before being stopped. Fortunately, only the suspect was wounded. When the Special Agent in Charge questioned the shooting, he suspected it was the 5.56 rounds that had over-penetrated. Turns out that the .40 pistol rounds were the culprits.

We want sufficient penetration without over-penetration.

Drug Enforcement Agency Wall Penetration Test also referred to by the ATF:

DEA Wall Penetration Test #1:

Wall #1 constructed of:

◆ 1 sheet of 1/16" plastic sheeting
◆ 2 sheets of 7/16" plywood
◆ 1 sheet of 9/16" hard insulation
◆ 2" of soft insulation

◆ 1 sheet of ½" drywall

Walls #2 & #3 were constructed of:

◆ 2 sheets of 7/16" plywood
◆ 2 sheets of ½" drywall
◆ 2" of soft insulation

Here Liberty Ammunition tests their 9mm rounds against standard wall board.

Penetration on ¼ inch plywood.

And sufficient penetration through interior sheetrock.

The average penetration listed:

◆ 9mm 147 grain Hydra Shock . . . . 3 Walls
◆ .40 cal. 165 grain Hydra Shock . . . . 2.5 Walls
◆ .223 55 grain Federal Tactical . . . . 1.5 Walls

Here we see the myth destroyed in two studies that handguns penetrate less than carbines. We can also say that penetration depends on bullet design and velocity but it is certainly true that rounds that expand the most penetrate the least through cover. This is a reason many tactical teams run a couple different loads through their 5.56mm M-4 rifles. They may have magazines stuffed with Hornady 223 Remington TAP® for entry work inside structures and Federal Tactical or Remington Core-Lokt for perimeter work where more penetration is required. *Note – Ballistic studies have been done which show that both the Federal Tactical and Remington Core-Lokt ammo have excellent penetration abilities, expand in ballistic gelatin well and don't over-penetrate. Both loadings in .223 are worthy of consideration. There is handgun ammunition which can accomplish the same thing, A) Penetrate through glass, sheet rock and sheet metal, etc., B) Expand in humans, and C) Not over-penetrate.

DEA Wall Penetration Test #2:
Consisted of firing rounds through 9 walls approximately 4 yards apart.
Walls #1 - #8 were constructed of 2 sheets of ½" drywall
Wall #9 – was constructed of:
◆ 1 sheet of ½" drywall
◆ 1 sheet of 7/16" plywood
◆ 3" soft insulation
◆ 9/16" hard insulation
◆ 1/16" plastic siding
*This simulates the construction of an exterior wall of a residence

The average penetration listed:
◆ 9mm 147 grain Hydra Shock . . . . 9 Walls
◆ .40 cal. 165 grain Hydra Shock . . . . 9 Walls
◆ M-16 55 grain . . . . 8 Walls
◆ M-4 55 grain . . . . 8 Walls

Vehicles

Laminated vehicle safety glass provides more of a deflection than resistance. When shooting out of or into a vehicle through the front windshield or back window, the tendency is for the rounds that hit the glass to follow the perpendicular angle of the glass. Rounds fired out through the front window will impact high on a target (the farther the distance, the higher the deflection). Rounds fired through the front windshield and into the car will deflect low. *Note – The deflection only affects rounds passing through the laminated glass not subsequent rounds fired through a hole you created.

Shooting through laminated safety glass causes deflection. In this case a Liberty round is fired through the windshield but deflects upward following the perpendicular plane of the glass.

CASE STUDY

A violent domestic dispute subject was attempting to flee the scene in his vehicle. One officer in the street on the passenger side of the vehicle was knocked to the ground as the suspect backed into and rammed the car behind him. The officer in the front of the suspect's car, fearing that his partner would be run over, fired through the front window at the suspect. The rounds deflected downward into the top of the dashboard and did not strike the suspect.

In a DEA training video members of that agency take a four-door sedan and fire through the vehicle with the handguns, subguns, shotguns, and carbines carried by that agency. From the side they shoot the tires, the car body, through the doors and windows. They then move to the front of the car and shoot through the grill, hood and passenger compartment. Yet, when all those rounds were fired by multiple agents at one time into the car, the vehicle still fires up and can be driven away (even with flat tire). More importantly, two cardboard targets that were placed in the front seat area under the dash and in the rear seat area, both simulating suspects taking cover, are checked, neither has been hit.

Remington tests their Golden Saber Bonded rounds against sheet metal.

This test indicates several points for you, the armed citizen. They are: A) Vehicles, despite their light metallic or plastic construction, can shield you somewhat from incoming fire. Remember my bank robber story earlier? B) That assailants inside an auto coming toward you are very hard to stop. Better to avoid the car if possible rather than trying to shoot the car to stop the assailant. And, C) Because of the kinetic energy impact of a car and the difficulty in hitting the driver, someone coming at you with homicidal intent is a serious threat and can be fired upon. This is the tough part of assailants in vehicles

The round still had adequate penetration against ballistic gelatin after shooting through the metal.

Here Liberty Ammunition is fired through a vehicle door.

The round penetrated the door with the inner core projectile able to hit the target beyond.

attempting to run you over. A car driven by someone attempting to hit you or run you over is a deadly threat, and stopping them is not an easy proposition – avoid/escape if possible, shoot when you must to stop the threat.

Body armor

Modern body armor using Kevlar was first patented by Richard Davis, formerly of Second Chance®. Mr. Davis's own history included being shot and wounded in Detroit by three armed robbers while delivering pizzas. Davis shot and wounded two of the robbery suspects. During his convalescence Davis began formulating the idea of concealable body armor and came upon a new synthetic material called Kevlar. Richard Davis was the first person to use multiple layers of Kevlar in a vest design to stop bullets. Marketing his vests to police officers, Davis would demo the vest by shooting himself with a handgun then turn and shoot several bowling pins off a table (to demonstrate that he could continue to fire to save his life after being shot).

The International Association of Chiefs of Police® DuPont Kevlar Survivor's Club® now numbers over 3,100 officers who have been saved from death or serious bodily injury. Two of my former coworkers are members of that club. Both were saved by body armor. Further, two other coworkers were saved by body armor: one by a Second Chance vest before the Survivor's Club was started and one from another type of ballistic fiber.

Vests are available to the armed citizen. Several companies manufacture body armor for citizens including designs for kids incorporated into backpacks.

Author's Second Chance vest purchased in the 1980s.

Guard Dog Security's ballistic backpacks feature Kevlar inserts for a student's back.

Available in pink for the girls as well.

I have two body armor designs from U.S. P.A.L.M. (Primary Armament Logistical Manufacturing) that I keep handy. In my office I have a Defender AR15 vest that incorporates two 11" X 13.5" NIJ Level IIIA ballistic panels in a quick don design. Should an active killer attack my building, which is secure but susceptible, I can toss the Defender AR15 over my head and then grab my DoubleStar Star15 carbine placed underneath the vest. This gives me four 30-round mags to respond with. At home, I have a Defender Handgun vest from U.S. PALM that has one .45 Wilson spare magazine and a Surefire 6PX 320 lumen handheld light. Grab the DoubleStar 1911 .45 that has a Surefire X200 weapon-light attached, from my quick access Sentry safe and I can respond to "bumps in the night" or a violent home intruder, a little better protected.

In my car I have a Blackhawk S.T.R.I.K.E. Level IIIA tactical vest with rifle rated plates fore and aft. As a full-time LEO it is my duty and sworn obligation to respond to active shooter calls or other violent incidents and armor helps me and other LEOs safely complete this task.

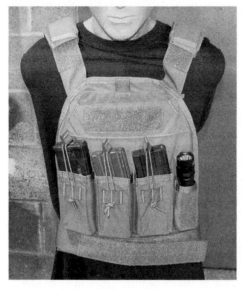

ABOVE: US PALM Defender AR15 is hung in the author's office.

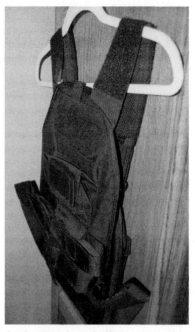

RIGHT: US PALM Defender Handgun ballistic vest set up for home response to unlawful incursions into the house.

Considering that taxi drivers and clerks at 24-hour mini-marts and gas stations are at a considerable risk, I would not want to do those jobs without wearing armor. The National Crime Victimization Survey clearly indicates the rate of assault in retail work as dangerously high. According to the U.S. Justice Report, Workplace Violence, 1993-2009:

Highlights

◆ From 2002 to 2009, the rate of nonfatal workplace violence has declined by 35%, following a 62% decline in the rate from 1993 to 2002.

◆ The average annual rate of workplace violence between 2005 and 2009 (5 violent crimes per 1,000 employed persons age 16 or older) was about one-third the rate of nonworkplace violence (16 violent crimes per 1,000 employed persons age 16 or older) and violence against persons not employed (17 violent crimes per 1,000 persons age 16 or older).

◆ Between 2005 and 2009, law enforcement officers, security guards, and bartenders had the highest rates of nonfatal workplace violence.

◆ Strangers committed the greatest proportion of nonfatal workplace violence against males (53%) and females (41%) between 2005 and 2009.

◆ Among workplace homicides that occurred between 2005 and 2009, about 28% involved victims in sales and related occupations and about 17% involved victims in protective service occupations.

◆ About 70% of workplace homicides were committed by robbers and other assailants while about 21% were committed by work associates between 2005 and 2009.

◆ Between 2005 and 2009, while firearms were used in 5% of nonfatal workplace violence, shootings accounted for 80% of workplace homicides.

~U.S. Justice Report, Workplace Violence, 1993-2009

It is clear after examining the workplace violence numbers that professions other than law enforcement are susceptible to armed and unarmed attack. Body armor is the last line of cover available to law enforcement and citizens and should be considered depending on vocation.

Cover is a life saver, period. Effective use of cover minimizes your exposure to your assailants fire while you are able to place accurate fire on him. Don't emulate the detective mentioned in the case study above and do a Sabrina from behind cover exposing yourself unnecessarily. Stay back away from cover, get the pistol or long-gun ready, roll out and solve the problem by putting rounds into the bad guy.

CASE STUDY

January 23, 2011, Detroit: Suspect Lamar Moore, wanted for kidnapping and rape of a 13-year-old girl, carrying a shotgun entered the Sixth Precinct of the DPD and opened fire. Captured on surveillance video, officers working the desk area took cover and returned fire. Very much like the "whack-a-mole" mentioned earlier, two officers popped up and fired. Four police officers were injured by the suspect who, at one point, dove over the counter to assault the officers' positions. At least one patrolman was unarmed having secured their pistol in a gun locker in a back room and had to hide under the front desk. The suspect though shot and mortally wounded by a plainclothes commander stayed on his feet and maneuvered on the police officer who used a counter area as cover. The suspect fired with this shotgun at the officer's outstretch hand/pistol, blowing off two of the officer's fingers and causing the commander to drop his pistol. Only after the commander scrambled from behind the desk did the suspect collapse. All police officers wounded recovered.

This video is available for your viewing at YouTube.com and is a very violent reminder of what cover is all about and how effective use of cover can save your life.

MOVEMENT

Taking root or not moving when bullets are coming in your direction is not a sound tactic in a gunfight. Imagine a train coming toward you and you're standing in the middle of the tracks. You don't want to move straight toward the train. If you attempt to backpedal, you'll soon lose your balance and fall. Turn and run on the tracks? You'll never be able to move fast enough to outrun the locomotive. So the answer is, get off the tracks as quickly and smoothly as you can without losing your balance.

We can begin moving off the "X" or the "train tracks" by incorporating a simple side step during our draw stroke or presentation of the pistol on target. Some have scoffed at the simple side step but realistically based on where you are right now while reading this, how much unimpeded room is available to your right or left – twenty feet? I seriously doubt it. How about ten feet of uninterrupted space with no chairs, tables of other obstacles in your way? As I write this, I could move only to my right and possibly just two adult steps before I hit a wall. Envision a gunfight in your living room, bedroom or rec room. Realistically, how much room is available? Why then do we practice techniques which only work on the flat wide open section of a pistol range?

Any controlled movement is better than no movement at all or standing stock still, but unrealistic movement can be dangerous as well. One tactic taught to police officers was to duck, touch the floor on the side you were moving to as you ran off the X. This technique would not work in a parking lot with vehicles let alone the interior of a residence. Developed and taught in an open gymnasium

the tactic was totally unrealistic. Sure, a turn and aggressive movement off the X for a couple steps will work but anything more than that and we are getting into tactics which work on the range, not realistic techniques which will work on the streets, or help an Armed Citizen win an armed encounter.

Another technique that has been advocated for private citizens is to aggressively move straight into a threat as you fire. The notion is that your aggressive movement and fire

Here student at Sig Academy evades rushing target while moving to the rear and laterally while firing.

Backing up will only cause you to trip and fall. Here lateral movement off the "X" gets the citizen off the line of attack.

Movement must be controlled of you can run into obstacles.

Step and drag movements can suffice in tight confines.

will somehow cause the threat to stop. As we noted in the previous case study about the Detroit substation shooting, the assailant was mortally wounded and for several seconds able to continue shooting and moving. Why on Earth would we want to make it easier for an attacker to be able to hit us with his gunfire by moving closer? Yes, police tactical teams teach to shoot while moving forward and to the rear but this is during narcotics search warrants or hostage rescue scenarios. Noted firearms and tactics trainer, and former U.S. Army Spec Ops operator, Paul Howe has stated that in combat operations he has been involved in such as Operation Just Cause, (the invasion of Panama), or the Battle of the Black Sea (Mogadishu Somalia combat operations reported in Mark Bowden's book and depicted in the movie of the same name, Black Hawk Down, he has never fired while moving. He has moved, then posted in position and fired, but never fired while on the move. That said, we still train for the ability to shoot on the move.

How much movement and what kind is the question. As we stated in the previous section on use of cover, if something solid is relatively close by and the threat is imminent, move to cover while or before shooting. If you have time, then get to the best covered position available. This may also mean that you cover the retreat of your friends or family as they move to cover or vacate the area. Teaching your family members how to move to cover safely, as well as moving from one covered position to another, is a wise tactical suggestion as well.

A lateral step/drag or two may suffice to get behind cover if it is close by. Turning and quickly moving allows quicker more aggressive movement off the attack line and maintains better balance.

We are designed to move best in a forward direction. Having toes, hips, shoulders and head pointed in one direction achieves better efficiency and reduces

bouncing which is deleterious to shooting on the move. Moving forward we advocate the "Groucho Walk" named after the famous late comic who crouched and glided as he moved forward. The heel/toe glide of the Groucho Walk is dependent

Here shooting great and master instructor Ron Avery demonstrates his moving and shooting technique at close range.

on the toe/knee/hips and shoulders being aligned. Having the toes pointed outward instead of forward as described, causes the hips to splay, resulting in a back and forth rocking motion that adversely effects accuracy.

When moving, the gun is at low, indoor or chest ready unless a specific threat area or person is being covered.

CASE STUDY

"C" is a governmental paramilitary operator with extensive experience in the world's hotspots in the Global War on Terror. He related a story where a member of his team was killed by a terrorist during a building clearing. The operator was moving down a hallway with his carbine held up at point shoulder position. An Islamic terrorist was lying on the floor in a doorway ahead and shot the American in the head, killing him. "C's" point was that if you move with a gun up at eye level you can miss threats at a lower level. Let us learn from this tragic lesson.

Try to use available cover when moving inside a structure or outside. When moving down a hallway in your home, why move straight up the center, when you can move to a doorway of another room or place some other type of cover such as a corner, appliance or piece of furniture between you and the possible threat.

When moving through a parking lot or other outside venue, you should place an obstacle or piece of cover between you and potential or real threats. As mentioned when we discussed use of cover, you don't have to be right on top of cover to protect yourself.

Lateral movement

Can be of two or three types. Side stepping we move one foot sideways then the other while facing forward, this is also known as a shuffle step or step/drag. We strive to have the best base or platform possible. We want to side step versus crossing the feet to reduce the likelihood of falling or stumbling. This type of movement can be used when a threat is encountered and you are out in the open but want to move laterally to a position behind a piece of cover.

If you want to move a distance and don't have a defined threat, just walk in that direction. A right-handed person can cover, and shoot if need arises, to the left using a two handed stance by swiveling at the waist. If a right-handed person is moving to the left, then it is easier to use a one handed position holding the handgun in the right hand and walking with toes pointed in the direction you're headed.

Step/drag is a more stable way to move forward or to the rear as well. When moving forward, the support side foot takes a step, then the strong-side steps. Once again, care is taken to have a stable platform when moving versus a narrow base. Flexing the knees aids in stability and reduces bounce. Stepping rearward

Step forward with your support side foot and then drag your strong-side foot

Then repeat the stepping. This allows for more control during forward or rearward movement.

when backing away from an assailant or threatening situation or area when using the step/drag technique, the strong-side footsteps back, then the support side foot drags.

Of course, if no imminent threat is presented, turning and moving quickly even running is a viable tactic. Do not run toward problems however. The rule as taught to me my members of LAPD-SWAT is that in tactical movement do not move any quicker than you can shoot accurately. This is frequently a problem when I've trained SWAT teams as a natural reaction, based on an SNS response is to run.

CASE STUDY

I was hired to train a county SWAT team. During narcotics search warrants they had been trained by their instructors to run into structures. A light snow had fallen and the team had wet boots once they hit the house and ran into the kitchen through the side door. Once the first two operators ran onto the linoleum they both slid and fell. In training this can result in injury. In a real encounter, this could result in death or serious injury and certainly does not equate to accurate fire if the need arises.

The reason we avoid rushing or running into a problem area is because we cannot visually see or mentally perceive and process any threats we encounter.

STATIC DEFENSE AND POSITIONING: BUNKERING OR ENSCONCING

If there is no reason, i.e. a family member that is downstairs or in a separate area of the house from you, there is a compelling argument for taking up a bunkered position and setting up what is essentially a hasty ambush or ensconcing behind cover and waiting for the threat to appear or the police to respond.

Searching through any structure, even if it is your own, is a dangerous tactic. In SWAT work, when teams do entries on narcotics or felony arrest warrants looking for dangerous subjects, the danger is extreme because you are entering into the "lair" of the suspect. They know the noises, creaks, light switches and layout of the rooms, hallways and stairs of their house. Despite using the tactics of speed, surprise and violence of action, a suspect only needs a few seconds to arm himself and respond.

"Bunkering" or ensconcing is a safer way to defend a structure if you don't have to rescue or move toward other family members.

CASE STUDY

My police tactical team made entry into a small house in search of a narcotics trafficker who was a violent three-time loser. The risk, as assessed during the research prior to the raid, was high. The team breached the front door, tossed in a flash-bang, which emits a blinding light and loud bang, and entered the house. Mike was point man and was moving down a hallway when he encountered a closed bedroom door. Mike opened the door and the suspect, who was lying on a bed against the wall to the left of the door, open fired with a revolver. One round struck the metal door frame next to Mike's head. The other two rounds hit him in his ballistic "raid vest" which saved his life. Mike pivoted and shot four two round bursts from his Heckler and Koch MP-5 9mm submachine gun striking the suspect with seven out of eight shots, killing him.

Searching has its risks but may be necessary based on the physical layout of your home, i.e. where other bedrooms for your children or possibly an elderly parent are located. It's kind of hard to bunker or ensconce in your bedroom when the intruder is between you and your children.

Further, ensconcing may not be possible if an attack occurs during the day when family is scattered about the house or property. This also creates a problem when your handguns or long-guns are not within arm's reach. Imagine sitting in the living room watching television, when an intruder begins kicking in your front door. Where are your guns? If the firearms are stowed in a safe downstairs in the den, or upstairs in a gun safe, how long will it take you to get to them? It is for this reason that many armed citizens elect to carry their handguns on their person within the home or strategically place quick access safes mounted on the walls in several rooms.

In the old television show Candid Camera the theme song stated, "When you least expect it, you're elected…" Violent crime happens everywhere at every time not just in the bad parts of town when you're armed to the teeth.

CASE STUDY

St. Louis, Missouri: Approximately 11pm on a Monday night a 17-year-old girl walks out to her car parked on the street in front of her mother's modest home. Two armed and masked gunmen seize the girl and use her as a human shield holding a gun to her head while attempting a home invasion. The girl's father is visiting however and draws his own gun shooting and killing one suspect and shooting and seriously wounding the other. The 17-year-old daughter was uninjured. The dead suspect had previously served time for robbery, the wounded suspect was once accused of murder but charges were dropped when witnesses to his crime would not cooperate.

Monday night at home, with a gunfight with two hyper-violent criminal suspects erupting, fortunately the father was prepared and accurate in his fire!

ACTIVE SEARCHING AND RESPONSE

Conducting what police call a slow and methodical search takes time and is certainly not to be conducted in haste. There are several different methods to search or clear your home or a structure.

Slicing the pie or quartering

Imagine you are approaching a room down a hallway. As you would normally walk down the hall toward the room, you can begin to see into the room. As you close in and pass in front of the threshold, you can see into the room except for possibly the corners but anyone in the room can see you. Further if the room is dark and the hallway lit up, they can see you but you cannot see them. This is not how you want to search a room or structure because anyone who can see you can shoot you if they are armed and so inclined. By slowing down, using available cover (such as a doorway) you can more safely search or clear a room. We do this by searching small sections or "slices of the pie" of the room.

As you move the pistol should move from a ready position such as low, indoor or chest ready up to point shoulder as unknown risks are approached. You must be prepared to fire if/when a deadly threat presents itself.

As in using cover, we want to stand back away from the doorway of the room we want to search. In most homes, this may not be very far.

As you "slice the pie" you "roll out" as previously described in the cover section. Only your eye and your handgun should be visible. We roll out from the waist, clear the visible section, then step slightly and roll out more, until the majority of the room is cleared in this fashion. Even after you have cleared the majority of the room from outside the threshold, the corners and areas behind furniture must be cleared. Once again, this is a game of angles and inches.

CASE STUDY

My team once searched an entire seven story apartment building room by room looking for a murder suspect who had run into the building. Using a body bunker we had to search each apartment that took hours and was exhausting considering the full SWAT kit (helmet, raid vest, duty belt) we had to wear and carrying the bunker that weighed in excess of 35 pounds. The stress level searching the last few rooms was certainly intense! We did not find the suspect that day but we certainly earned our pay.

Care must be taken to not lead with a foot, your shoulder of other parts of your body. For example, don't expose a foot by stepping out too far, to a subject in the room. By leading with a body part rather than rolling out ready to shoot, you expose your position. All an assailant has to do is aim at the doorway and wait until you come into view, or shoot through the wall for that matter.

When you search, don't anticipate seeing an entire person if the person is hiding. You will see a tennis shoe sticking out or part of a shoulder or top of their head. You may not see their entire body.

If you are responding to calls for help from a family member, this quartering or slicing the pie tactic can be employed more quickly to safely clear your way.

"Slicing the pie" refers to quartering or segmenting the room into pieces of the pie.

A small step is made, then you roll out to clear, then another step and so forth.

Using this technique the bulk of a room can be cleared without making entry.

The same stepping and rolling out is down, just in a quicker fashion. In this way, you are not blindly moving into gunfire in your haste.

Remember to breathe a few deep breaths before you start searching and during your search. That will help control the inevitable SNS response and improve your performance.

CHALLENGING AN INTRUDER

If during your search you encounter an intruder who does not pose a deadly threat, then you must give them verbal commands. Do not approach them to put hands on. If they don't have their own gun or other weapon, by closing the gap and getting within arm's reach, you are giving them the opportunity to attempt to take your gun.

Your job is to protect your family's life
and your life – not apprehend suspects.

Also don't be shocked if the assailant does not follow your commands to get on the ground even when you are pointing a firearm at them. As stated, I've pointed guns at hundreds of people on the street and in confrontations indoors. Many were so unimpressed with my shiny pistol, steely-eyed countenance and loud repetitive verbal commands that they turned and fled. In an armed citizen confrontation, this is a good thing. He runs away and you just wait for responding police to search for him. A tactic might be to order the intruder to "Get out of my house!" Your job is to protect your family's life and your life – not apprehend suspects. That choice of holding them at gunpoint or telling them to beat feet and get out is up to you.

When challenging a threat, give them short, repetitive verbal commands such as
"Drop the crowbar! Drop it now! Get down on the ground!"

CASE STUDY

An off-duty police lieutenant comes home and after entering the house realizes that there is a burglary in progress. The lieutenant draws his pistol and begins searching, encountering the burglar who, is pointing his own gun at the off-duty cop in plainclothes. This armed stalemate could have ended in a terminal way for both citizen and criminal. Finally the lieutenant says, "This could end bad for both of us. Why don't you just take off?" At which point the suspect runs from the house. Some would argue the police officer should have shot but they weren't in his shoes at that moment facing death. On that day, the lieutenant survived and that is the number one mission.

The best way to reduce the threat to you is to order the assailant, "Get down on the floor! Arms out to the side, palms up! Spread your legs! Don't look at me! The police are on their way! Don't make me shoot you!"

Do all this from a position of cover such as from a corner, behind an appliance or doorway minimizing your exposure. As in preparing for the police response after a shooting, which we will cover later, if possible prepare for the officers arrival. Unfortunately there are "blue on blue" shootings each year where off-duty or plainclothes cops are shot by responding officers in the chaos of an armed encounter. Reduce that likelihood by lowering or re-holstering your firearm prior to contact with them. Be advised that if you or a family member cannot open the door for them then they will probably kick the door in.

RETREATING

Just because you start clearing and searching doesn't mean you have to continue. If at any time you feel the risk is too great, retreat (back up) to a position of cover and "hunker down." In this way, you can set up that hasty ambush we talked about for any intruder who elects to continue forward toward you. This is exactly what that Detroit female homeowner did, mentioned in an earlier case study when three intruders kicked in her back door. She bunkered and shot at them as they came toward her. All three retreated, then one intruder drew his own pistol and attempted to enter again only to be met by more of her gunfire, after which he quickly gave up anymore thoughts of invading the home, and then all three ran off into the night.

COMMUNICATIONS

Police officers will make all possible haste toward a "burglary in progress armed homeowner" call, a robbery or shooting. But when you are the one involved and forced to wait, it can seem like hours. You want to call or have someone else call prior to contact, if at all possible and when it is safe to do so. If the threat is imminent, then take care of business, control the threat, and then call the police.

You getting shot while talking to police dispatch instead of taking care of business and possibly shooting the intruder is not a viable approach. The dispatcher will probably warn whoever calls to "put the gun down." The dispatcher is trying to protect the responding officers but not you. Don't listen to this advice if it puts you and your family at risk. Have your family member, or you if you're calling, stay on the line with police dispatch until such time as police arrive and begin communicating directly with you. This open line is recorded by dispatch and can serve as evidence if your verbal orders are not followed and the intruder begins to attack. Remember to keep your language powerful and direct but not threatening, i.e. "Don't move or I'll blow your head off!" or other threats. A declaration such as, "Don't make me shoot you!" can be used in your defense.

ATTACK SCENARIOS

As you go about your daily routine, envision attacks that come from different directions or in different environments you might travel. Constantly play the when/then game to think about what you will do when "it" happens.

Criminals have forced entry to commit burglaries, rapes, home invasions and all manner of criminal activity in a vast number of ways. Potential armed confrontations or attacks may happen:

- outside (front)
- outside (rear)
- front door
- back door
- other door(s)
- garage
- other outbuilding
- windows
- sliding glass door(s)
- in your auto
- parking area
- business location
- public location
- even at a public park or other non-developed area

The number of locations or the environments where you might have to engage in a fight for your life are limited only by the places you go or travel. Each one has different physical layouts, structures, available cover and areas of concern to deal with. Some of which you and your companions or family may be isolated in dealing with the attacker(s). Others, such as malls, football stadiums or other public areas, may have a large number of other citizens. You have to safely traverse or work within whatever structure or environment you're in and win the day.

Smart and common sense tactics can make that winning possible.

TIME

Many tactics are dependent or reliant on the amount of time available. A spontaneous assault right now may give you only time to respond. Hopefully this response will be based on your training and preplanned, pre-thought out responses.

Other scenarios or confrontations may have some time to allow you to better prepare or operate. If time permits, of course, await the police and let them handle the situation or avoid the confrontation altogether by possibly retreating to cover or getting out of the area. Quite possibly drawing your handgun, covering the threat, ordering the assailant(s) to "Stay back!" and then getting the heck out of Dodge!

DISTANCE

Maintaining your distance from a threat is a sound tactic. We have already shown that an assailant armed with a contact weapon – knife or bludgeon, at 30 feet or so – can close the gap between you and he in less than a couple of seconds. Staying back and covering them with your firearm from a distance is sound strategy. Be advised that while in an SNS response, closeness is equated with control. Armed citizens and law enforcement officers oftentimes rush into or close distance with a threat because they believe that going hands on or being close means they are dominating the encounter.

Even in "felony car stops" where LEOs are chasing felons in a vehicle pursuit and officers announce on the radio, "If the car stops, let's use felony stop tactics!" one officer or more will run up to the car, recklessly endangering themselves. The result is that other officers who were in more control and behind cover, have to run up to protect their brother.

We shoot better at a distance, so why "storm the beaches"?

CASE STUDY

On SWAT when dealing with violent felon searches in homes, we would establish an outer perimeter that was manned by patrol. In one memorable incident we had pushed "Al" a seasoned SWAT operator up into an attic crawl space to search for a suspect. Much like the work of the "tunnel rats" of Vietnam, searching a crawl space is very dangerous. After Al located the suspect and we broadcast an apprehension, we turned around and all the officers from the outer perimeter were now standing in the house. The outer perimeter had collapsed.

Closeness does not equal control. When possible maintain your distance.

WEAPON ACCESS

Storing and securing a weapon and access during an emergency situation is about finding a balance. The more secure a firearm is to prevent theft and to keep it out of the hands of non-authorized persons such as children, the less accessible it is. Big heavy safes are a great way to protect firearms from burglars and damage or loss due to fire, but are often slow to open and are often placed in rooms such as basements or dens with solid floor versus upstairs bedrooms or living rooms.

The answer and a good balance between speed of access and security is one of the modern safes from Sentry or Gun Vault. I have used the Home Defense Center from Sentry Safe for a couple of primary long-guns and a pistol for armed response in my home. It is a decent sized safe that fits in a corner. It cannot secure all of my firearms but it takes up very little space and keeps the guns out of the hands of my growing grandchildren.

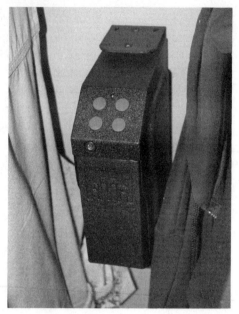

GunVault Speed Vault mounted in closet. Press the combination and the door drops down offering quick access.

For handguns I use a Sentry Digital Safe and a GunVault Speed Vault. Both feature access combinations that are a quick series of button pushes you select from the four combo buttons. Both either open on a compression gas strut (Sentry Safe) or drops down from gravity (Gun Vault).

My recommendation if you have a firearms collection is to secure most of your guns in a large safe and one or more secured in quick access safes.

My travel safe used when flying is a NanoVault 300. To comply with fed-

Sentry Safe Digital allows quick access with pneumatic door.

Press in your code and the door pops up and open.

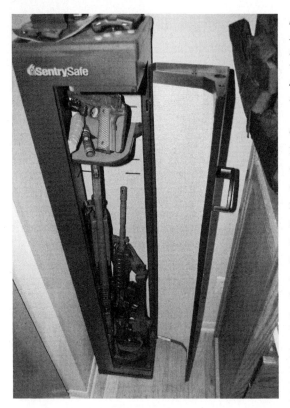

Sentry Safe Home Defense Center secures two long-guns, pistol with weaponlight and spare Surefire handheld light as well.

eral law, you must declare a firearm when flying which can only be transported in checked luggage. To find out more, visit the TSA website at http://www.tsa.gov/traveler-information/firearms-and-ammunition there you can find out more about how to transport firearms and ammunition while flying. The NanoVault 300 has a push button combination so it can still be accessed if you lose or misplace your keys. It also features a cable that can be run through the hardware of my suitcase to prevent easy theft by pulling it out of my luggage.

Prevent two types of tragedy:

1) Prevent an accidental shooting by securing your firearms, and

2) Prevent a tragedy of being unable to access a gun during an armed encounter or intrusion into your property.

For these reasons many armed citizens are electing to carry a handgun on their person, while at home. It's easy enough to do with so many quality holsters. I've heard of a "game" played by friends who carry concealed. They have a standing bet of $5.00 if they can catch their friend without a firearm on their person. To some, it may seem over the top. I was once accused by an acquaintance, actually a friend of a friend on Facebook, of being a "Jack Bauer wannabe." There are two points I want to relate here: 1) I pointed out that I was not paranoid, I was experienced. I have spent the time from age 18 until now, some 34+ years dealing with violent people and seeing the results of their acts, and 2) That this same anti-gun "let's all hold hands and sing" person almost lost an eye when criminal suspects attacked him and he was stabbed in the side of the head.

The wise man learns from others mistakes and experiences – the ignorant man fails to learn from his own.

LOW OR ADVERSE LIGHTING AND TACTICAL OPTIONS

Criminals seldom, if ever, look for a fair fight. They avoid confrontation and the armed citizen like the plague. They therefore ply their trade under cover of darkness, low or subdued lighting that can conceal them and their actions until they attack or complete their criminal acts.

> ## CASE STUDY
> My father passed away several years ago. His obituary ran in the local paper with the announcement detailing calling hours as well as the funeral date, time and location. I was asleep the night before the calling hours when I received a call from my police department's dispatch center stating that an alarm drop had occurred at my father's house. Officers were on scene, it was an apparent false alarm and I should respond to secure the house since the front door had apparently been left unlocked.

When I arrived on scene, still rubbing the sleep from my eyes, the officers said that they had checked the house and apparently my brother or I had left the front door unlocked and the wind must have blown open the door causing the alarm. I thanked them as they departed.

I then looked around the house since both my brother and I are very careful about locking up. In a back bedroom I found a window leading out to a screened in porch pushed up and a small statue knocked over on the floor under the window. I then walked out to the porch and examined the screen. A suspect had slit the bottom of the screen with a razor blade, had entered the porch and then pushed open the window to the house. Once he exited the back bedroom he had initiated the motion sensor in the hallway causing the alarm to go off.

It was then that the burglar unlocked the front door and left the house.

I had to call the officers back to the scene to make a burglary report and show them the evidence. They had stopped at the easiest conclusion – homeowner error – and had not looked beyond that. In the cover of darkness a serial burglar had picked an easy target based on reading the obituaries. My father's home could have been ransacked, family heirlooms lost or damaged. The only thing that stopped the burglar was as an alarm, which a loving son and police officer had paid for years ago as a Christmas present.

At night, all the monsters come out to play…

According to the FBI's Law Enforcement Officers Killed and Assaulted for 2012, examining the years 2003-2012, 55% or 295 officers out of the total of 535 which were feloniously killed in the line of duty were killed at night. 55%.

The FBI has stated, "historically most line-of-duty deaths and serious injuries take place during the hours of darkness." And yet, very little if any police firearms training takes place in low or subdued lighting. For instance, in my state for years basic police academies were allowed to train recruits for "low light" by having them wear welding goggles. The state qualification course for pistol and shotgun for in-service officers allowed the same welding goggles to be worn. Since welding goggles only impair vision there was no training in the use of flashlights or weapon mounted lights.

Many agencies nationwide still do not conduct meaningful low light training for their officers and many officers have little to no knowledge of how to work and operate safely, in low light conditions.

THE EYES

When I started working security in 1980 while attending University, most of my work was conducted at night in low or subdued lighting and I was ill-equipped to deal with these conditions. I can remember working a small community theatre that is unfortunately situated in a deteriorating section of town. The first night I worked in the parking lot, I had no flashlight and my employer did not provide one. The second night I took an old Radio Shack® plastic flashlight the store chain used to give away for free. It was a six cell D battery light but it was worth little more than what they gave it away for. Sometimes it would light up and sometimes it would not.

It was then that I decided that I would have a decent working flashlight and how most of my police equipment purchases were subsequently made – out of necessity. I bought handcuffs because I figured I couldn't sit on a bad guy until the police arrived, a raincoat because I got soaked one night working outside and a decent flashlight because I wanted to be able to see and operate in the dark.

CASE STUDY

As a Field Training Officer I once trained a rookie who arrived on my shift after working 12 weeks on afternoon shift. He didn't have a flashlight and I asked, "Where's your flashlight?" He said that he had left his Streamlight® SL-20 light in a patrol car and someone had taken it (yes, we have thieves in law enforcement. Why do you think we have locks on our lockers?). I asked him what he was planning to do if we had to search a darkened factory or house. He said he would stay with me… I asked if he still had the flashlight – three cell D battery light which the department had issued him. He said, yes but that it wasn't too bright. I pointed out that any light is better than being in the dark… And believe me, he was in the dark. He didn't make it through probation…

Over the years I've worked on nightshifts extensively, spent hundreds, no thousands, of dollars on flashlights, weapon mounted lights and have had some of the best training in low-light operations as well as training hundreds of LEOs, SWAT operators and private armed citizens in low-light operations, tactics and shooting.

Much of this research comes from a friend of mine, Marshall Schmidt. I met Marshall, a law enforcement trainer, years ago at a police conference in Dallas, Texas. Marshall was a trainer for the Kansas Bureau of Investigation and specialized at that time in low or subdued lighting training for officers. Marshall now works as a trainer for Glock USA.

The retinas of the eyes are made up of rods and cones. The rods are more photosensitive and number at around 120 million. The cones number at around six to seven million and are used for daylight or photopic lighting conditions. Mesopic vision is in intermediate light and a combination of rods and cones are used for vision. Scotopic vision is at low or subdued light levels.

It is wrong, however, to think of low, subdued or adverse lighting as only occurring outside and at night. Even during the height of the afternoon sun, low or subdued lighting can be found indoors. Black-holes, as Ken Good refers to darkened areas or spaces such as closets, interior rooms without lighting, or under desks or anywhere in a room where light does not penetrate, may even be found in an otherwise well lit room.

Author lectures law enforcement students on how the eyes are affected by low light.

CASE STUDY

I've conducted hundreds of narcotics search warrants as a team leader or team member on SWAT. Most of these were conducted in the height of the "crack wars" of the 1990s. Each team member carried a H&K MP5 submachine gun with a Surefire® white light integral forearm. In addition team members carried at least one handheld flashlight with many carrying weapon-mounted white lights on their pistols. We used to joke that in a dope house the only light bulb that worked was in the kitchen and frequently we conducted raids on houses where the only illumination was the flicker of light from the TV set, which always seemed to have cable. But I digress… It paid to have at least one quality light if not multiples to look for possibly armed dope dealers.

LOW LIGHT ADAPTATION

When you move from the sun lit exterior of your home (photopic vision) to a darkened area (scotopic vision) you cannot normally see well and it takes a period of time until you can safely navigate inside.

In an SNS response vision is affected as well with more loss of night vision and the ability to distinguish shapes and colors further impaired – the cones of photopic vision are what the eyes use to see colors.

◆ If you have normal vision of 20/20 when you enter into a low light environment, your vision deteriorates to a level of around 20/800 or about 5% of your normal visual acuity. Consider that legal blindness equates to a visual acuity level of about 20/200. This means that your vision is four times worse than that of legal blindness.

◆ At 15 minutes your eyes adapt to a point your vision will be about 20/300.

◆ At about 32 minutes your vision improves to about 20/180 and is the best that it will get.

Put simply, your night or scotopic vision right off the bat can leave you vulnerable and, in most situations, who has time to wait 32 minutes for their vision to improve?

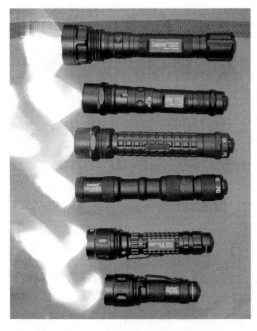

Blackhawk's excellent handheld flashlights.

HERE COMES THE LIGHT

I progressed in my equipment upgrades to what, at the time, was high-tech lighting, Kel-Tec Flashlights, then Maglites. I saw that in the hands of officers, they improved police night operations substantially. These lights offered better/brighter bulbs and reflectors as well as durable aluminum bodies that could double as impact weapons for law enforcement officers.

The problem with these flashlights is that they used disposable batteries that could cost you a few bucks and had the tendency to die when you needed them most.

For this reason, most of us used to carry small AA battery Streamlight® or Maglite penlights. Although these lights offered little illumination in comparison with their larger brothers, they were better than being in the dark.

Streamlight solved the problem with the introduction of their line of rechargeable flashlights. It was at this point in time while carrying an SL-20 with 20,000 candlepower, while working security at an outdoor concert facility that light could be used to distract or disorient subjects as well. Frequently we were required to move large groups of concert-goers who were under the influence of alcohol or drugs. Shining my flashlight at them when they would not cooperate was a way to prompt them to move away from the blinding light towards areas they were permitted.

Since those days more and smaller rechargeable flashlights have come on the scene as well as the use of LED – Light Emitting Diode bulbs. The benefit of LED's in flashlights is the thousands of hours of burn time possible versus standard incandescent bulbs and they are more rugged as well. The first LED flashlights emitted a light that was kind of bluish in color but today's high quality LED's are great lights very white and extremely bright. Another nice feature of LED bulbs is that you have more run time as the batteries die versus little warning with incandescent bulbs.

Surefire came on the scene with their 6P two cell CR123 battery lights which introduced the term lumen. The original 6P was 65 lumens. Lumens, according to Surefire, are a better indicator of overall light beam brightness than candlepower.

Today's small, single CR123 battery and double battery CREE LED lights from Surefire, Streamlight, Blackhawk®, Brite-Strike®, Insight®, NovaTac® and many more quality manufacturers, allow the armed citizen to always have a light with them – in a pocket, purse or carried on the belt. Further, modern mini-lights such as the Executive Precision Lighting Instrument light from Brite-Strike uses two AAA batteries but produces 160 lumens of light and only weighs next to nothing.

Lineup of micro lights from NovaTac, InSight, Surefire and Blackhawk. Any of these are suitable for everyday carry for the armed citizen.

Today in uniform I carry two rechargeable lights from Streamlight, a Dual Switch LED Stinger® flashlight as a primary and a smaller Strion® flashlight as back-up, following the old Navy SEAL motto – "Two equals one, and one equals none." Redundancy in safety equipment is always nice.

Off-duty in a jacket or vest pocket and available at the house for self-defense, I carry lithium battery lights from Surefire, Blackhawk, Brite-Strike and No-vaTac.

Factors to be considered when purchasing a flashlight are:

◆ Throw – The distance the beam can travel and illuminate a target.
◆ Corona – The wider area of a beam that encompasses the entire lit portion.
◆ Hot Spot – This is the intense circle of light within the corona where the beam is at its brightest.
◆ Side Spill or Side Splash – Is the unfocused light that is emitted from the bulb or LED and lights up areas around the circumference of the lens.

For defensive purposes, you want a flashlight, and all of the aforementioned lights are capable, which can punch through the darkness to intensely illuminate a target area or intruder from head to toe, at a distance with minimal side splash. A beam which is so intently focused that the hot-spot does not allow you to see the threat's hands, or what's in them, is of little value, so too, a flashlight which cannot penetrate the darkness with white light to be able to identify a threat should be avoided.

Activation switch

For most defensive purposes, a tail-cap switch is preferable. In this style of switch, a rubber button switch is on the end-cap. To activate the light, the user must press the light inward.

◆ "Click" switch – When the user presses inward the switch "clicks" on and stays on until you press the switch again.
◆ Click switch for different light levels – Another type of flashlight click switch is a click on for high lumen level, click again for low level and then click off. I am not fond of lights with this style of click switch for self-defense.
◆ Momentary switch – When you press the button, the light illuminates. You release pressure, the light goes out.
◆ Rotary switch – Many flashlights feature a momentary on button switch that can be left on for extended time by rotating the switch clockwise.
◆ Multi-Purpose switch – In these flashlights there is a momentary on button at the beginning of the press. Pressing further clicks the light on. Double or triple pressing the button can elicit a strobe feature or even a Morse code blink for S-O-S.
◆ Rotary selection switch – Some flashlights have a rotary switch that

selects function but does not turn the light on and off. The Blackhawk Gladius® for instance, has a rotary switch which features: constant on, momentary on, strobe, and lock-out. With the Gladius you select the feature and then press the momentary tail-cap button to actuate. I usually leave mine in momentary on mode.

For general purpose, I prefer a flashlight that has only a momentary button switch or a combination switch that has momentary button that presses farther to click and stay on.

Strobe capability is nice and can be very distracting on the subject. Having run hundreds of personnel through low and subdued light level shooting programs, most people do not have the skill level with light to double or triple click the light to actuate the strobe. A rotary switch such as on the Gladius takes more practice as well. Unless my light was previously set to strobe function, I've found that I don't normally use this on the street or in training.

Lumen level

For most general purpose flashlights, I believe a lumen level above 100 is necessary. Fortunately most lights exceed this level. The rule is that the higher the lumen level, the lower the runtime or time until the LED begins to fade. Many lights have two light levels, one at their highest and one substantially reduced.

The excellent Surefire 6PX Tactical is a great light featuring 320 lumens. At this light level, the beam can disorient or temporarily distract a threat. The 6PX Tactical is selling for around $63.00 right now from Amazon.

High intensity white lights allow you to work behind a "wall of light." When I've acted as a bad guy role-player in use of cover drills in low light I can attest to the blinding nature of these modern high lumen level lights. When an intense white light hits you, it is virtually impossible to ascertain where the student is located, the lower the overall ambient light level, the more intense this effect. The longer the light is left on, the more an antagonist can adjust but the concept of the "wall of light" is tactically effective.

Fortunately there are some great products out there, many available at great prices and most are available at the company's website or Amazon.com. Check-

Surefire's excellent 320 lumen 6PX Tactical handheld LED flashlight.

Author's partner Jeff Tyler uses the neck index shooting position.

ing Amazon you can read the products reviews so you're not getting an inferior or cheap product. Remember the admonition, "Buy cheap, pay twice!" when buying self-defense equipment.

FLASHLIGHT USE

There were law enforcement myths surrounding the use of flashlights, such as officers shouldn't use flashlights because it would attract gunfire. Truth is, as law enforcement trainer and researcher Tom Aveni has pointed out, that this is a LE myth but more importantly, "Low light shootings account for at least 60% of police applications of deadly force. They seem to diminish police hit ratios by as much as 30%. Low light also accounts for as many as 75% of all mistake-of-fact shootings."

Yet, as previously mentioned few agencies train extensively in low-light operations, adverse light shooting or the coordinated use of handheld light and handgun.

You use a flashlight to:

- ◆ Navigate – Flashlights are used to find your way and avoid physical hazards such as obstacles, drop-offs or holes.
- ◆ Locate – Lights can be used to locate both friend and foe. Searching through your house in the middle of the night, a handheld light can help you locate the sound of the noise you heard.
- ◆ Identify – Once you find your way and locate the person(s) you're searching for, a light can help you identify them and ascertain if they present a deadly threat.
- ◆ Engage the threat – And we mean that not all "engagement" is deadly

Here student uses Harries technique behind low cover.

in nature. If the subject poses no threat to you and you are not in fear of your life, then engagement may be verbal as in, "Get out of my house," or "Stand back!" It may also mean non-deadly force engagement, i.e. spraying a subject with pepper spray or using your C2 Taser®. When it comes to deadly force, as Tom Aveni has pointed out, police accuracy in low-light situations deteriorates by as much as 30%. Flashlights, when used correctly and with training, can improve this hit percentage substantially.

CASE STUDY

A Colorado man shot and killed his own 14-year-old daughter who was sneaking back into the house through a basement window in the early morning. The father thought it was a burglar breaking in.

FLASHLIGHT TACTICS

Operational under-standing and tactical training using handheld white lights has im-proved tremendously over the past few years. Sadly if you watch many (most?) law enforcement

Neck index is used to roll out from weak side of cover.

officers operate with flashlights it is pretty dangerous. During a building search, for instance, many LEOs will simply walk around with their lights illuminated the entire time. As they walk and raise/lower the light while searching, each time the light comes back to point at the ground by their feet, they illuminate/expose themselves to any potentia assailant hiding in the darkness. Regardless of lumen level, this has always been a problem. It is especially true with modern high-capacity lights that can reflect off the surface of the floor, completely illuminating the officer and any other officer standing in the area. This "tracking back" can and should be avoided by only using the temporary or momentary activation button on the light.

Another issue in this regard is "side splash" from the light. In some flashlights this is more pronounced but side spill can throw enough light to the side to illuminate you.

Concepts I've learned over the years when using white lights are:

◆ Use a flashlight grip which coordinates the light beam and handgun when you can.
◆ Usc a two-handed stance whenever possible.
◆ Use the momentary button when searching or operating with the light.
◆ Keep the flashlight placement ahead of your body to minimize side splash.
◆ Try to use cover as you normally would. More on cover tactics with the light later.
◆ "Paint" the area with light. Light on, sweep the area with the light's beam. Light off.
◆ Move after illuminating an area to make a harder target.
◆ If you locate a subject who does not present a deadly threat, keep your light on. If you turn the light off, he can run or move which may require you to search again.

When I first started in law enforcement the most advocated tactic was the FBI flashlight hold. In the FBI hold, the flashlight is extended out to the side at arm's length. The theory here is that attackers may

Author demonstrates the strongest flashlight technique, the Harries method.

shoot for the light and if it is held out to the side the agent/officer will be safe. Once again, Tom Aveni's research has put this myth to bed.

We want to have a few different skill sets in our repertoire and different light techniques as well.

FBI technique – The FBI technique can still be used and is a viable tech-nique if searching for an armed attacker from behind short cover such as over a low wall or vehicle or with narrow cover such as a tree less than arm's reach wide or a utility pole. The flashlight is held up and away from you with the sup-port hand while the pistol is covering the threat area with the gun hand. Remem-ber that the gun should be up and within line of sight. You aim the handgun. You search with the light.

Negative aspects of this technique are a lack of coordination between hand-gun and flashlight. With modern high lumen lights, however, you usually will get enough light downrange to be able to see a wide area. Shooting accuracy is adversely impacted based on the use of only one hand. Side splash and re-flection off ceilings and floors usually illuminates you regardless of the side placement of the light.

New York or Stack technique – Is assumed

A simple way to use a flashlight while working with a handgun is to "stack" the mag baseplate on the flashlight tube. Simple but it offers little recoil control.

The Chapman technique coordinates the light and handgun and is good for large flashlights with side switches.

by simply holding the flashlight in your support hand and stacking the baseplate of the magazine of the pistol held in your gun hand on top of the flashlight tube. For close in work with the pistol, decent accuracy can be achieved if the pistol is brought up to the line of sight.

Negative aspects are a lack of recoil control during firing as the baseplate/flashlight tube match-up is not conducive to control movement or bounce. Further, there is the tendency to point shoot with this technique rather than bring the pistol up to eye level and aim. This technique is better to employ with an activation switch that is located on the side of the tube.

Chapman technique – The late great International Practical Shooting Confederation Grand Master and World Champion demonstrated this technique when I attended an Advanced Officer Survival course that was taught by Mas Ayoob and Chapman years ago. This technique works best with larger tube flashlights such as D cell Maglites or the Streamlight SL20 with switches located on the side of the tube (works with smaller flashlights as well). In the Chapman technique the flashlight is held with the thumb or index finger on the button. The knuckles of the shooting fingers are indexed on the tube and the support hand fingers wrap around to complete a solid two-hand hold. This is a very solid technique and the hands can be pulled back to chest ready with the forearms resting on the ribs for extended periods.

Negative aspects are the more complex nature of the hold and that the pistol is held in the center of the body which necessitates more roll-out from cover. Because the grip is different than the following two techniques, you cannot easily transition to other techniques. Still the Chapman technique is a solid two-hand technique worthy of consideration.

Harries technique – The Harries technique is the premier two-handed flashlight technique. Isometric pressure is used to control the pistol by pressing the back of the hands together at the wrist. In this posture the Harries Technique very much resembles the Weaver shooting stance. The flashlight is held in a "reverse grip" i.e. – lens or bulb end at the pinky. The technique is assumed by extending the shooting hand/arm out, wrapping the support hand under the extended gun arm and mating the two. To achieve isometric pressure, roll the support elbow under.

Negative aspects are a more complex platform that takes more training and skill maintenance to maintain proficiency. You must be careful to extend the gun arm first and then wrap the support hand under, otherwise you "flag" or "laser" your own forearm. The Harries technique should not be used when rolling out from the "weak" or support side of cover because you expose more than one half of your body before the pistol clears cover.

The Harries method is the preferred method when shooting with two hands and working from the strong-side of cover.

Neck-Index technique – This technique was designed by Ken Good of Strategos International and is the best one handed flashlight shooting technique. The pistol is extended up to eye level but the flashlight is indexed at the neck or under the ear at the jaw. The light is held

Neck index places the flashlight on your weak side so it exposes less when shooting around cover to that side.

in the reverse grip as well. This is the best way for a shooter to roll out from the weak or support side of cover.

Negative aspects are the tendency for shooters to place the tube of a larger light on the shoulder. Doing so tends to aim the light toward the floor and not on a co-axis with the barrel. Another error is the tendency to bring the light toward the chin, which illuminates the rear/top of the slide. This oftentimes prevents the shooter from seeing the assailant/target. Finally, the light is placed close to the head/body. If the light is left on, then the assailant may shoot toward the light.

There are other techniques such as the Ayoob technique, the Roger's or Syringe technique and more. These techniques are worthwhile and mastery depends on how much time you have to train and develop them as skills. In my experience, the two basic techniques I would recommend are the Harries and the Neck Index.

RELOADING WITH LIGHT IN HAND

There have been a lot of overly complicated notions and ideas put forth as to what to do with your handheld light while reloading: place the light in your gun side arm pit, push it through your belt, clamp it between your knees, kneel and place it on your foot, use an aftermarket lanyard or ring on your finger or wrist, and more. My experience on this matter is that the more complicated a skill set you use or releasing your grip on the light – the more chance you'll fumble the reload or drop the flashlight.

Years ago I remember firearms trainer Chuck Taylor recommending that you just keep the flashlight in your hand and reload. Since I have been practicing and teaching this technique, I've not had any students fumble or drop flashlights or magazines. While it certainly works easier if you have a smaller flashlight like an N sized 3-volt lithium, it works with C size flashlights like the Safariland Stinger as well as D sized flashlights.

Simply keep the flashlight in hand, reach to your spare magazine carrier, grab the new mag and then reload. Have doubts? Double and triple check you have an unloaded pistol then try this technique. I think you'll be surprised.

Shooting from cover with a flashlight

As in our previous recommendations on cover, when using a light stay back from cover so that you can extend the pistol and have the sights at eye level prior to rolling out as well as having the flashlight in position to instantly illuminate the area.

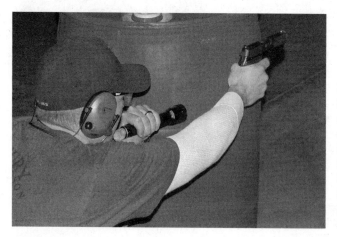

This is why training is so important. Here student is too close to cover and his flashlight is held improperly. When he illuminates the light he will not be able to see past his own gun hand.

The correct procedure is to roll out then illuminate. If you activate the light prior to rolling out, you will blind yourself from the backsplash reflected off the surface of your cover, as well as illuminating yourself to the assailant. Additionally, don't track the light back to your position. Roll out, light on, search by "painting the area" with sweeping motions of light, then light out and roll back behind cover. Think about the "whack-a-mole" game mentioned and possibly change your position or elevation. If you locate, identify and then neutralize a threat by shooting until they are down, then you can keep the light on. Some will tell you to turn the light off and move in the dark after shooting. This is a task requiring high order control. My personal opinion is that it is a lot to ask someone to turn a light off when a threat is found and shot. Movement is good, but if you turn the light out and move, the subject may move and then you have to re-search to locate him.

As mentioned the Harries is best assumed from the gun or strong side of cover, the Neck Index on the support or weak side, e.g. a right-handed shooter uses Harries shooting around the right side of cover, and the Neck Index around his left side of cover.

If short or low cover is used, i.e. a vehicle or low wall, then the FBI technique of extending the flashlight out away from cover is a viable tactic.

WEAPON-MOUNTED LIGHTS

CASE STUDY

August, 2014 (LoudounTimes.com): An off-duty sheriff's sergeant shot and wounded his 16-year-old daughter when he mistook her for an intruder in the home. The daughter had apparently snuck out earlier in the night and was sneaking back into the home at 3:30 a.m. when the sheriff's deputy responded to the burglar alarm going off in the garage area. The deputy shot and wounded his daughter in the darkened garage when he believed an intruder was coming at him.

Surefire's excellent DSF Series Shotgun forearm with over 600 lumens of white light. Mounted on Vang Comp tuned Remington 870 it is a formidable shotgun set-up.

Do I like them? In a word, yes. Operationally over the years running a submachine gun with a Surefire forearm, a Colt M4 with a white light attached and working SWAT and patrol carrying a Blackhawk Xiphos pistol light as well as having run Low Light Pistol courses and training SWAT operators in low light ops over the years, there is a distinct advantage to weapon mounted white lights. Executing search warrants on countless dope houses in the middle of the crack cocaine wars and slow/methodical home searches for murder suspects, I can attest to the value of being able to have two hands on a weapon system pointing at a threat while illuminating them with a high intensity white light. Furthermore, when mounted on a handgun, a weapon-mounted light allows the user to point a firearm and illuminate a target area or suspect with one hand. Consider the offhand being used to stabilize or balance yourself while ascending or descending stairs, opening a door or positioned to fend off an unseen or seen attacker. In law enforcement, K9 officers who frequently hold a dog leash in their offhand, can effectively search and cover with a weapon mounted white light. On police uniform patrol and SWAT my Glock 19 was outfitted with a Blackhawk Xiphos light (180 lumens) and carried in a SERPA Level 3 holster.

Running low light pistol "scramblers" which require students to move through a field of cover with or without partners against a role-playing suspect using air soft pistols, paintball or marking cartridges, I can attest to the effectiveness of weapon mounted light with so equipped students oftentimes dominating the force-on-force encounters.

This is not to say that you should only have a weapon mounted light and not a handheld. You can never use the light on the firearm as a flashlight only because…it's attached to a firearm and everywhere you point it, you are pointing a live handgun or long-gun. While using weapon-mounted lights for SWAT, I

would have a white light around a lanyard on my wrist. Yes, I had a white light on my MP5 or M4 and a Xiphos on my Glock 19 in my holster, but I also had a Blackhawk Gladius on my wrist. In this way I could search or illuminate an area without pointing a firearm.

Glock white light mounted on author's G19, perfect for home defense.

This set-up is excellent for low or subdued lighting. Crimson Trace Lasergrips and Surefire X200 white light. Best of both worlds.

For home defense, I have a Sentry® quick access Home Defense Center® in my bedroom. Inside I have a DoubleStar 1911 .45 pistol with a Surefire X300 weapon light (500 lumens) attached, a Remington 870 shotgun custom crafted by shotgun master gunsmith Hans Vang from VangComp sporting a Surefire 600 lumen forearm light, and a Colt 5.56 M4 carbine with a Viridian Green® X5L-RS white light/green laser combo light (190 lumen white light). I also have a U.S. Palm® Defender body armor carrier which features front/back IIIA ballistic panels, a spare Wilson® eight round magazine for the pistol and another Surefire 6PX Defender white light. You can see I value quality lights on both handgun and long-gun.

Fortunately many concealed carry holster manufacturers such as Blade-Tech® and Raven Concealment Systems® and others make holster manufacturers have begun making scabbards for pistols with weapon mounted lights. These rigs include inside the belt holsters as well as belt mounted concealment scabbards.

CASE STUDY

We were chasing robbery suspects in the city's eastside where I patrolled on a sunny afternoon. They bailed out of their vehicle and we began a search on foot of the backyards and potential hiding areas. I was by myself searching a garage using a flashlight with my handgun, a Smith and Wesson 5906 9mm pistol in my gun hand. Despite the garage door being up, I had to use my Streamlight SL20 light to penetrate the shadows and adverse lighting under the car. There he was! I could only see the bottoms of his tennis shoes since he lie away from me with his head under the engine. "Hands, show me your hands!" I yelled at the suspect. I had him crawl forward out from under the front of the car with his hands outstretched overhead. I was ordering him to walk toward me when another officer, under the adverse influence of a Sympathetic Nervous System response and "John Wayne'ing it", ran in front of my muzzle and grabbed the suspect forcing him to the ground.

Sunny day outside but under and in front of that car in that garage, I needed a flashlight to safely perform my job.

Life has taught me many hard lessons, having at least one quality flashlight, day or night, is one of those lessons. Increase your odds, purchase a high lumen, quality hand-held flashlight and then train. Put some range time in on a regular basis while working with these flashlight techniques. Even if your local range does not permit working in low or subdued lighting, you can still practice the techniques.

Dry fire (with a safely unloaded and double-checked pistol or long-gun – even though it's still "unloaded" don't point the firearm at another person, flat-screen TV or your wife's Pekinese…) in your own home will certainly improve your performance.

Better yet, seek out quality instruction from a vetted instructor.

LASERS

CASE STUDY

Early in my SWAT career, weapon mounted lasers were introduced into law enforcement and my commander at the time became enamored with them (quite honestly I think it was because he wanted to improve his shooting without practicing…). He ordered lasers that were about the size of a pack of cigarettes and had our armorer install them on our MP5 subguns. Norm, our armorer and a friend of 24 years, complained that the units were fragile, hard to zero and easily knocked off zero. Never the less, this commander had his lasers despite the fact that there were no white lights on the submachine guns. Oh, you could see these little red dots dancing around but not the suspect in the darkness. I could tell you that this same commander would get in some trouble for "playing" with his laser on an op but I won't…

Viridian Green white light and green laser combo. Definitely an improvement over earlier designs.

Suffice to say, that I was not enamored with lasers for some time. But my old buddy Marshall Schmidt began working for Laser Max and persuaded me to try one of his company's lasers in a low light pistol class. Oh, the design and practical use started to make more sense. Then Crimson Trace sent me one of their designs, which attach to the grip of my Glock 19. Okay, you now had my interest especially when Crimson Trace sent a training DVD on how to work with lasers. It seems to always be the way that once you educate yourself and train with the gear or tactic, all of sudden truth is injected into the equation, either supporting the equipment or proving it worthless.

Just last year I ran a Law Enforcement Carbine Instructor course in the fall. I had a Viridian Green white light / green laser combo, the excellent X5L-RS mentioned earlier. On the evening of the third day of training, I run a low-light training portion. Shooting the Colt carbine with the Viridian Green long-gun system, I was actually giggling while shooting on the move. I could clearly locate and identify my target with the white light but I was also making head shots because of the strobing green laser dot – all while shooting on the move!

Some will say that lasers offer a deterrent effect with the assailant freezing or submitting to the red or green dot placed on his chest. To this I say – don't count on it. If pointing a firearm in general does not result in surrender or submission, a laser dot won't make them curl into a fetal position. Cops point Tasers with laser red dots at bad-guys every day without instant success, don't expect laser-mounted firearms to do any better.

Do you absolutely need a laser? No, but lasers can improve shooting in certain conditions and for shooters who have trouble seeing the sights due to deteriorating eyesight, a laser may help. Other shooters with good eyesight may benefit as well. If you are contemplating purchasing a laser product, go to YouTube and check out The Art of Survival video series or the Viridian Green video series featuring my buddy Rich Nance at viridiangreenlaser.com.

Lasers, or any device or piece of equipment, will not make you a better shooter, period. They can be used to improve your performance, but no piece of kit can replace time in training.

"It's almost like cheating!" Certainly a top performer in low light.

This holster from Viridian Green turns on the white light or laser as you draw. Innovative and quality product.

LONG-GUN TACTICS

Since the old West, Greener 10 gauge and scatterguns of 12 and 20 gauge, lever-action rifles, even single-shot bolt action rifles have been used in personal defense by armed citizens. Clint Smith of Thunder Ranch fame has a saying, "We carry a handgun to fight our way to our rifle!" And indeed Clint, the father of the modern urban rifle concept, should know. Yes, handguns are convenient to carry but compared to shotguns of 20 gauge or larger, or rifles of .223 or above, have significantly less ballistic impact on target.

That said there are instructors who steer citizens away from using long-guns in personal and home defense. Many of the critics of long-guns in armed defense have little experience with them. We hear these complaints about long-guns:

◆ Are not necessary for armed defense
◆ Are too long and hard to manipulate in close quarters
◆ Over-penetrate through common interior walls
◆ Take time to access
◆ Require two hands to manipulate

Funny, most of my teammates and I carried long-guns on hundreds of tactical operations I was involved in. Further, when we knew we were going up against a serious bad actor, we almost always gravitated toward a shotgun, subgun or carbine. Yes, we carried a sidearm in a holster and would transition to the handgun when entering small areas or when one-handed manipulation was dictated by the environment, but we all carried long-guns. And it seems to me that members of our military when conducting house or building clearing operations in far off hostile locations carry carbines or shotguns.

Let's address some of these issues.

Carbines or shotguns are simply not necessary – This comes from the land of "this is all you need." Indeed states like Colorado and New York have implemented completely ignorant and illogical magazine capacity laws based on "this is all you need." Ten-round magazines with seven bullets in them or 15-round magazines in pistols designed to hold 17 rounds, you pick the law which is

Long guns improve performance in armed encounters based on many different factors.

more devoid of common sense. The facts are that I cannot tell you how many rounds you will need, nor what your armed encounter will look like. Just this week armed citizens, including off-duty police officers have gotten into armed confrontations nationwide.

CASE STUDY

In Pennsylvania, an off-duty officer was being beaten by five occupants of a vehicle involved in a road rage incident when he fired a shot, wounding one of his attackers and causing the others to scatter.

CASE STUDY

East Peoria, Illinois: An off-duty F.B.I. Agent shot and killed a gunman who had walked into a sports bar and shot both his ex-wife and her current boyfriend to death.

Yes, both of these incidents involved lawmen but both incidents had nothing to do with their law enforcement vocations and they are first and foremost citizens of this country, lawfully carrying concealed.

I can't tell you where, when, how many assailants or how long the incident will take. I can only tell you that you want the most effective weapon available and that long-guns have more ballistic impact than pistols and revolvers of even the same caliber.

The mere fact you're in an armed confrontation is an anomaly. After we get over that reality we should develop plans and contingences to solve the problem in the most efficient and expeditious way possible.

Too long or cumbersome for close quarters – Is simply not true. If you were to stand with arms outstretched holding a pistol and stand with a 16-inch carbine both in a combat platform or stance, you would find the overall profile very similar. Further, if approaching a door or smaller room, you don't have to have the carbine or shotgun at point shoulder position. You can transition to a tuck po-

With proper techniques long guns can be used in home defense.

sition wherein the butt-stock is clamped under your arm, in your armpit or use indoor ready wherein the muzzle is canted down and outboard to the weak side, inside your "safety circle."

Working with a carbine or shotgun conducting searching, room entry and clearing is a question of training and experience because it is certainly true that they are valuable tools in those kinds of armed scenarios.

Long-guns over-penetrate – As mentioned in the ballistics and caliber section of this chapter, when a DEA operation resulted in gunfire in a trailer park, it was the .40 which over-penetrated not the 5.56 carbine rounds.

Having responded to countless shootings, I cannot remember a case where a shotgun over-penetrated and wounded innocents. There have been cases where rounds fired from bad guys with AKs have sent rounds into other structures but these were gangsters spraying the area.

Will OO buck penetrate through a sheetrock wall and possibly injure others? Yes but so will pistol rounds when we look at the tests we cited earlier.

Do I want to fire a 12 gauge Brenneke® slug designed for hunting in my home in a self-defense scenario? No, but Federal Reduced Recoil 12 gauge fodder, absolutely.

Take time to access – Well, unless you walk around with an M4 or 870 on-sling, this is a quote from Captain Obvious. But if we go back to the fact that we cannot predetermine what your encounter may look like, we cannot say how much time you'll have to access a more efficient weapons system. I previously mentioned one incident I experienced at my home when a shotgun was multiple times and pellets whizzed through the trees above our house. My response was to grab an M4 and call the police.

Certainly if your only home defense long-gun is stored in a large, slow to access safe, then this point may have more import. But even then, if you have a minute in an event that is building in intensity and you're waiting for a police response, why not up-armor?

Pistol grip on M4 allows armed citizen to use support hand to open doors. Slings allow both hands to be used.

Requires two hands to operate – Once again, we say, "It depends." Can you fire a shotgun or carbine one-handed from an armpit tuck position? Yes you can. Can you go to indoor ready to free the off or support hand for things like opening doors? You bet. Can you even run the gun including reloads with one hand? With training, it can be done.

Equipment wise, we always suggest two or three point slings for long-guns. A sling to a long-gun is like a holster for a handgun. The sling enables the user to go hands free or "on sling" if both hands are needed.

Certainly we shoot better with two hands on the long-gun but we shoot better with both mitts on the handgun as well. Training and practice improves performance generally and it is certainly true with long-guns.

ACCESSORIES FOR LONG-GUNS

Red-dot sights – My M4 carbines all field red-dot or holographic sights like the excellent Aimpoint T-1, H-1, PRO – Patrol Rifle Optic, EOTech sights, In-Sight MRDS or Redfield Counterstrike, because they improve my performance with the carbines.

Years ago the United States Marine Corps conducted a test with red-dot sights to see their value and impact on accuracy as well as time on target. When running qual courses they found that the collimator sights were just as accurate

Left to right: EOTech, Trijicon ACOG, Aimpoint T-1 and H-1, Sig Sauer Red Dot, InSight MRDS, Trijicon RMRs

Viridian Green makes an excellent white light, green laser combo for a carbine.

Here author works out with Rock River carbine, InSight MRDS-mini red dot sight and their white light, and Blackhawk two point sling.

but faster on target. Because the red-dot or holographic sights only require one visual index, the red-dot or reticle on target versus aligning the front sight post within the rear sight aperture. The USMC has found their RCO – Rifle Combat Optic, Trijicon's ACOG – Advanced Combat Optical Gunsight, so battle proven that when a friend's son recently went through Marine Corps boot-camp, he did not even train with iron sights.

White lights – For the same reasons I've already mentioned, white lights allow you to navigate, locate, identify and engage armed criminal assailants.

Slings – No, they don't get in the way. Modern two point slings like the excellent Vicker's Sling® from Blue Force Gear improve performance and allow the armed citizen to operate better with a carbine.

THE CAR GUN

Since we've put many of the myths on long-guns in armed defense to rest, let's introduce a very valid concept, the car gun or truck gun. I have retired Detroit PD Sergeant Evan Marshall and the fine folks at the Stopping Power forum online StoppingPower.net for solidifying this concept for me.

The idea is to have a carbine or other long-gun in your vehicle that is more effective than a handgun. As I remember, Evan was doing some contract work for a U.S. Government entity and was asked by an old LE friend if he had a long-gun in his vehicle. He stated he did not and was reminded about the road he was traveling "Ev, some of the nastiest people in the world live off I-40 between Fort

Smith and Oke City. Don't ever come over here again without a rifle." After that, he got a carbine that he carried in his vehicle.

As a LEO carrying off-duty in my state or out of state under LEOSA – Law Enforcement Officers Safety Act, I carry a Level IIIA raid vest with rifle plates installed in case of response to an active killer scenario on or off-duty. In addition, I have a carbine accessible. For my own Car Guns I've outfitted two different carbines, which I've carried locked in my vehicle.

The first is an Auto-Ordnance M1 .30 carbine with a folding stock. I've attached a picatinny rail on the top of the barrel and mounted an InSight MRDS – Mini Red Dot Sight. On the off-side I mounted a single cell CR123 battery NovaTac flashlight. A bungee sling rounds out the package with 15 round magazines stuffed with excellent .30 100 grain DPX ammunition from Cor-Bon. I've worked with this carbine and it is fun to shoot, exceedingly accurate and with the Cor-Bon a solid performer on target. I'm able to make head shots with the MRDS from 50 yards standing with no problem. I have a small chest spare mag carrier from Blue Force Gear where I carry my spare mags. When in the passenger compartment of my vehicle, I carry the M1 in a nondescript double tennis racket bag I picked up from Play It Again Sports®.

The second carbine I've set up for the car is the one I'm currently using. It is a Rock River 5.56 lower on which I've mounted a Del-Ton® full upper, adjustable stock and parts kit. The Del-Ton/Rock carbine features an Aimpoint H-1 red-dot sight, Magpul – short vertical foregrip, and a Blackhawk white light mounted using a Command Arms Accessories light mount. Like all my carbines, the Del-Ton/Rock River carbine has a two-point sling attached. This carbine rides in an excellent product the Trojan Horse Gun Case® from Comp-Tac®. This case looks like a tennis racket bag but can transport a 16-inch barrel M4 with magazine inserted.

Care must be taken to secure your car gun carbine or shotgun from theft or unauthorized access. In this regard several new products address this such as the AR-Solo Vault® from ShotLock®.

The current car gun is this DelTon upper and parts package on a Rock River lower. Aimpoint H-1 red dot and white light complete the package carried in this discreet Trojan Horse Gun Case by Comp-Tac.

TACTICS WRAP-UP

There is no such thing as "cheating" in a gunfight. Just like the Marquess of Queensbury Rules don't apply on the street to "fisticuffs," an armed encounter has no "rules." Yes, you must obey the laws on the use of deadly and non-deadly force but when it comes to the two-way range and shots being fired there is no requirement that you be fair. As we say in law enforcement, "Fair is where you ride the rides, eat cotton candy and walk in Monkey sh*t" it does not apply to violent encounters.

When carrying concealed, you must always weigh the "risk" of getting involved with the "need" to do so. Most times you want to be the best witness you can be and avoid involvement. But as we say in LE, "on-duty you go to the calls, off-duty the calls come to you..." Some times when rounds are going off and innocents are endangered good men must stand up and put themselves in danger. We try to do this without recklessly endangering ourselves and we never give the bad guy a fight chance when they are actively trying to kill us and others. As one trainer put it, "They are one who put their arm in the lion's cage. They are the one who started it." Dominate the encounter and win. Later chapters will deal with the aftermath but for now understand that the mental aspects of winning are so more important than the gear.

> ### CASE STUDY
> Just recently two Las Vegas Metropolitan Police Department officers – Officer Alyn Beck and Officer Igor Soldo were shot and killed in ambush as they were eating their lunch at a pizzeria. After the male and female suspects killed the officers, they took their sidearms and went to a WalMart in the same plaza, where they fired a shot. Armed citizen Joseph Robert Wilcox confronted them. While challenging the male suspect, Wilcox was shot and killed by the unseen female suspect. Police responded to the store, engaged and wounded the male suspect, who was then shot and killed by the female after which she committed suicide.

This chapter is dedicated to Officer Beck, Officer Soldo and to Joseph Robert Wilcox who stepped up to the plate when it counted and was killed.

How do you deal and stop hyper-violent assailants like these two? You mentally prepare and physically train for it. Let's now look at the training aspects of being an armed citizen.

CHAPTER SIX

TRAINING

Quite simply, training is the engine for winning a violent encounter. Whether we go home, to the E.R. or to the morgue, or instead send our assailant seeking medical care or a body bag, is dependent on the "sweat equity" we have paid in training. Yes the mental issues of our survival and the tactics we use are vital to 1) Avoiding a confrontation in the first place, 2) Observing the precursors and pre-attack indicators and warnings of an imminent threat, and 3) Effectively responding when faced with a deadly threat – whether with communication to the authorities leading to a law enforcement response; with non-deadly force such as pepper spray, a Taser or other less-lethal device; or with deadly force. Training is the key.

We will not "rise to the occasion" but rather "default to our level of training."

CASE STUDY

"Dan" was a uniformed police officer responding to a domestic disturbance call. The incident involved a grown son and his parents. The son was a convicted felon who was assaulting his parents with his prosthetic arms/hooks. The reason he wore these prosthesis was that he had accidentally blown off both hands with a homemade hand grenade in a confrontation with state police in another state. After serving eight years in prison, he was released and moved into his parent's home. After the parents called in to police announcing the domestic assault, the son had armed himself with a .308 bolt action deer rifle which he had

Firearms instruction and training can start on a static line but it must progress to be relevant.

taught himself to operate with his prosthesis. He took up an ambush position prior to the officer's arrival on scene. As Dan emerged from his patrol car, the suspect shot him through the abdomen above his duty belt. The .308 round expanded and blew a fist-sized hole out Dan's back, severing his duty belt.

Dan never stopped and never dropped. Though his belt was hanging down, only held on by "keepers" attached to his trouser belt, he successfully drew his duty pistol and he and his partner returned fire, killing the assailant.

I received a call from another officer who wanted me to know that Dan heard my voice in his brain yelling, "Stay in the fight! Get to cover! Get your gun out and rounds on target!"

It was a humbling experience in my training career. It wasn't the first and sadly won't be the last time some man or woman I've trained put their training and themselves to the test in a life or death encounter. Fortunately it won't be the last time that the law of realistic training saving a life will be proven.

Make no mistake, I stand on the shoulders of giants, but more importantly those lessons passed on to me that have saved my bacon more than a few times, that I have passed on to countless officers I've trained, are now being passed on to you.

TRAINING MODEL

I've used a model originally given to me by noted trainer Bruce Siddle, which I modified and expanded over the years, in training firearms instructors as well as basic cadets and new officers. The model illustrates the training flow we employ to properly train men and women to work the street.

The proper training flow takes a student who is motivated to learn, and gives them:

Proper firearms training content – Content that gives them proper firearm

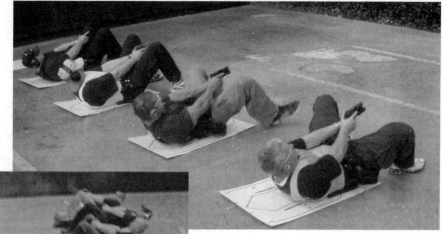

You must be able to fight regardless of your position. It is the trainer's job to prepare you.

Training gives you the skills you need to win, regardless of what level you're shooting from.

skills they can actually do in a stressful situation. Skills that actually have been proven to work or be worthwhile on the street or in actual violent encounters during an SNS response. Motor skills are broken down into classifications. The majority of our skills should be gross motor skills. Gross motor skills require large muscle masses to accomplish, versus fine motor skills. Fine motor skills require eye/hand coordination, such as precision shooting, and deteriorate in a SNS response. Complex motor skills, also known as serial motor skills, require the upper and lower body to work in concert. Driving, for instance, is a complex motor skill. Gross motor skills actually improve with stress, and since fine motor movements go out the window under stress, we want to revolve our self-defense and armed response strategies around gross skills as much as possible. I have actually seen more than a few shooters stumble and fumble actions such as reloads in just the stress of an agency qualification event. Shooting in defense of your life on the "two way range" of the street only magnifies this lack of coordination and inability to perform fine motor skills.

Proper motor skill development – We want to follow a sound methodology of skill development based on motor learning science. As we begin training in a new skill, static training in a closed environment is required. In static training and blocked practice, we isolate a specific motor skill to practice, the draw-stroke or presentation of the pistol from the holster, for instance. We may segment the skill into three parts, i.e. the beginning, middle and end. This segmentation is called chunking. The closed environment pertains to the fact that we are not reacting to changes in our environment or simulated threats. We are isolating and practicing a specific skill. As we begin to flow movements together we have entered the fluid training stage. The instructor may begin using stimulus/response training at this point. He may match a simulated threat, e.g. when a threat target turns, to a response, i.e. draw and fire two rounds. In the fluid stage of training it is seldom necessary to go full speed and power but rather to work on technique and smoothness. As my late Filipino Martial Arts Instructor, Suro Mike Inay used to say, "Let's work on technique, speed and power will be out on the street." The next level of training is to venture into open environment training wherein the student must react to simulated threats versus "On the whistle, draw and fire two rounds." The student shoots when he perceives a threat, i.e. a picture threat target, and keeps shooting until it is no longer a threat, such as when the target turns or falls. Random training is often ignored by many programs. In random training, rather than do what the instructor calls out or instructs, the student downloads or retrieves the necessary skills to solve the problem or save the day. The student is forced to download the skills from short-term memory and this is a vital part of learning. Dynamic training need only compose a small part of training but is vitally important. We will deal with dynamic training later. A good way to illustrate proper skill development is using the British model of training which was taught to me by my friend and fellow trainer Hertfordshire Constable James Dowle: Explain, Demonstrate, Imitate, and Practice. The instructor should follow this flow throughout firearms training.

High repetitions – "Repetition is the mother of all skill" is a quote I'll attribute to the late Filipino Master Edgar Sulite. Put simply, if you want to get good at anything from badminton to bowling, you've got to practice. We used to think that it took thousands of repetitions to get what laymen call "muscle memory," what is now referred to as a Motor Program by Richard Schmidt, PhD the author of the seminal book Motor Performance and Learning (1991; Human Kinetics Books). What modern science has shown us is that these motor programs, think of a pistol draw-stroke as an example, even for the most complex motor skills, only require about 250 repetitions for smooth, fluid movements. It should be noted as Malcolm Gladwell has pointed out in his book Outliers: The Story of Success (2011, Back Bay Books) that mastery takes far longer and the best performers in any field of endeavor practice hard to get there and practice hard to stay there. We have to be careful that we don't fatigue in our live-fire firearms training by training too long. This can lead to unintentional discharges and other safety issues.

Skill competence – Means that with proper and regular training, you get good at performing the skills whether it is the aforementioned draw-stroke, reload, use

"Do it again, and again, and yet again!" If you want to be good, you've got to practice.

of cover, etc. Shooters whether new or old want easily obtained and attained skill levels. It is simply not that easy. Although, introductory skill levels of the fundamentals of shooting can certainly save your life. Indeed the difference between basic and advanced training are the speed, power and intensity of the output. They are the same skills. You want to achieve and maintain skill competence then put in the time and reps. In the beginning stages of motor skill development we must actively think about how to do something. With training we can progress to the point that once we get the "go" signal or stimulus we just respond with a successful motor program.

Skill confidence – The more you do something and the better you do it, the more confident you become and this confidence leads to control of the SNS. We know, for instance, that with our shooting and tactics training we begin to feel more competent which reduces our anxiety and helps control our fear. Essentially our brain feels like "this ain't heaven, but I can operate here…" Meaning that we can focus less on our response and pay more attention to threat assess-

Cover is a lifesaver but in order to feel confident in its use, you must gain competence in training.

ment, our tactics and controlling the threat. The first time a police cadet clears a house in training he feels totally out of control and out of his depth. With time and training however, he begins to learn the skill and begins to feel confident. In short order after doing the skill repeatedly he cannot become overconfident, but should feel in control.

Confrontation simulation – The last part of our training flow chart is confrontation simulation or simulated encounters. When I began my police career we used role-players armed with cotton ball rounds or balls of cotton stuffed into plastic casings with large pistol primers inserted and loaded into revolvers. Eye protection was mandatory in these scenarios. If and when the suspect or officer fired, the cotton ball would fly out and impact the target, within ten feet or so. Nowadays these types of events are known as force on force and are an integral part of most basic training programs.

The training flow circle leads back to a motivated student since, in order to stay good, you have to practice and follow the never ending circle of training.

CASE STUDY

A police captain once commented on in-service training and the requirement that officers continue to train throughout the calendar year and throughout their career. "When will they ever be trained enough?" He lamented that his officers were being pulled off his shift for firearms and assorted training programs…

Here a student engages in force on force using airsoft. It is not enough to engage in static line work, you must apply the skills in confrontation simulation.

The answer to this question is that training never stops. It must be ongoing and must be a dedicated part of your decision to be armed.

STALE BEER

The concept of skill degradation over time is known as the stale beer concept. The truth is that the further you get from a training program the more you lose. As police trainers we now acknowledge that you are better off giving officers eight different one hour training programs during a calendar year than one eight-hour program. The "one time in time" training program leads to too much loss of abilities and skill. Can you imagine a Navy SEAL or Delta Force operator who only shoots once a year for a few hours? I was once told by a member of SEAL Team 4 that when these Naval special operators shoot, the military ships their ammunition on pallets and for eight hours a day during that training block or cycle all they do is shoot.

> ### CASE STUDY
> Over my police career I've seen countless officers who come to the range, for shotgun training specifically, who have lost most of their abilities or skills. Simple tasks such as loading, unloading, clearing, firing and cycling the 12 gauge pump shotgun have been lost since they last touched the gun.

The counteraction or preventative for skill degradation is practice. Simple practice on a regular basis keeps the skills sharp. Short of live fire there are many ways to train on a regular basis which we'll cover shortly.

The 12 gauge pump is an awesome firearm but only through training can skills stay sharp.

THE THREE R'S OF TRAINING

Relevant – Training must be relevant to the task. The notion that you can engage in non-relevant firearms training and still be properly prepared for a violent encounter does not hold water. As an analogy, let's examine boxing. You do not walk off the street and into the ring facing your first skilled opponent in a match. You would start with the basics of stance, movement and punches first practiced in shadow boxing. You would then progress to power development on the heavy bag and speed development on the speed bag. A coach would work with you using focus mitts while you learn slipping, bobbing and weaving as well as combinations. Interspersed throughout would be fitness work to develop stamina, wind and strength. Only then would you step into a ring for sparring work with protective head and body gear. This training would commence over time to get the required skills and then improve upon them. Boxing is, after all, the sweet science.

Unfortunately the training that most CCW permit holders go through is better described as an introduction rather than serious worthwhile training. Training preparation for the armed citizen need not be as intensive as a Olympic athlete or Navy SEAL, but good fundamentals practiced on a regular basis will certain improve your chances.

Realistic – In order to win the day in an armed encounter, your training program must be realistic, meaning the skills learned must be translate to the street or environment you're in. There is a tendency nowadays for armed citizens to seek out "high-speed low drag" folks or alleged former operators for firearms training. Is it really necessary to train under one of these guys to achieve the level of ability to save your life? Not really. Sometimes we have to ask ourselves, does their job experience and the training they give translate to the armed citizen on the streets of America?

That said, standing in a booth at an indoor range or on a line at an outdoor range and loading only when the instructor tells you, slow fire shooting, not moving off the line of attack, etcetera is not conducive to winning on the street as well. There is a lot of realistic training that can be conducted without playing urban commando.

Repetitive – Sufficient repetitions to achieve "myelination." As reported by Bobbi DePorter in her Quantum Learning book (DePorter, Hernacki; 1992; Dell), our brains have millions of nerve cells called neurons. Connecting these neurons are branches called dendrites. Myelin sheaths cover each of the dendrites. As you practice your armed response motor programs, this myelin sheath increases improving performance.

Professional shooters shoot a lot and practice a lot. I've been told that one early three-gun master class and champion shooter went to the range with a five-gallon bucket of ammunition every day! Certainly we don't want and cannot commit that

Encounters take place at "bad breath distance." Training must include those realities.

amount of time and ammunition to our pursuit of effective armed response in our homes, at work or in public, but we can and should practice sufficiently to improve our tactics and shooting. How much time, energy and ammunition are up to you? Officers who have survived a life-threatening encounter tend to take their training more seriously than those who haven't because they realize the importance of relevant and realistic training repeated on a regular basis.

THE FUNDAMENTALS OF MARKSMANSHIP

"Some people try to find things in this game that don't exist, but football is only two things – blocking and tackling."
~Vince Lombardi

Many people and some trainers will try to circumvent the fundamentals by attempting to use shortcuts. They will say, "In a real confrontation, you won't see your sights so you don't need to learn to use them," or "In an actual shooting you'll get a convulsive grip on the pistol and slam the trigger so, you don't need to learn trigger manipulation or a correct grip."

I have a saying I've used for years, "We strive for perfection but we'll settle for excellence." We understand that there will be skill degradation based on an SNS response but we need to learn how to do things correctly. Just like football in the Lombardi quote, we understand that shooting and tactics fundamentals will allow us to dominate and win an armed confrontation.

Platform or stance

Years ago I began using the term platform versus stance because stance in my

The fundamentals must be developed in a repetitive way. Without solid fundamentals, success is a wish away.

mind equates to a fixed non-fluid position. In truth we strive to have the most balanced position or platform available but we don't want to "grow roots" to the ground or floor during an armed confrontation. We need to get the best base possible since like buildings, everything starts from a "firm foundation." By and large our shooting platform is with feet shoulder width or slightly wider with the support side foot slightly forward. Our knees are slightly flexed to act as "shock absorbers," in general our toes, knees, hips and shoulders are oriented toward the threat. Shooting instructor Ken Hackathorn refers to this as our "natural fighting stance." The platform we use to shoot a pistol can with slight changes be used to defend ourselves with empty hands, a shotgun, carbine or submachine gun. The late-great close quarters fighting instructor Colonel Rex Applegate noted that

when threatened, man had an inclination to square off to the threat.

The key to controlling footwork is a simple weight transfer to the balls of our feet. My friend and fellow instructor Chris Cerino, from Top Shot® Season One and Top Shot All Stars equates this weight shift to attempting to pin a piece of paper to the floor. Imagine a note was passed to you in school and a teacher was coming toward you. You shift your weight slightly to pin the note to the deck. This subtle little movement permits recoil to flow up your arms, down your body and into the ground, versus hav-

Toes, knees, hips and shoulders squared to the threat with weight on the balls of the feet.

ing your weight on your heels and even slight recoil pushing you around. Proper weight distribution keeps the pistol down in recoil, allowing quicker follow-up shots. You don't want to lean too far forward so that you are off balance.

When stationary, moving or behind cover we strive to achieve the best base or platform possible but like most things in combat there is some compromise at times.

Grip

Most modern competent instructors prefer a thumbs high forward grip on the semi-auto pistol but many don't know how to explain or demonstrate how to correctly grip the handgun. World-class champion shooter and instructor Ron Avery states that in order to control the pistol you need both leverage and friction. Leverage is obtained by being high on the back-strap of the handgun so that the impetus of recoil while shooting transfers into the forearms versus causing muzzle flip, the higher the shooting hand is on the back-strip the more recoil control and less flip. The pistol or revolver is controlled with a "pincer type" grip of the two middle fingers of the shooting hand, curling and pressing rearward on the front of the grip. Although you grip with the pinky finger, very little pressure can actually be developed and most of our grip is with the middle and ring fingers. Grip energy is directed back into the "drumstick" of the thumb, so that pressure is front to back. The thumb is up or pointed toward the target in line with the barrel.

The 360-degree thumbs high and forward grip helps control the recoil and keeps the pistol on target.

The trigger finger is indexed alongside the frame/slide area of the pistol, above the trigger guard. It does not enter the trigger guard until you are committed to taking a shot. Dr. Bill Lewinski and Force Science have done research on trigger finger placement using training pistols mounted with sensors. Although we instruct students to not place their fingers inside the trigger guard or make contact with the trigger, the reality is that in stressful situations we do. As Mas Ayoob once told me, "When stress goes up, the finger migrates to the trigger," that said, this is a good reason to not have a "hair trigger" or light trigger in a defensive pistol.

As Ron Avery points out, we "set" the shooting hand wrist, we don't lock it. By curling the shooting hand thumb downward and locking the wrist we actually lose trigger finger manipulation and dexterity.

The support hand is the majority controlling hand during two-handed shooting. Whether it is 50% of the grip, 60% or as high as 80% as instructors such as Kyle Lamb suggest, the support hand grip is vital to control the handgun (and it's hard to determine what percentage the support hand versus gun-hand offers since pistols don't come with meters). Friction in shooting the handgun is obtained by a 360-degree grip around the pistol. With the shooting hand thumb positioned high and not curled downward an opening for the support hand is made on the grip. This is filled with the support hand. The wrist of the support hand is canted so that the thumb is in line with the barrel. If you were to point downward toward the deck with the index finger of this hand, the finger would point to the ground at a 45-degree angle.

The fingers of the support hand press into the fingers of the gun hand. Pressure is side to side.

A firm handshake type of grip is exerted on the pistol. Too little and you'll be readjusting your grip after every shot. Too much and you'll exhibit shaking

of the hands and reduced ability to manipulate the trigger.

Note – The handgun should properly fit the shooter. I've seen male and female officers have problems with handguns which were too large for their smaller hands. They would have to move their

Friction and leverage help control recoil and improve shooting.

gun hand around the gun in order to press the trigger. This is most pronounced in higher capacity double stack pistols with double-action triggers.

Trigger management

The manipulation of the trigger is the most vital piece of shooting. We can have a poor stance or platform, bad grip, fail to breathe or follow-through and ignore the other fundamentals – we may still hit. But if we slap the trigger we will deviate the muzzle to such a degree that we can completely miss the target. Even at close range.

I prefer the term trigger press. We are attempting to press the trigger straight back. The term "trigger squeeze" seems to connote a squeezing motion of the whole hand. This is not conducive to accuracy.

Years ago, I, like many other shooters and police cadets was directed by my instructors at the time to place only the tip or the pad of my trigger finger on the trigger. The problem with this is that, for me, it led to muzzle deviation by way of angular pressure on the side of the trigger. I have long ago changed to placing more trigger finger on the trigger, up to the first distal joint of the index

Groups happen based on the application of the fundamentals. Here the author works on bar target.

Results based on application of the fundamentals.

finger. For me this positions the finger better on the trigger and offers better biomechanics. Where should you place the index finger on the trigger? Wherever it feels comfortable and natural and where you can best manipulate the trigger without angular pressure.

Parts of trigger manipulation

Many shooters, even many cops who've been on the job for years, don't touch the trigger until they fire the shot. To fire a shot they go from outside the trigger-guard to making contact with the trigger face, through the trigger take-up or slack and then firing the shot, all in one movement. This oftentimes results in trigger slap. If we are committed to a shot, i.e. a deadly threat is presented by a suspect, or an instructor gives a fire command, then the trigger finger makes contact with the face of the trigger.

With an empty handgun, which you have double and triple checked, and no ammunition in the room, pointing at a safe backstop, you can try the following.

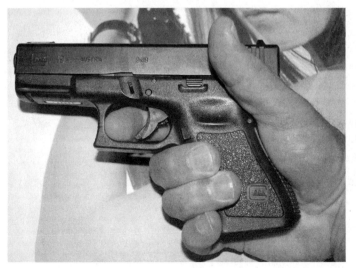

Finger completely off the trigger.

Take-up or slack

Each handgun trigger has an amount of movement prior to the striker activating, hammer falling or firing pin being released. This is called take-up or slack. Some pistols such as double-action/single-action pistols such as the Sig Sauer P226, Beretta 92, S&W 5906, etc. have a heavier weight and further distance until the shot breaks. Even the Glock series of pistols have as much as 3/8" of travel before the striker fires. My G19 pistol with its eight-pound New York trigger still has some take-up before the break of the shot. Single action pistols like the excellent DoubleStar 1911 have less movement or slack in the trigger and a lighter trigger weight but still have some.

Pressure wall

As you "bump" up against the point where the sear breaks the shot, you are "up against the pressure wall." Which means further pressure or movement will fire the shot. With an unloaded pistol and pointing at a safe backstop, i.e. a Safe Direction® wall pad or concrete block wall, you can learn where this pressure wall is on your pistol.

Trigger reset

In dry fire mode with an empty pistol, after you have pressed the shot, while holding the trigger to the rear, manually

Trigger finger at first touch.

Trigger finger at "pressure wall."

Trigger breaks and shot is fired.

Trigger has been reset and is ready for follow-up shot.

rack the slide. If you then slowly release the trigger you will hear an audible "click" when the trigger "resets." This means that another shot can be fired from this point with another press of the trigger. There are a couple of bad habits here. Many neophyte shooters remove their trigger fingers completely from the face of the trigger between shots. Once again this is trigger slap and is to be avoided since it adversely affects accuracy.

Shooting to reset

This is a term that many instructors improperly use. Two techniques some instructors teach can become training scars and are to be avoided: 1) Holding the trigger to the rear after each shot. The notion here is to follow-through on the trigger prior to releasing for better accuracy. 2) They then suggest after pausing and holding the trigger to the rear, you only then release/reset the trigger and press the second or subsequent shots off in this manner. This poor technique can often result in a student under SNS not firing more than one shot because they don't release the trigger or poor accuracy because of so much movement of the pistol to fire one shot.

We all shoot to reset since we have to move our trigger finger enough for reset to occur. When shooting, I would recommend resetting the trigger on recoil and bumping up against the pressure wall to be ready for follow-up shots. Shooting great Todd Jarrett says that most tops shooters are trigger "slappers" and let their fingers fly off the face of the triggers between shots. I respect Todd's abilities but don't know if I would recommend slapping the trigger to new shooters. That said I do let my trigger finger fly and then take the trigger back to the pressure wall. If no further shooting is necessary, the finger is removed from inside the trigger guard and indexed at the slide/frame point.

Out of all the fundamentals as we have indicated, trigger manipulation or management is the most important. We can literally hold the gun upside down with one hand, stand on one foot, but if we smoothly press the trigger, we will hit our target.

Sight alignment

Sight alignment is placing the front sight within the rear sight notch so that it is even at the top with equal light on both sides. Some sights, such as the Smith and Wesson M&P pistols have a smaller front sight so that there is more room on either side within the rear sight notch. Some pistols such as the Glocks have blockier front and rear sights so that there is little room on either side. As I have gotten older, I've been looking for better sights than are offered by most factories. I've had Lasik surgery with my dominate right eye corrected to 20/20 and my left eye at 20/40 to read with, this is called "mono-vision." (Note – This was a mistake in my opinion and I should have had my left eye corrected to 20/20 because my sights are always blurry now. So if you are contemplating Lasik, and it is a great thing, and are a shooter, talk to your eye surgeon about this.)

Because of vision issues, I currently use a factory Glock rear sight but a green fiber optic front sight from Hi Viz® Shooting Systems. This allows my front sight to "pop" a little easier on target. I have also begun using an S&W M&P340 as a back-up gun. This five shot scandium frame revolver is outfitted with XS Sights 24/7 Express Sights. The big front sight featuring a Tritium insert is so much easier to see than my old Chief Special sights.

As part of Jeff Cooper's Modern Technique of the Pistol we find the term "flash front sight picture," meaning that at most combat distances one only has to flash or lightly focus on the front sight on target to achieve solid hits. Cooper wrote in his excellent book, To Ride Shoot Straight and Speak the Truth (1998; Paladin Press) that "the body aims and the eyes verify" which means that once natural point of aim is found and additional training obtained (a successful motor program is achieved) then the pistol is presented to the target and the eyes verify this alignment prior to shooting.

Cooper's statement falls in line with modern research on what the eyes can focus on during SNS. My friend Randall Murphy from Meggitt Training Systems (the makers of the FATS® – Firearms Training Systems) has conducted state-of-the-art research using headsets which can track what a test subject's eye focuses on during a stressful simulated armed confrontation. Murphy's research clearly demonstrates that the eyes tend to focus on the threat but as Randy points out, that doesn't mean we ignore the sights in training. As he has said to me, the sights are the training wheels with which the shooter learns alignment. We train using the sights to achieve a successful motor program so that in an actual armed encounter we raise the pistol to the same spot.

CASE STUDY

Over the years I've dealt with "point shooting" and point shooters ad nauseum. My experience and those of my fellow trainers is that point shooting at below eye level leads to misses even at close range. In countless confrontation simulation scenarios we have noted time and time again students missing at distances as close as five feet when their pistol is held at chin or chest level or lower. However once the student brings the pistol up to eye-level where you have the eyes, pistol and target in a straight line, hits are achieved.

I am a fan of red-dot, i.e. holographic or collimator sights. These sighting devices have been around since the Vietnam era with Bull Simons' Son Tay raiders using them in their attempt to rescue American POWs held in North Vietnam. The raiders were troubled by their ability to hit targets in low or subdued lighting. They found the answer in a shooting supply catalog with the Armson

Trijicon RMR red dot sight mounted on Glock 17.

O.E.G. – Occluded Eye Gunsight. The OEG superimposed a red aiming dot on target. Although the raiders did not rescue any POWs, who were moved prior, they did engage North Vietnamese and Cuban military personnel in a gunfight and were very successful with their red-dot sights.

It took a long time for the military to widely adopt red-dots but in today's military every service uses some type of holographic or collimator sight. They have been so successful that the technology has shrunk and is now being applied to pistols with Trijicon's RMR – Ruggedized Miniature Reflex sight being used among others.

The nice thing about reflex or holographic sights is that one only has to "float the dot and take the shot." Just superimpose the red-dot aiming point, chevron or reticle onto the target and press the trigger. There is no need to align the front and rear sight. As the United States Marine Corps found out years ago when testing these sights, there is no accuracy fall-out but there is an distinct improvement in speed on target.

A couple of truisms here: 1) Everyone's sights move. Even the top shooters in the world cannot hold their pistol completely still. That said many shooters will attempt to rush or slap a shot when "everything is perfectly lined up." This leads to trigger slapping or jerking and poor accuracy. 2) In order to hit, perfect alignment is not necessary. You can, at most handgun shooting distances, hit within an eight-inch circle if the front sight is bumped up against the left side of the rear sight, the right side, is barely visible above the bottom of the rear sight notch or is completely above the top of the rear sight.

A good saying in terms of sight alignment is, "See what you need to see to make the shot." Meaning that at relatively close range shooting aggressively once the pistol breaks the line of sight will result in center mass hits on target. My corollary to this rule is, "The further the distance, the smaller the target, the more you have to pay attention to your trigger and sights."

Sight picture

Taking sight alignment and placing it on what you want to hit is sight picture. As we have already stated, a strict focus on the sights or even front sight although desirous is not required at most handgun ranges. We bring the pistol to eye-level and can, using the entire rear frame of the pistol as a sighting system, achieve decent accuracy.

CASE STUDY

Howard Wasdin, Navy SEAL Team Six member and author of "SEAL Team Six: Memoirs of an Elite SEAL Sniper" (2011; St. Martin's Press), once told me and a class of SWAT operators during a hostage rescue training class that when he was involved in the infamous Mogadishu, Somalia, combat operation that the hardest thing to do in combat when rounds are coming at you like a hornet's nest is to pay attention to your sights to get rounds on target.

We can use the entire pistol as an aiming sight out to decent distances. Noted firearms trainer Bill Burroughs (Talon International) has commented that the entire pistol can be used as an aiming aid or sight until it no longer fits within the target area. Once the pistol is seen as larger than the target area, the sights must be referenced. Remember though, "The farther the distance, the smaller the target, the more you have to pay attention to sights and trigger," headshots or small target areas at close range, require sight alignment/sight picture.

Breathing

Every warrior class from the Spartans to the Samurai and Miyamoto Musashi, including our modern warriors in military and police uniform, have come to find that breathing specifically what trainers now call autogenic or tactical breathing has direct impact on performing well under stress.

CASE STUDY

As a veteran of hundreds of SWAT narcotics search warrants, I would take the research that as few as three to four deep breaths can reduce your stress (take control of your SNS response) to the point that you can perform complex motor skills, and recommend it to our team. While riding in the SWAT raid van prior to enforcing a search warrant I would say, "Breathe to reduce your stress and focus on your task."

Autogenic breathing simply means breathing in through your nose for a four count, hold for a count of four, breathe out through your mouth for a four count and hold for a count of four, then repeat. Anytime I'm aware of an increase heart rate during stressful times (I usually feel this in my neck) then I start using tactical breathing.

Over the years when I've faced dangerous of stressful situations or conditions, I'll take a few deep breaths and immediately feel the stress and symptoms of an

SNS response such as – tunnel vision, auditory exclusion, hands trembling, lack of cerebral cortex processing, all reduce or come under my control again.

Follow-through

This means staying on the sights and trigger through the break of the shot. Most times I've missed at small targets or during multiple targets events are because of I've failed to follow-through. Tactically there is a danger to relaxing too soon or coming off the gun and giving attention to persons, areas or things other than the threat. Once you come off the threat or attend to other things, the threat may attack or move.

It is generally suggested that you continue to shoot until the suspect is no longer a threat. This has been summarized by the statement, "Shoot them to the ground." There can be a danger with putting a large number of shots on one suspect when dealing with multiple adversaries, in that it gives time for the other suspects to recover and attack. We do not want to fire only one shot at each suspect based on the realities of low hit probabilities in actual shootings (in police shootings hit rates average 20 to 40%). However, we do not want to give our other assailants the time needed to react and respond. Two to four rounds may be a decent number per assailant. The notion that under an SNS response you can: shoot one on bad guy #1, one round on bad guy #2, two rounds on #3, then come back and shoot #1 & #2 again some more, is not realistic and may not be even possible.

Accuracy wise in that brief period you are no longer paying attention to the sights, the pistol may be moving. On the range I've seen many students toss shots two and three on a first target when shooting two or more targets due to lack of follow-through.

It has become "tactically cool" to come off the sights, trigger and target after firing. Instructors who advocate this technique do so with a "snap" back to a ready position. Looks cool but in real life, don't you want to stay on target to make sure he's down and out before coming off target? Of course, in my life and career I've never been described as "cool."

To hit you've got to apply the fundamentals including follow-through. Coming off target too early leads to misses.

Recovery

Firearms instructor Chris Cerino and I began adding the recovery phase to the fundamentals years ago. We noted that far too many law enforcement officers were rushing to re-holster after encounters. The truth is that no one ever won a gunfight by being the first one to put the pistol or revolver back in the holster. I began using the phrase, "Reluctantly re-holster," to describe this process after all, you've had this gun out of the holster or in a ready position for a reason, you need to be sure that the threat is down and out and no other threat exists before you relax. Even then, it is entirely possible that the suspect is just feigning incapacitation and playing "opossum."

This recovery phase has several parts. The first is to counteract against the effects of the SNS and tunnel vision. We do that by lowering the pistol slightly and starting to expand our vision. We compensate for tunnel vision by turning our head.

We move to change our position to make a harder target and if cover is within steps, we move behind it. If a tactical retreat is advisable and possible we safely move away from the threat.

If the threat is down and out or under control we may hold on the suspect's hips or a position if the suspect is prone, which allows us to see his hands.

If shots have been fired, we glance at the pistol to see the condition. Many times in high stress shootings or scenarios students will not give conscious

No one ever won a gunfight by being the first back into the holster. Reluctantly reholster and break that tunnel vision.

thought to the condition of the pistol, i.e. they shoot to slide lock back and are standing, post incident, with an empty pistol in hand.

We can also conduct a "tactical reload" also known as a "reload with retention" to ensure that our pistol is topped off with ammo and ready to go.

Regardless of whether we've have fired or not, we want to look around for other citizens or police personnel, witnesses and possible other threats. The eminent firearms instructor John Farnam states, "Life is a live-fire, 360-degree environment."

If and then we determine that it is safe to do so, we reluctantly re-holster.

GIVE AND TAKE

A number of years ago firearms instructor Andrew Blubaugh, former Recon Marine, police trainer, and director of Apex Shooting and Tactics, applied the concept of "index and trade" to the fundamentals of marksmanship. The concept was name changed by Chris Cerino to "give and take," and subsequently incorporated into firearms programs we taught for the state LE academy.

Give and take means that if one or more of the other fundamentals of marksmanship are not as strong, then a shooter must focus on the others to achieve accuracy. For example, if a shooting platform or position is not what it should be because of terrain or movement, then the shooter should focus on the other fundamentals. Remember my example of shooting a pistol upside down on one foot, with one hand? When I do this in basic programs or with new shooters, the emphasis has to be on the trigger and sights to make the hits.

Give and take. If some of the fundamentals are not available, like platform, focus on the others.

THE BASICS

The basics of shooting are the fundamentals of marksmanship (FOM) and they need to be trained and competently attained and attended to with regular practice. Students always want "advanced" or "high-speed low drag" training. The problem with this notion is that they have frequently not competently attained the basics. In truth, "Advanced techniques are the basics mastered," and like focus on the basics in football, focusing on the fundamentals of marksmanship wins gunfights and armed encounters. You will often hear a coach tell his team after a disappointing loss, "Monday, we'll be focusing on the fundamentals." You never hear a coach say, "We need to get more complicated and intricate."

How then can we attain competency in the basics? Proper training, time, repetition and practice are the methods we use.

DRY FIRE

All shooters, regardless of competency levels, benefit from dry firing their handgun as well as engaging in dry (unloaded) weapon manipulation drills of the firearm. Few of us can afford to live-fire on a regular basis to maintain proficiency with our skills. Dry-fire is an important way to develop the myelination I talked about earlier and successful firearm motor programs.

Use a Safe Direction Composite Armor Board from my buddy Steve Camp at Ravelin Group, or an ammo can filled with sand, or a safe backstop such as a cinder block wall. Double, then triple check to make sure your handgun is unloaded and no live ammunition is in the same room.

> ### CASE STUDY
> The Federal Air Marshal's management gave instructions for their personnel not to engage in "dry fire" in hotels while on assignment because they had to pay for too many big screen TVs and plumbing repairs in the walls of hotel rooms where some of the marshals had stayed.

Engage in dry-fire sessions working on the FOM including trigger and sights. Striker-fired pistols will have to be manually racked after each trigger press. Some instructors have called this action a "training scar" since the typical response to a "click" and not a "bang" is to engage in malfunction clearance drills. However, in all the incidents where I have re-

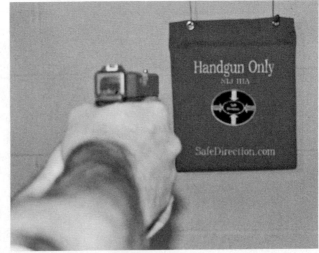

Safe Direction makes an excellent dry fire product to lessen the chance of an unintended discharge injuring someone.

sponded to a threat on the street and range work, I've never seen this become a problem. In training we are isolating a skill such as trigger press and we can do that without adverse impact on our defensive pistol work. This is one of the ways that shooters have improved their FOM since man has been carrying firearms.

We can practice various aspects of our combat handgun skills – the presentation of the pistol from the holster, reload with retention, reload without retention, use of cover, movement, etc. To improve our performance the purchase of dummy training rounds is recommended. I prefer the metal case and orange plastic simulated bullet. The metal case will stand up to the rigors of repeated use and the orange plastic faux projectile is easily seen and hard to confuse. That said, inspect each dummy cartridge prior to loading in a magazine. These dummy rounds allow the slide to go into battery when conducting reloading drills.

As a way to improve your training, use a simulated target such as an actual Shoot-N-C target or even a photocopy of a threat target.

Let's examine a dry-fire presentation of the pistol from the holster with a four-count draw-stroke.

Count One: Obtain a solid three finger grip of the pistol in the holster, while deactivating any safety mechanisms such as thumb breaks or other retention devices, the off-hand is placed center palm on center chest to facilitate a block, parry, or strike.

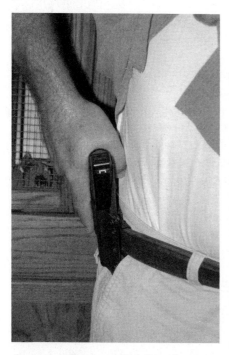

Count 1: Achieve a solid three-finger grip of the pistol in the holster.

Count Two: Rock & Lock – As soon as the muzzle clears the top of the holster, rotate or rock the muzzle forward and toward the threat while locking the wrist. Properly done, the thumb of the shooting hand is indexed on the outside of the pectoral area with the pistol slightly canted outboard so that in live-fire the slide can properly reciprocate. Some trainers advocate a muzzle canted downward position but this can lead to misses at distances as close as five or six feet and even hits may be in soft tissue in the belly. As Dr. James Williams states in his Tactical Anatomy class, "Between the naval and nads there's nothing good to shoot."

Count Three: The support-hand and gun-hand meet at center chest at what is high-ready position with muzzle oriented toward the threat. From here the

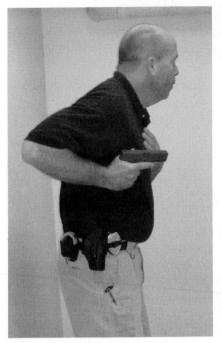

Count 2: Rock the pistol out of the holster and lock the wrist, indexing the thumb of the shooting hand at the outside of the pectoral.

Count 3: The hands meet at center chest, pistol pointing toward threat.

pistol is lifted up to eye-level, pressed outward toward the threat, while the trigger finger begins applying pressure to the trigger.

Count Four: The arms are at full extension, the pistol is held at eye-level with soft or hard focus on the front sight and all slack is taken out of the trigger to fire a shot.

Note – If a shot is not necessary, the trigger finger does not enter the trigger guard. It is fully anticipated that the armed citizen will have a greater possibility to draw and point the handgun at a suspect to stop a developing threat, than actually drawing and firing.

Note – As master shooter and instructor Bill Rogers of the famous Rogers Shooting School states, the time difference between placing the trigger finger on the trigger and keeping it outside the guard in a shooting scenario is substantial. I would recommend without hesitation Roger's book Be Fast, Be Accurate, Be the Best (2010; Rogers Shooting School Publications) and his Panteao Productions training DVD Reactive Pistol Shooting.

RECOVERY TO THE HOLSTER

To recover to the holster we recommend the following procedure. Lower the handgun to the subject's hips and begin to scan the area by turning your head,

Count 4: Handgun is lifted up and pushed out toward the threat. Shot can be fired, if necessary, as handgun breaks the line of sight.

Handgun is returned to placement at Count 3, then Position Sul is used as 360 scan is commenced.

return to Count 3 of the draw-stroke with the forearms resting on the floating ribs. Transition to Position Sul and move your feet to check the areas to your right, left and behind you. Re-holster with the support-hand indexed on the chest to protect yourself.

To add realism via a time constraint, you can use your smart phone as a shot timer. Surefire has a free app that you can download to engage in worthwhile structure practice. Remember be smooth in your movements.

Hundreds of these presentations and recovery to the holster can be practiced in the safe confines of your home if the safety protocols are followed! By clearing the pistol and engaging in safe practice you won't shoot your plasma TV or your wife's Pekinese.

TRAINING GEAR

S.I.R.T. training pistol

The Shot Indicating Resetting Trigger Training Pistol from Next Level Training (NLT) is a training device that I've come to appreciate more and more. Originally introduced to me at the annual conference of ILEETA, the SIRT pistol allows realistic training via the use of a laser training "pistol." Replicating a Glock 17 sufficiently that it will fit in my Blackhawk SERPA duty holster, the SIRT PRO model which I have been working with is a completely non-firing training device with all the controls where my G19 are located. With a removal and weighted simulated "magazine," I can practice reloads as well (although the slide does not move at all). The weight is right at 28.9 ounces for the SIRT and 30.7 ounces for my loaded G19 with a 15 round magazine.

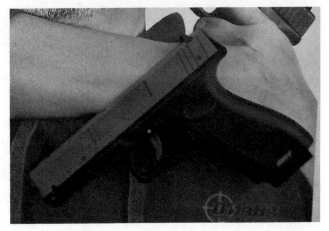

The excellent S.I.R.T. training pistol. Simply nothing else like it.

The SIRT PRO model features dual lasers. When your finger begins to apply pressure on the trigger a red laser beam is projected from the lower laser (where the guide rod would normally be located). This red laser is adjusted by NLT to impact lower than the sight line. This would allow an instructor monitoring a student's use of the device in training to track if the student has his/her finger on the trigger, where the SIRT pistol is pointing and movement pre and post trigger break.

A green laser is sighted in dead-on with the sights and "fires" when the trigger is fully pressed. If the trigger is held to the rear and not reset, the green laser stays on.

These green and red lasers can be reversed by an internal switch, so that the green turns on first, then the red.

Training opportunities are endless because, unlike air soft or marking cartridges, there is no danger to the environment. No safety equipment is necessary and targets can be simply copied from the internet and printed, standard paper or cardboard targets, martial arts striking bags like a boxing heavy bag or a Body Opponent Bag (which simulates a real man), or even an innovative target of a plastic sealed bowl filled with water (I've done this with a one gallon jug of spring water from the store). In this way you can train by yourself with a resetting trigger pistol (unlike dry firing with an unloaded pistol which needs to be reset after every shot). I've used all of the above as targets. In combination with a SHOT timer such as my Competition Electronics Pocket Pro, I can work on my draw-stroke, multiple targets, use of cover, on and on. Just last year while convalescing from knee surgery, I set up some training using a SIRT pistol and other laser training technologies in my den. Gave me something to do, opportunities for practice from concealment and more, as well as beating the heck out of watching TV on a cold fall day when trips to the range were not recommended.

Just yesterday I consulted with three trainers from the state police academy who were interested in improving their firearms and officer survival training

Body Opponent Bag can be used with SIRT pistol to incorporate empty hand striking as part of drawstroke.

for their students. What I recommended was the purchase of SIRT pistols and then progression through air soft drills conducted with an instructor, before they introduced confrontation simulation. Does this sound like the boxer analogy we used earlier? You bet.

Another option for SIRT work is the training pistol used in conjunction with a free smart phone or iPad app called Ubersense which is a "video analysis & sports coaching app." If you have a beginning student or student experiencing problems and would like to diagnose their movements, just video their FOMs and review it. Many shooters don't understand how a trigger jerk or slap can throw them off target or how they are failing to follow through while shooting multiple targets, etc. You can even draw lines or other shapes to focus their attention and ship the video to an email address for further review. Pretty cool technology that can be used out in the field for shooter training.

LaserLyte

LaserLyte makes some neat and fairly low cost training devices as well. In my officer at work I have a LaserLyte plastic trainer pistol (Model LT-TT), a LT-PRO red laser that works in pistols and revolvers from .38 special (minimum two inch barrel) to .45 semi-auto pistols. The device is sized by tightening or loosening the adapter and "fires" a laser dot on target when it "hears" the hammer drop. The LaserLyte training pistol has a trigger that resets after each shot.

Although this pistol has more of a "toy" feel to it, the sights are good and the ergonomics well designed to recreate a modern striker fired semi-auto pistol. I simply install the laser LT-PRO in the barrel of the pistol and am good to go with training.

LaserLyte has several laser training targets that are pretty cool. The TLB-1 is powered by three AA batteries and has a circular five-inch red target area. Simply turn the target on, and "fire" the training pistol at it. To see your hits, fire a shot at the one-inch "Display" target and LED

LaserLyte Laser Target and LT-PRO laser for use with standard handgun.

Airsoft pistol powered by "green gas."

lights will illuminate where you hit. For subsequent strings, just hit "Reset" and you can do it all over again.

New training targets from LaserLyte include the Reaction Tyme targets that will flash and beep a target light in random three to seven second intervals and then beep twice if struck. The laser Plinking Cans are a lot of fun with three can shaped targets. Simply turn them on and set them down on a flat surface. Strike the one and half inch oval target area and a little piston topples the plinking can over. The last new target is the new countdown target which has a larger target screen, and gives audible beeps to start time and another beep to stop at either three or seven seconds, whichever you select.

I've got the Trainer Target and Plinking cans set up in the armorer's room across the hall from me. From my office I can easily hit the target and cans with the trainer pistol, which allows me to work on my sight picture and trigger press as well as the other fundamentals of marksmanship.

Airsoft

Several years ago I became aware of a new "toy" called airsoft that looked to have some interesting applications for training. The original manual cocked airsoft pistols were strictly toys, as were the original electric pistols. But soon "green gas" airsoft pistols hit the market and I purchased a couple to play with. Green gas is actually propane, and the interesting thing about the new air soft pistols is the accuracy potential. The .20-gram plastic "BBs" fly down the barrel at a decent velocity and a "bump" in the barrel imparts a backspin on the projectile. The result is some exceptional accuracy from pistols that closely resemble the actual handguns out there. I happened upon a DVD by an innovative trainer named Rich Daniel out of Oregon (Fist, Feet, Knife, Gun and The Place to Shoot indoor firearms range). Rich was taking air soft to new levels by using them in conjunction with live-fire firearms training. You can do training drills with airsoft indoors using cardboard targets that you simply cannot safely do life-fire, as well as teaching shooter new material in a safe way prior to live-fire. As long as eye protection is worn, the possibilities are endless.

I had the opportunity to meet and train with Rich Daniel when members of the Seattle Police Department who had trained with him, instructed at an international police training conference I attended. Seattle was rotating all of their personnel at the time through a firearms training program which used air soft as the training modality.

Since then I have used air soft in basic training programs with police cadets as well as advanced officer survival programs with veteran officers. We've used airsoft against cardboard targets, boxing focus mitts to work on the transition for empty-hand to handgun, other students, and role-players in confrontation simulation scenarios. For work against cardboard targets, as long as eye protection is worn (the BBs tend to bounce around) students and instructors are fine. In scenario-based exercises, throat protection and a heavy garment and gloves as well as eye pro should be worn. Rich Daniel uses street hockey helmets modified with mesh to protect the face and eyes. The helmet is to protect the student from impacts with objects, walls and other students.

The only negative aspect of airsoft training is the reduced sturdiness of the pistols and magazines. The magazines cost about $30.00 each and will invariably break if dropped on a concrete floor.

For more information and some really cool training check out Rich Daniel's DVD Legitimate Training with Airsoft.

CONFRONTATION SIMULATION TRAINING

A lot of proper preparation for armed confrontation can be accomplished at home conducting dry fire or by using any of the modalities mentioned above. There is still a missing element, in my opinion, which is confrontation simulation training, also known as force-on-force, adrenal based training, shoot or don't shoot, stress inoculation or scenario based training. The notion here is to take the student out of the classroom or off the live-fire range and put them into scenarios in which they have to interact with role-players and make correct tactical and force decisions using inert, airsoft or marking cartridges. As I previously mentioned, early versions of this type of training used cotton-ball projectiles that were only used in revolvers LE carried almost exclusively at that time. The next step for me was using Code Eagle paint or marking cartridge rounds then Simunitions, which were developed in Canada, and with conversion kits could be used in the S&W 5906 semi-auto pistols my agency carried at the time. These new marking cartridges had a thin skin plastic projectile that was filled with inert marking compound and powered by large pistol primers. Make no mistake, these projectiles can hurt you traveling at 400fps or thereabouts.

CASE STUDY
I can remember getting some Code Eagle in and asking my then training Sergeant Dave Van Pelt to "shoot me in

the back." The good sergeant had some understandable trepidation about doing this but relented. Yes, it stung and left a red mark but wasn't debilitating. When I called Simunitions about safety equipment a short time later and asked, "What safety equipment do you recommend?" He said, "Well, it depends on how tough you are. The Norwegian Jaegers (their special operations troops) wear shorts, sandals and eye protection." I freely admit after years of Sim use, I'm not that tough...

Simunition marking cartridges can be used in pistols with conversion barrels attached or for the Glock pistol, a dedicated training pistol. Sim makes protective suits for scenario based training which protect against injury to eyes, face and body. The only detriment is that Simunitions are not available for civilian use and cost about 50 cents per round.

UTM and Speer's Force-on-Force are other brands of marking cartridges but are restricted to the military and law enforcement only. That said, airsoft has been successfully used in armed citizen confrontation simulation training for a while now. Once again, if other students or role-players are to be targeted then appropriate

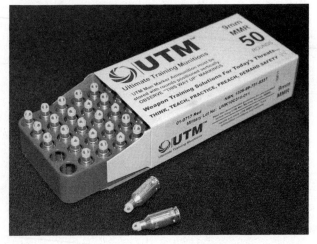

UTM marking cartridges fire paint rounds.

eye, face, neck, hand and body protection is mandatory.

STRESS INOCULATION

The idea of this type of training is to introduce the student to the stressor, cause a sympathetic nervous system response, and teach them how to deal with and overcome the brain and body's response to fear. The inoculation concept simply means that by exposing yourself to the stressors or fears in training, and all the physiological, physical and psychological responses involved, you'll be able to operate better when it happens for real.

After years of running these types of drills I've found them extremely valuable and worthwhile. That said there are some important rules and safeguards that need to be in play.

1. The training must be designed to empower and lift the student up, not trash them.

2. The scenarios must be "winnable," no ninjas rappelling out the ceiling.

3. Sufficient safety equipment must be worn. Damaging a student's eye or chipping their teeth or physically injuring them is not acceptable.

4. A safety officer must be present who can halt the proceedings to protect both student and role-player.

5. It is recommended that the scenario be videotaped for debriefing.

6. Debriefings should be positive in nature and not trash the student's performance.

7. The student should always win, even if promptings must be given by the instructor on how to win or what to do. I have literally had to position a LE student and a role-player and then give prompts such as "Forearm strikes, knee strikes! Front takedown!" it is vitally important that the student become empowered in training even if they are scared, timid, or lack self-confidence. If the student leaves training doubting their ability to win an encounter, then it has been a failure. There have been several basic academy students who decided that law enforcement was not for them after this training.

8. Multiple scenarios should be given. In this way a student has sufficient number of reps to become inoculated to the stress.

Everyone gets nervous when running a confrontation scenario. The training value is learning to operate while stressed. As Colonel Dave Grossman, author of On Combat (Grossman, Christensen; 2004; Warrior Science Publications) points out in his lectures it's not that military special operations personnel don't feel fear or aren't stressed, it is that they based on their training, have expanded their comfort zones so that they can operate at a higher level, under worse conditions and longer than the average person. Though you and I will never operate at the level of a Delta Force member or Navy SEAL, we can expand our own comfort zones and increase our ability to deal with our own SNS response through scenario-based training.

I came across the Hooded-Box Drill® while watching a documentary about training that Department of State Security agents go through. Trainer Duane Dieter trains Naval Special Warfare operators as well as DSS agents. He developed the Hooded-Box Drill and I have used a modified version ever since. The idea is that the student comes into a specially prepared room where role-players are already located behind a wall. We usually lower the lighting level and play loud music in the background. A hood is lowered over their head with instructions to react and appropriately respond to whatever threat they are confronted with. Could be a drunk in a park, a domestic disturbance, a fight in the parking lot of a bar, etc., when the hood is lifted they must control the threat.

We have just talking drills where verbal direction is the only requirement, man with a knife, man with a gun, hostage incident, a physical fight between two role-players, on and on. Once the student controls the situation we call, "Break!" and position the hood back over their head. In this way, we can give one student five or six scenarios in the space of two minutes or less. The idea is to introduce max stress but enable the student to win the day. Our LE students are armed with a marking cartridge or airsoft pistol, Hydro-Shot which is an inert water spray which simulates pepper spray, and a Blue Baton which is a training baton simulating an expandable metal baton.

Borrowing and modifying Mr. Dieter's training has increased the reality-based training we offer our law enforcement officers. I have run similar programs for armed citizens training with similar positive results.

CASE STUDY

The first course I ever used the Hood Drill on was a Female Officer Survival program. One of the most rewarding programs of my career, the ladies really "opened up a can of whoop ass!" as the saying goes and were very aggressive. Part of this was because they stated they didn't have to "Compete with the testosterone in the room," like normal in-service but rather felt they could get suitably aggressive without being judged. In consideration, maybe we as a society should ponder this... I'll cover more on this topic in Chapter Nine – Ladies, Guns and Armed Defense.

For more information on this type of training, I would recommend Ken Murray's book Training at the Speed of Life (2004; Armiger Publications). Although geared for the military and law enforcement, there is a treasure trove of information on this type of reality-based training.

TRAINING SUMMATION

I've lost track of the number of officers who have stated that training saved their life. Even at this stage in my long law enforcement career, I spend thousands each year on books, DVDs, training courses and training equipment. I learned early on how important the training I received was as well as the practice I give myself to learn new skills as well as maintain those I already have.

It doesn't take hours per day or even hours per week but it does take some time and due diligence to learn those skills and tactics which will save your life, train to perfect them and continue to work to maintain them.

Armed confrontations or even potentially violent confrontations can make you weak-kneed, shaky and gasping for air – that's even after you've won. Give yourself and your loved ones the best chance possible – train like your life depends on it, because it does...

WHAT IT TAKES TO HIT

Kevin R. Davis

Originally published in SWAT magazine, October 2008

What will it take for you to hit and stop your assailant in a deadly force encounter? Will the assailant be under the influence of extreme rage or drugs and hard to stop? Will one shot drop the suspect or will it take an entire magazine or more? What will that encounter look like? Will it be at close range or at 50 feet or more? Will you have a front, back or side shot? Will he be moving toward you or laterally or standing still? Furthermore, will you be moving "off the X" as you shoot? All of these intangibles and many more such as adverse lighting, innocent civilians in the background must be prepared for in your training.

If we can't say what your encounter will look like, then we cannot say what skills you will need to win the day. This is the case with the use of the sights on your pistol as well. For someone to say that you won't use your sights because of fight or flight or that you shouldn't need to see your sights to hit at close range belies the fact that you don't know what you will need to do to "make the shot." Since misses do nothing to aid in the fight for your life (indeed misses compound your problems) and we can only count on decisive hits to stop an assailant, it is imperative that our rounds be on target. Further, on the square range our targets don't move and innocent bystanders don't get in the way. Sadly when it comes to those "bumpy things on the top of the slide" (sights) we are subject to dogma from so-called "experts" who tell us what we will need to win the day, that misses are not a factor or that "any" hit will do. We must instead look at what it takes to hit and how we can correctly develop the motor skills conducive to winning a violent encounter.

Automatic motor programs

According to movement expert Dr. Bill Lewinski of Force Science Research Center, a skill such as the presentation of the pistol from the holster, also called a motor program, must be practiced until it becomes automatic. Given a stimulus such as a suspect armed with a pistol or a knife, you must be able to draw your handgun without conscious thought to the process. Your grip and stance must be also practiced to the point that it is automatic. "Running the gun" must be second nature. Only by training to such a level can you expect to be effective. This includes sight alignment and sight picture. The sighting process – bringing the pistol to eye level and aligning the front sight within the rear sight notch and centering that on the target – must be developed as a part of the draw stroke. The presentation presents the pistol to the target so that the sights are aligned. As Col. Jeff Cooper said, "The body aims, the eyes verify." Oftentimes we have shooters who report that they "didn't see their sights" in combat however Dr. Lewinski submits that if the act was an automatic motor program, in most cases you wouldn't remember seeing the sights, you would do as you've trained to do.

Are there advantages to not bringing the pistol to eye level? The late Col. Rex Applegate, who himself advocated eye level shooting, suggested a continuum of shooting from one handed "hip" shooting to two handed eye level shooting with sights aligned. Col. Applegate believed that man had an internal clock and would shoot based on his perception of time needed to bring the pistol to eye level. Applegate was not a fan of hip shooting commenting that it was too inaccurate outside five feet based on the inconsistent wrist and elbow bend.

If we accept that eye level shooting and sighted fire is the ultimate in terms of accuracy potential, anything less is what Applegate called "a compromise."

Those bumpy things on the slide

I grow tired of the whole point shooting issue. I've had to spend too much time fixing shooters who were told, "At this distance inward you don't need to see your sights," or "Just shove the pistol out and fire" (some instructors even taping over the sights because students were referencing them while shooting?) neither is conducive to good accurate fire and I've seen both fail in training scenarios and force on force. Recently I had a range officer (I will not use the term instructor because…he isn't) tell a shooter I tried to correct "We don't teach flash front sight picture." When I informed him that the majority of the instructors do, he said "We don't teach that, we teach point shooting." Question: If you don't refer to the sights, how do you improve accuracy? Another co-worker said that these people believe it's like the movie Star Wars, "Luke…trust the force." I've heard point shooting instructors say, "From thirty feet inward you don't need your sights." Thirty feet? Well that might work on the square range at a wide target that isn't moving but when these same students try it on force on force, they fail. But then again many PS Koolaid® drinkers never let reality get in the way. Realistically, when should you use the sights? Whenever you perceive you have enough time. When should you use a "rougher" alignment i.e. Applegate's admonition to "shoot through the weapon system"? Whenever you perceive you don't have enough time to do otherwise. When should you shoot at a hip, chest tuck or CQB position? When you believe you don't have enough distance to extend or time to bring the pistol up higher.

The object of the endeavor

The object of your gunfire in a deadly encounter is to score decisive hits on target. Decisive hits that cause your assailant to stop or impair his attack on you. The most decisive hits in this context are, according to Dr. James Williams of Tactical Anatomy Systems™, the Mediastinum (upper center mass in the body targeting the heart and major blood vessels above the heart), the Lateral Pelvis and the Brain Stem. These are specific targets not just anywhere from topknot to toenail. Hits on these targets are more effective than shots elsewhere on the body and are aided by accurate fire. Accurate fire is aided by sight alignment / sight picture and trigger press. Alignment and sight picture are aided by an automatic (well developed) stance, grip and presentation of the pistol from the holster. Start by developing the basics and work from there. If the suspect is close and you don't perceive enough time, well trained compromise positions can be effective. Let's stop telling out students based on our biases what they will need and instead develop shooters who can hit.

WHAT APPLEGATE SAID

Originally published in The Firearms Instructor, the magazine for IALEFI –International Association of Law Enforcement Firearms Instructors, Issue 4

Rex Applegate. The name conjures up images of some OSS operative cloaked in secrecy being trained for some classified mission behind enemy lines in WWII. The name connotes a lifetime of study in armed and unarmed combatives. The name also is associated in the field of firearms training with point shooting, something that Applegate believed and instructed in until his death. Since Applegate's passing the direct line to his beliefs and teachings has been lost. But fortunately we have a body of work that articulates what the good Colonel believed and instructed. It is to this material that we will quote and to his "disciples" that carry on his work to this day.

The development of point shooting

Applegate was tasked by "Wild Bill" Donovan commander of the OSS to learn all he could about close-quarters combat. When it came to use of the pistol which clandestine operators relied upon as the primary weapon in many cases, he and other instructors at Section VIII, Camp Ritchie, Maryland began with a system of combat shooting developed by British commando trainers W.E. Fairbairn and E.A. Sykes. This is not to say that this program was a static one. Applegate states that, "we added our own real-world experience and continued to validate and refine point shooting technique even more. The result was a method of combat shooting which allowed the effective delivery of fire at close range in virtually any light conditions with the use of sights this method was ultimately taught to thousands of U.S. and allied operatives and successfully applied in combat countless times during the war". These techniques were taught in range sessions with static target but were built upon in realistic sessions using bobbing and moving targets and the infamous "house of horrors."

Martial scientist

Col. Applegate looked at the effects of a deadly threat on performance. He said, "Statistics have consistently shown that the typical gunfight occurs at close range, in low light, and under conditions of extreme stress. The closer and more imminent the threat, the more immediate your need to fire. In these circumstances, the body's instinctive reactions to stress take over and only natural movements can be performed reliably." He outlined these reactions to a deadly threat as follows:

- ◆ crouching to present a smaller target
- ◆ squaring your body with the threat
- ◆ focusing your vision intently on the threat
- ◆ convulsive muscle contractions

It is interesting to note that these reactions have been backed up by state-of-the-art research. In 1998 Bill Burroughs completed a study of reactions of officers in Simuntions® dynamic training events. His study involved 157 officers participating in 188 life-threatening scenarios. Burroughs found that participants reacted in the following ways:

Squaring the body to the threat 59%
Focused vision on the threat 93%
Used binocular vision 88%

Oftentimes armed and unarmed tactics are developed in the comfort of the training hall. Applegate was not interested in what worked in competition or under controlled conditions. He was interested in what worked in mortal combat. If a student could not replicate his training in combat or if the techniques didn't work, they were thrown out. When talking about techniques developed primarily in competition he had this to say, "The problem with these interpretations of combat shooting is that none of them bother to consider what actually happens to a shooter when the target is shooting back. There is a tremendous difference between shooting methods that work well when you're simply trying to put holes in the target and those that work well when the target is trying to put holes in you." These responses are instinctive gross motor movements that will almost always override your ability to perform finely coordinated actions.

The Applegate Method

The "Applegate" method differs from the original Fairbairn technique. Essentially Applegate took Fairbairn and Sykes's techniques and modified them. In the Fairbairn/Sykes method the gun is raised to chest level and held directly in front of the centerline of the body with the wrist canted. Said Applegate, "One variation of pointing shooting is the original method developed by Fairbairn and Sykes. This technique involved bringing the pistol up to chest level and pointing from the center of the body. This is more difficult to master and inherently less accurate than bringing the gun to eye level, therefore it is not recommended." The mechanics of instinctive pointing (Applegate method) are very simple: the eyes focus on the target, then the arm is raised until the hand breaks the line of sight…keeping the elbow and wrist locked and raising the arm like a pump handle, a very accurate and consistent alignment of the pointing hand and the line of sight can be achieved. Contrary to popular belief, Applegate did not believe that shooting was as easy as pointing your finger. He believed that the eyes, pistol and target must be in line. "The mechanics of instinctive pointing are very simple: the eyes focus on the target, then the arm is raised until the hand breaks the line of sight." Applegate said of the original Fairbairn technique, "Since this technique does not take full advantage of the body's instinctive eye-hand coordination, it is inherently less accurate than bringing the hand to eye level. The point shooting method you have just learned is an improvement upon the original Fairbairn/Sykes method that was found to be even more effective in actual shooting incidents. It is also easier to learn and master and is therefore preferred to the original technique." Applegate student and survival skills pre-eminent instructor Bruce Siddle, who studied extensively with the Colonel states Applegate advocated to "always" bring the weapon to eye level and use the whole weapon system as the front sight. He would state to "keep your eyes on the target and shoot through the weapon system" to illustrate his point. Furthermore, Applegate believed the key to accuracy was based on simple principal of alignment; the officer's eyes, the weapon system and center mass of the threat should align in a straight line. While he did believe in keeping your eyes focused on the target, he did not believe in looking over the weapon, but through the weapon.

Hip shooting

The Applegate method is not hip shooting. "Although the method of shooting by instinctive pointing has been called hip shooting, it is not. A pure definition of the term hip shooting is: "the type of shooting done when either the wrist or the elbow is pressed or held tightly against the side or center of the body at hip level at the time of firing." Applegate covered all contingencies from touching distance wherein the officer or soldier could not physically raise the pistol to techniques where more time and distance allowed bringing the pistol up to eye level, using two hands and using the sights, "Realistic combat shooting technique therefore becomes a continuum that ranges from contact distance (so-called "hip shooting") to two-handed, sighted fire. Where you fire along this continuum is based on your distance to the target, the perceived threat, and your ability to control the instinctive physical response to stress." Yes Col. Applegate taught the "body point" his version of hip shooting. But he described these techniques as compromise positions often necessary when it was not possible to raise the gun to eye level. However, the good Colonel believed that the pistol should be brought to eye level if at all possible. "Shooting with the gun-arm elbow resting against the side, or hip, is a poor alternative to the instinctive pointing, straight arm shoulder-pivot method. If the officer and criminal are almost in body contact, or if it is impossible to raise the weapon to eye level to fire, this type of firing may be the only expedient. However, it does not take much practice to jam the muzzle into the criminal's body during a struggle."

The Colonel commented on the limitations of hip shooting in his book Killed or Get Killed, "It is difficult to master this method of shooting, where the elbow is bent as much as shown above, or when it is resting on the hip. It is hard to achieve, through practice, the ability always to bend the elbow at the same angle under combat conditions. There are many who can shoot accurately at targets on a horizontal level from the hip position, but it is not a method by which the ordinary individual can achieve proficiency without a prohibitive amount of practice." Furthermore, Applegate wrote and stated that the body point (hip shooting) method was limited in its effectiveness to 5 feet, (according to Steve Barron, Applegate said 10 feet with practice). Bruce Siddle studied with Colonel Applegate for several years prior to Applegate's passing. As a matter of fact, Siddle and Applegate were working on an article together during the Colonel's final days. Siddle states, "he (Applegate) believed man had an internal clock that estimated the amount of time needed to raise a weapon to eye level. If the threat was close and imminent, he felt the weapon would start to be discharged the second it cleared leather and would continue to discharge to shoulder or eye level if time allowed."

One-handed shooting versus two-handed shooting

Col. Applegate was primarily a one handed shooter. He clearly described his opinions on the matter:

"The single-handed carry in the instinctive method is superior at close quarters for a number of valid reasons. The gun-free hand is useful to hold a flashlight, open a door, fend off an attacker, maintain balance, feel along walls or up stairs, help conduct silent movement, and to maintain contact with other officers in dark conditions. It is also much easier to shoot objects above eye level and around obstacles with less body exposure." He did state, "Everybody knows that you can shoot a handgun better with two hands-if you can use the sights and have time to aim-than you can by using one hand.

Applegate does comment on the validity of the two handed isosceles stance, "However, World War II combat experience and recent police reports indicate that the two-handed Isosceles stance, with both arms fully extended, is usually instinctively resorted to by the officer/soldier when the target is shooting back." Modern research has validated the effectiveness of the isosceles stance. In 1989 Harland Westmoreland published Isosceles vs. Weaver Shooting Stances: The Selection of a Shooting Stance Under Stress (1989; PPCT Research Publications). Westmoreland surmised that, "when suddenly attacked especially in close quarters, is to face our opponent squarely with our hands and arms extended out in front of us." Furthermore, Westmoreland noted that oftentimes a one handed stance is utilized as well. The Burroughs study noted that in dynamic events wherein officers responded spontaneously that the Isosceles stance was used by the majority of participants (59% Isosceles, 19% Weaver and 7% Natural).

Applegate knew this commenting, "In its basic form, the isosceles stance is nothing more than point shooting with a slightly more stable platform."

Applying Applegate's lessons today

Yes, we have come far in terms of technology and training for today's modern warriors. Developments in armament, equipment and training methodology have improved over the years (change for the sake of change is not an improvement, however…). The nature of pistol encounters has pretty much stayed the same. The pistol is a close range defensive arm, after all, if you know you're going to be in a gunfight get a long gun. Within these close range violent encounters Col. Rex Applegate's methods still make sense. Col. Applegate understood that the nature of pistol engagements is really about two different scenarios with distance and time being the deciding factor. In other words if the officer perceives they have time and distance they will bring the pistol to eye level and utilize the sights. This internal clock as Bruce Siddle is quoted earlier referring to is based on a sympathetic nervous system reaction to a violent encounter. What Applegate and his students referred to based on actual shootings has been quantified and qualified using modern research methods. We now have reasons why based on physiological effects of stress that officers may not be able to see their sights. Although all agree, including Applegate, that an officer is far better off bringing the pistol to eye level using two hands and verifying the sight alignment prior to shooting, we understand the limitations of the human animal in times of peril. It then becomes a question of improving performance under stress. Applegate attempted to do that with his "house of horrors" and modern firearms instructors attempt to do that with Simunitions®. By doing all we can to properly develop firearms motor skills, to teach threat cue recognition and inoculate our students to the effects of stress we can hopefully prepare our people for winning an armed encounter regardless of the conditions. That is what Col. Rex Applegate wanted and attempted to do in his time and what we must endeavor to carry on today.

The author wishes to thank the following for their contributions to this article: Bruce Siddle, Mike Janich, Lou Chiodo, and Steve Barron.

CHAPTER SEVEN:

POST-INCIDENT POLICE INTERACTION

CASE STUDY

A uniformed officer responds to a call of a possible burglary in the middle of the night, at an apartment building. As he arrives, he observes a subject and challenges him at gunpoint from a position of cover, "Police! Don't move!" the subject draws a handgun and says, "Sheriff's Office! Don't you move!" The potentially lethal stand-off continues until the on-duty officer shines his flashlight at his uniform and says, "No, I'm really the police!," at which time the off-duty deputy holsters his handgun.

Yes, it really did happen and yes, it could have ended tragically for one or both in an incident in which the off-duty deputy was pulling his waterbed outside because it had sprung a leak. The police officer used cover but shining the flashlight on himself was a tactical blunder. Certainly the deputy was a victim of lack of train-

Good, aggressive law enforcement officers are responding. How you mentally and physically prepare is vital to a safe interaction.

ing in this area and violated the most important rule:

Rule #1: On-duty officers are in charge! Do what they say, or you may get shot!

The dangers of intervention are highlighted by the Las Vegas incident where an armed citizen intervened in a big box store after a subject, who had just shot and killed two LVMPD officers, entered and fired a shot. But if you've intervened or if you've brandished your handgun in response to a threat, then the local police or sheriff's office deputies are on the way, and failure to mentally and physically prepare many end in tragedy, including you being shot.

Just this year at the International Law Enforcement Educators and Trainers Association conference during the "Deadly Force Panel of Experts" chaired by Massad Ayoob, this question was posed by the audience, "How should a police officer deal with an armed man who refuses to obey a police officer's orders to drop his gun?"

My response was that there are no easy answers. From what we know about response time, an armed man can fire before an officer reacts and responds. Even lucky shots such as the "Gunman in the Lobby"

If a police officer arrives on this scene, even though this armed man is a police detective it can end tragically. He is holding his badge in his right hand where it cannot be seen by responding officers.

we detailed in Chapter Three can occur and have fatal consequences.

Police are likely experiencing an SNS response after receiving a call such as "shots-fired, man down, armed citizen involved." Remember that this sympathetic nervous system response may include: tunnel vision, auditory exclusion, reduced cognitive processing, inability to perform fine and complex motor skills. They are in a "fight or flight" mode, and since they're coming in your direction the flight isn't a concern, the looking for a fight is, and guess what? You just pointed a gun at someone, had a violent altercation or shot someone, and these hyped up officers are coming your way.

Even plainclothes, undercover or off-duty officers are not immune from this danger. In the 1970s, plainclothes cops in New York City were being shot by responding uniformed officers. This resulted in the "Color of the Day" being briefed at roll calls. "The color of the day is blue," which meant that undercover or plainclothes officers would pull out blue armbands or headbands when taking enforcement actions on the street. Verbal responses such as "I'm on the job!" were used with possible precinct assignment, etc., being asked by responding uniformed officers. With an authorized strength of over 30,000 cops, one can easily see that not every officer could possibly know every detective or plainclothes officer.

Fratricide or "blue-on-blue" shootings continue to be a problem to this day.

In 2010 the State of New York convened a task force on police-on-police shootings after several off-duty or plainclothes officers were shot by uniformed officers responding to or involved in "man with gun" calls, shootings or violent crimes in progress. Unfortunately, the task force had few police firearms and tactics instructors, and much of their work veered off course into the area of racial stereotyping and other issues of race. That said, their report Reducing Inherent Danger: Report of the Task Force on Police-on-Police Shootings contains some interesting points.

From that task force here are some proposed protocols:

For officers taking action out-of-uniform

1. Only intervene to protect personal safety or another's safety: otherwise, be a good witness.

2. Inform the police dispatcher or call 911 if you are taking action, armed, and in plainclothes.

3. Display your shield prominently prior to taking action.

4. Identify yourself frequently and loudly as a police officer.

For confronted officers

1. Don't move.

2. Avoid reflexive spin.

3. Identify yourself loudly as a police officer, using specific coded language.

4. Obey the commands of the confronting officer.

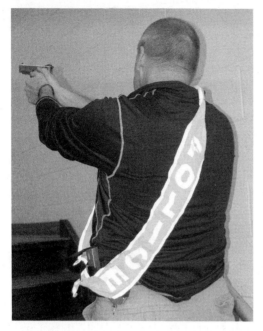

For off-duty cops, I recommend the DSM – Don't Shoot Me banner which is carried on the belt.

The CCW DSM model is a smart addition for any concealed carry permit holder.

For officers challenging an armed individual

1. Don't stereotype.

2. Take cover.

3. Shout clearly and repeat, "Police! Don't Move!"

4. Broaden your focus from the gun to assess the situation.

If we insert the phrase "armed citizen" or "concealed carry permit holder" or even "law abiding armed citizen" for "police officer" in the Confronted Officers section, we have some decent recommendations to follow.

Further if we identify ourselves visually with a DSM – Don't Shoot Me Banner from dsmsafety.com, we can lessen the chances of getting shot as well. These banners are worn in a small ballistic nylon carrier on the offside waist. You simply reach down; grab the loop at the top of the carrier and pull. The banner deploys and can be easily pulled over your head so a green high visibility banner with CCW or ARMED is prominently displayed across your chest and back.

Don't think these issues are not important. Even members of the Secret Service and other state, local and federal plainclothes agents and officers have purchased the banners, some with money out of their own pocket. I have a couple of these DSM banners and wouldn't hesitate to deploy in my own city, let alone out of town or out of state.

CASE STUDY

I worked as an undercover street narcotics detective for a number of years. My job was primarily to conduct surveillance of drug dealers and run "controlled buys" using confidential informants, but every once in a while I would have to take action to aid uniformed officers. Ditching my undercover car around a corner or out of sight, I'd pull my badge, which was on a chain around my neck, and proceed to help out.

I was fully conscious that even officers from my own agency could mistake me for a suspect in the dark.

CASE STUDY

Jim was a detective assigned to the vice unit. One time he was pursuing a suspect on foot through backyards. He was aggressively tackled by a uniformed officer who didn't know him.

Don't pursue a suspect on foot. That's not your job, and with responding officers experiencing an SNS response and you in fight or flight as well, you may get shot.

RECOMMENDATIONS POST INCIDENT

1. Communicate your status via phone calls or have someone call for you. "Armed innocent citizen on scene."

2. Describe your attire or have a caller describe you.

3. Holster your handgun or set down long-gun if at all possible.

4. Display your Don't Shoot Me banner

5. Take some deep breaths (autogenic breathing) and start thinking

6. Expand your vision. It is entirely possible a plainclothes or off-duty officer may be on scene.

7. Anticipate that you will be challenged at gunpoint by aggressive uniformed officers under an SNS response.

8. Anticipate being ordered to a prone position and handcuffed. Do not resist!

9. Do exactly what the officers order you to do, including dropping your handgun.

10. Do not pursue the assailant on foot.

Massad Ayoob talks about sending out a "meeting party" away from you who can meet the police, advise the officers of what has gone on and what the current status is. This person should stand out in the open, under a light with arms raised. They too should expect to get proned out and handcuffed.

Dispatch will invariably ask you to put your gun down or secure it prior to the uniform response. This could be catastrophic if an attacker seizes that opportu-

Reholstering is safer than standing with pistol drawn (if at all possible).

nity to disarm you or attack with their own gun. If you are holding a subject at gunpoint, communicate this to dispatch. Keep the line open even if you have to set the phone down. The open phone line will record any verbal orders or challenges from you to the suspect such as, "Don't move, I told you not to move!" or verbal threats, scuffles, commands, shots, etc. that occur. Only when it is safe for you to holster should you do so.

Don't relax too soon. As in the tragedy in Las Vegas, bad guys can have back-up too. Many law enforcement officers have been shot and killed or wounded by suspects lying in wait and protecting the "six o'clock" of their henchmen.

Just like the off-duty cop who has been involved in a shooting or violent confrontation, you must overcome the effects of the SNS response by autogenic breathing and then start thinking and preparing. Far too many law enforcement officers undercover, in plainclothes or off-duty have been shot in these types of scenarios. We need to learn from these tragedies and plan and prepare for it.

COMMUNICATIONS

If you make the call to dispatch and the assailant is still on scene, you want to give a clear description of yourself and other family members or friends on scene so there is no confusion. Much, not all, of this information will be sent to the responding officers via their Mobile Digital Terminal (in car computer) on "call notes." Unfortunately, you cannot expect officers responding to a hot call such as "shots fired" to read these notes on the way. They may get a little info, i.e.:

Dispatch: "Car 15"

Uniformed Officers: "Car 15, go ahead, Arlington and 5th."

Dispatch: "Car 15 and any car in the area, Signal 33 (Shooting), 999 Baird St. Caller states that suspects kicked in the rear door and entered the residence and he fired shots at them. One suspect down, two other suspects left the scene on foot, unknown description."

Uniformed Officers: "Car 15 copy."

Dispatch: "Zero, One-Fifteen" (Time)

I can't tell you how many times I've responded to shootings or other violent calls with this little information relayed. MDTs have improved communications and information transfer from dispatch to the patrol officer, but you can't count on it.

If the assailant has left the scene, information that should be relayed is:

◆ Where attacker is
◆ Whether they are armed
◆ If they fled the scene
◆ Direction of travel
◆ Physical description
◆ If they are down – have been shot
◆ Need for EMS or paramedics

Understand that paramedics won't enter what they consider a "hot zone" without police presence.

CASE STUDY

My partner and I responded to a shots fired call and found a victim out in front of a tattoo business with apartments above it. There had been some kind of altercation and the tattoo artist had shot him from a window with a rifle. His femur had been broken and he couldn't move and was bleeding pretty bad. With my partner providing cover, a civilian friend of the wounded man and I ran behind the car where he was hiding, scooped him up and ran back behind a brick building next door. The fire department paramedics had arrived and were half a block back. I waved for them to come up (we were completely hidden next to a brick building), but they wouldn't do it. We had to carry the guy out to them.

Got to love fireman, the don't want anything to do with bullets and gunfire (who does?) but they'll still run into a burning building…

Massad Ayoob clearly makes the case for early communication post incident. His excellent book Gun Digest Book of Concealed Carry: 2nd Edition clearly indicates that oftentimes the first person to call the police is construed as the victim. I could not agree more. Further, police often respond to fight calls or incidents where both parties involved claim innocence and insist the other side started it.

If the other party has friends or witnesses and you don't, expect them to all point the finger at you regardless of your assailant's guilt. If you have witnesses as well, police will take statements from both sides but unless there was a bus full of nuns who witnessed the incident, you will likely be treated as a suspect until your innocence is proven by investigators.

You have to understand that police have a very jaundiced eye and that everyone claims innocence. Even suspects with guns or dope found in their pockets exclaim, "Those ain't my pants!" or "That's not my gun!" Because of this, uniformed responding officers treat everyone in a shooting as a suspect at first. It is in their vital interest to secure and stabilize the scene.

You need to respectfully articulate, "I am the victim! That man tried to rob me!" or whatever the crime may be. As Mas Ayoob points out stating, "I will sign charges!" is a good thing because many police deal with uncooperative "victims" (usually bad guys themselves) who refuse to prosecute their assailants.

Avoid statements such as, "I didn't mean to shoot him" or, "The gun just went off…" These types of statements indicate the shooting was not intentional or was accidental, which destroys an intentional self-defense claim later. These types of statements are made by law-abiding citizens who are not used to violence. What they really meant to say was, "I didn't want to have to shoot him. He left me no choice." These spontaneous utterances will be recorded by officers in their Action Taken reports or addendums to the investigator's report and can hurt you later if/when you make an official statement.

Keep your mouth shut except for the following. Officers frequently get in trouble when they shoot their mouth off or make statements indicating anger. It is completely understandable why you might be fairly well upset about a man who just tried to kill you or your family but making statements such as, "F*ck you! You got what you deserved! I hope you f'ing die!" indicate anger to most witnesses. Verbal parting shots as the suspect is wheeled away on a paramedic gurney such as, "See you later sucker!" or similar will not go over well with a possible jury later.

Limit what you say to uniformed police on the scene or to investigators who show up. You do want to clearly state:

- ◆ You are the victim
- ◆ Where any evidence might be located such as empty casings
- ◆ You also want to indicate where you were, where they were and in which direction you and he fired
- ◆ Ask for a "victim advocate." Most cities have victim advocacy programs that actually help victims of crime. They can provide emergency housing, advise you on the legal process and even provide funds for new deadbolts or a new door, for instance, if you cannot afford them. Victim advocates will "hold your hand" during the trial of your suspect and the involved legal process. Victim Assistance has been a long supported charity of my wife and mine, because they really help the victims of crime. That said

some may be anti-gun, so they may elect not to aid you after a shooting.

Remember that everything you say will be recorded, and anticipate that everything will be captured on video tape as well. We'll deal with the adverse impacts of memory and video evidence in the next chapter.

CASE STUDY

We had been chasing a B&E suspect from a business in our city through a swamp/wooded area to another town. One of our officers and one of their officers was hot on the suspect's tail when our officer yelled, "Stop or I'll shoot!" as a feign or fake to get the suspect to stop. (By the way, this never worked and frequently resulted in the suspect hitting "over-drive" and taking off.) The rookie officer from the other agency fired, however, missing with one round and striking the suspect in the buttocks with the other. I arrived on scene right after the shooting. After I left officers traced the line of fire and found a citizen dead, killed with a shot to the head, which came through the side of his house as he slept on a sofa in the front room.

The city where the other officer who fired worked was sued and settled out of court for a serious sum of money. The officer was terminated from the agency. In a serious miscarriage of justice, our officer was fired as well, even though threatening to shoot suspects who were running away had been done for years.

OTHER TYPES OF POLICE CONTACT

In over 32 years of carrying concealed, my armed status has never been detected by another non-law enforcement citizen.

Many times CCW permit holders, even off-duty LEOs are paranoid about being detected. To the point of some permit holders not carrying because of this possibility. There may be a time, however, that despite properly concealing your

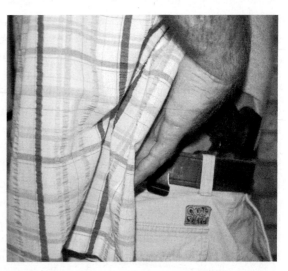

Occasionally your pistol grips or holster may be seen and a citizen may call the police. Remember to keep hands away from the holstered handgun when they approach and follow their commands.

firearm, another citizen detects your handgun based on "grip printing" (where the grips push out from the concealing shirt when you bend over), etc. With the proliferation of concealed carry throughout the U.S. this is certainly less of a problem than it used to be.

CASE STUDY

A coworker, a fully sworn police officer, was carrying openly on his belt after work, with his police badge pinned next to his holstered handgun. He was carrying out of the city at a soccer match where his daughter was playing. A school administrator approached him and stated, "The carrying of firearms is not allowed on school property." The off-duty officer stated, "I'm a police officer." The school principal said, "That doesn't make any difference." (One wonders what type of threat the principal must have felt to approach the officer to begin with, but understand that many anti-gun folks just don't want guns around.) Despite the incidence of active killers on school properties and that this officer represented a protective option for the children at the game, the principal didn't care. He walked off, got on his cell phone and called the local PD. When the police arrived, the off-duty officer walked over and identified himself and the on-duty copper told the principal the officer had every right to carry on school property.

An important note here is that the officer was prepared to leave the premises or secure his handgun in the trunk of his car, despite the legal right to carry on school premises, because he wanted to avoid a confrontation. This is one of the reasons open carry should be avoided, if at all possible.

It is interesting to note that police officers carrying under the Law Enforcement Officers Safety Act, which allows for nationwide concealed carry, must abide by the state laws where they are carrying. For instance, prior to Christmas a detective I worked with asked me about carrying in New York City. I pointed out that the S.A.F.E. Act in New York State restricts magazine capacity in that state for retired LEOs or officers from carrying from out of state. At the time of this writing, in New York state you cannot have magazines that can hold more than ten rounds. Further, only seven rounds can be loaded into these ten round magazines. That would prohibit my 15-round Glock 19 mags and I would be forced to carry my Glock 26 downloaded to seven in the magazine or my DoubleStar 1911 with only seven in the eight-round Wilson mags I carry. Now under the S.A.F.E. Act laws you are not limited in the number of seven round magazines you carry…? Go figure…

In my state when concealed carry was first passed, the law required that permit holders expose their handgun after they got into a motor vehicle. The entire

New York state compliant handgun, magazines and ammunition. DoubleStar 1911,
Wilson mags loaded with seven rounds, carried in Crossbreed Holster.

time they drove around, permit holders had to leave the gun exposed. Getting in/
out of the car they had to remember to cover it or lift the garment over the holstered handgun. Fortunately in my state, the law has been changed. Know what
your state law indicates and make sure you comply with it.

Further, my state still requires that:

"If a person is stopped for a law enforcement purpose and is carrying a concealed handgun as a CCW licensee, whether in a motor vehicle or not, he shall
promptly inform the law enforcement officer that he is carrying a concealed
handgun. In a vehicle, the licensee shall remain in the vehicle and keep his
hands in plain sight at all times. Violating this section of law is a first-degree
misdemeanor, and in addition to any other penalty handed down by a court, may
result in the suspension of the person's concealed handgun license for one year.
A permit holder is not required to inform law enforcement of this status if he is
not carrying a firearm.

If a person is stopped for a law enforcement purpose and is carrying a concealed handgun as a CCW licensee, whether in a motor vehicle or not, he shall
not have or attempt to have any contact with the handgun, unless in accordance
with directions given by a law enforcement officer. Violating this law is a felony
and may result in permanent loss of the person's handgun license.

If a person is stopped for a law enforcement purpose and is carrying a concealed handgun as a CCW licensee, whether in a motor vehicle or not, he shall
not knowingly disregard or fail to comply with any lawful order given by any

law enforcement officer. Violating this law is a first-degree misdemeanor and may result in the suspension of the person's concealed handgun license for two years.

If the CCW licensee surrenders the firearm, then the following applies:

◆ If the firearm is not returned at the completion of the stop, the law enforcement officer is required to return the firearm in "the condition it was in when it was seized."

◆ If a court orders the firearm's return and the firearm has not been returned to the licensee, the CCW licensee can claim reasonable costs and attorney fees for the loss and the cost of claiming a firearm.

If you are pulled over while carrying a concealed handgun, remember the following:

◆ Before the officer approaches, roll down your window and place your hands in plain view on the steering wheel.

◆ Calmly tell the officer that you have a license to carry a concealed handgun and that you have a handgun with you. Ask if the officer has particular instructions concerning the handgun.

◆ Do not touch or attempt to touch your handgun unless specifically told to by the officer.

◆ Do not exit your vehicle unless specifically told to by the officer.

◆ Comply with all lawful orders given by the officer.

Ohio's Concealed Carry Laws and License Application, Attorney General Mike DeWine, 4/7/14

These recommendations are what I would do and have done as an off-duty police officer carrying concealed during a traffic stop, and what I have recommended to police and private citizen students alike during these types of police contacts.

CASE STUDY

About a month ago I received this email from a former student of mine advising me that he had followed his training after he was stopped for speeding through a school zone:

"After pulling me over, the officer took my license back to his car. He showed back up at my driver's side window several minutes later and his first question to me was, "who taught your CCW class?" I answered that it was a man named Kevin Davis that taught me back in 2008. The officer asked, "Kevin Davis from the XXXX Police Department?" He told me that he knew you, and wanted to let me know that you did an excellent job at instructing the CCW class as I performed properly as a CCW holder during the traffic stop."

The student was released with a warning.

Note that these directions apply within the State of Ohio and pertain to CCW permit holders acting within the state as well as permit holders from other states with which Ohio has a reciprocity agreement or other states which Ohio recognizes for CCW. You are responsible to know the laws of any state where you carry and your responsibility to advise law enforcement personnel of your status if applicable.

For more information, check out the National Rifle Association's Institute for Legislative Action, Gun Laws section for a compendium of state firearms laws, or to view "State Laws at a Glance" at nraila.org/gun-laws.aspx or a variety of sources that show reciprocity maps and links for state laws.

CHAPTER EIGHT

THE INVESTIGATION

CASE STUDY

A police officer is forced to shoot an armed robber after the suspect leaves a bar he has just robbed, walking out a side door directly into the officer with gun in hand and money in a pillowcase. The robber is shot and killed. The officer has his pistol taken by a supervisor, is taken to his station and locked in a suspect holding room until investigators interview him.

CASE STUDY

A police officer has just shot and killed a man who answered the door with gun in hand at an apartment on a loud music call. The rifle looks like an AK-47 but turns out to be a BB gun. The officer is disarmed at the scene, taken back to the station, placed in isolation in a suspect holding room, and interviewed immediately after the shooting.

CASE STUDY

A veteran police officer with over 25 years of service is criminally indicted for felonious assault after a shooting involving a crack-head who attempted to rob the department store the officer was working off-duty security. After the suspect commits a strong-arm robbery of the 16-year-old female cashier, the officer grabs him from behind. The suspect still high after an all-day cocaine binge tosses the large officer around "like Hulk Hogan." At one point, the exhausted officer, feeling he is losing the battle, draws and fires two rounds. One of his bullets misses. The second round goes in and out the suspect's cheek, creating just a flesh wound. In the words of the officer, "the suspect fights harder," picking the stout officer up and throwing him through a glass exit door. A video shows the suspect attempting to run away, and the officer attempting a tackle, which misses. The suspect is moving away through the parking lot, the video shows the officer raise his handgun and the suspect sustains a wound to his thigh that shatters his femur. The suspect hobbles to the rear of a parked car where he is taken into custody.

The officer is interviewed by his agency. The detective commander who interviews him compels the statement in what in law enforcement parlance is a "Garrity Statement." During this "use of force investigation" instead of obtaining the "totality of the circumstances" and the officer's perceptions as to what happened, the police commander focuses in on the department issued handgun the officer used versus the legalities of his use of force. In their agency, the officer is not permitted to work an off-duty job and carry the agency handgun. *Note – A Garrity Statement is a compelled statement that means that what the officer said is for internal investigation only and cannot be used against the public employee at a criminal trial. Unfortunately this Garrity Statement is taken into the Grand Jury along with the videotape. The officer is indicted.

I am retained as an expert by the officer's defense team. During the course of the interview on everything the officer saw, heard, smelled, felt and perceived (an interview, the likes of which he had never been give prior) I learned that the suspect had attempted to disarm the officer during the fight in the store checkout area. The officer told me that the video used by the prosecutor to indict him was not even the shooting. The actual shooting occurred when the suspect threw him through a glass exit door and then rammed his hand into his pants pocket as if to draw a gun. The officer fearing the suspect, who had already attempted to disarm the officer, was drawing a handgun. The officer had opened fired at his point and then attempted to tackle the suspect who was still trying to get away. The video the prosecutor had only showed the officer raising his handgun from low ready to point-shoulder and then lowering it.

Armed with this new knowledge, I went home and imported the video in question into my laptop and a program called Microsoft Movie Maker®. I broke the video down into frames per second and could only find the officer had four tenths of one second from which he raises his pistol from a 45-degree angle downward, toward the suspect, and then lowers it. Could the officer fire three shots in this time frame? I went to the range with a PACT timer, got on my knees like the officer involved in the shooting, and attempted to raise the pistol and fire as fast as I could.

Here are my results:

First String

.72	First Shot
.83	Second Shot
.97	Third Shot
1.08	4th
1.22	5th
1.33	6th

Second String of Fire

.60	First Shot
.72	2nd
.83	3rd
.94	4th
1.06	5th
1.17	6th

Put simply, there was no way our officer could raise his pistol and fire three shots in .40 of one second. I put this information into an opinion and submitted it to the defense team. At that point, a new video emerged which actually showing the femur shot and supporting the officer's statement.

In the interim the officer had to go through hell, the possibility of losing his job, going to trial and maybe even going to prison for doing his job.

THE ARMED CITIZEN COROLLARY

Now, this is a book for the armed citizen, why would I start this chapter on post shooting investigations talking about shootings involving police officers?

Because these same detectives and police supervisors may be investigating your shooting.

Here are some facts about law enforcement use of force:
- Most police agencies within the U.S. are 40 officers or less.
- Most police agencies don't experience officer-involved shootings or even serious use of non-deadly force with any regularity and may have never investigated a police shooting.
- Most administrators have little knowledge about the legalities of use of force.

- Most chiefs of police are politicians who serve at the whim of their political masters.
- Most investigators have little training on how to investigate police shootings, how to investigate and document "the totality of the circumstances."
- Although most agencies have policies on use of force, many fail to follow their own policies.
- Most agencies are unaware of the effects of the sympathetic nervous system on a person and their performance, post-critical incident amnesia, inattentional blindness, sleep cycles and memory, Miranda and Garrity, cognitive interviewing, scientific research on performance and movement, response time versus reaction time, and more.

Couple all of the foregoing facts with a police officer who has had marginal training on the legal aspects of use of force and you have the recipe for a poor outcome. Officers are empowered by their city, county or federal government to use deadly and non-deadly force in the performance of their duties, but may not have a solid legal understanding of when they can and cannot use force and are subject to a poor use of force investigations when they do so.

The result is that police agencies frequently throw their own officers under the bus in a shooting or serious use of non-deadly force or improperly discipline them, even criminally charge them based on lack of knowledge about use of force law. The driving force for this, in years past, was "vicarious liability" – agencies, supervisors and even officers were afraid they would be sued in civil court. The truth is that I don't know of one officer who has ever paid out of his pocket in a civil suit on a use of force. That's not to say that busy agencies don't experience lawsuits but in truth, most civil litigation is not from the big cases say, a police shooting, but rather on minor injuries in the little uses of force.

The big liability today is political liability. Agencies are more afraid and are more likely to toss an officer under a bus out of the reaction to the politics of force than for the monetary fears of a civil suit. Think about Reverend Al Sharpton or Rev. Jesse Jackson or a slew of "community activists" coming to a city after a cross-racial shooting. This will only be magnified if the suspect was unarmed or had an airsoft pistol versus a real firearm. These activists will organize marches and exert tremendous political pressure on the agency. Seldom will a chief stand-up to such pressure, because they are more worried about their job and their career than taking care of their officer. There are exceptions but few and far between. The officer is more dependent on their police union or association and their attorneys to protect them than they can count on the leadership of their own agency.

Indicative of this difference between the ranks and the feelings of most chiefs of police to citizen armed self-defense, is the comparison of line officers support of the 2nd Amendment and concealed carry by citizens versus police chiefs in most major cities. In April of 2013 PoliceOne® released a survey of over 15,000 officers on gun control and concealed carry. From that survey:

Question: Do you think a federal ban on manufacture and sale of ammunition magazines that hold more than 10 rounds would reduce violent crime?

Survey Results: 95.7% "No"

Question: What effect do you think a federal ban on manufacture and sale of some semi-automatic firearms, termed by some as "assault weapons," would have on reducing crime?

Survey Results: 71% "None"

Question: Considering the particulars of recent tragedies like Newtown and Aurora, what impact do you think a legally armed citizen would have made?

Survey Results: 80% "Casualties would likely have been reduced"

Question: Do you support arming teachers and/or school administrators who volunteer to carry in their school?

Survey Results: 76.6% "Yes, if they are vetted, trained and qualified annually"

You can go to PoliceOne.com to view the complete survey results.

Compare this with police chiefs in Chicago, Baltimore, New York City, Washington D.C. and other large American cities. Legislative Chair Tom Manger stated on C-SPAN® in December 2013, that The Major City Chiefs Association has come out in support of the assault weapons ban, and the ban on "high capacity" magazines. In addition they've supported the asinine S.A.F.E. Act in New York state as well as supporting other gun control issues making statements such as "Assault weapons are enablers of violent crime and mass murder."

Of course, we are comparing 15,000 working police officers with 64 chiefs who are appointed to office by politicians, most of whom are vehemently anti-gun. We only have to examine the effects of gun control and crime by taking a look at Chicago and Washington D.C. The exception is Detroit Police Department Chief James Craig who has stated "If more citizens were armed, criminals would think twice about attacking them. When we look at the good community members who have concealed weapons permits, the likelihood they'll shoot is based on a lack of confidence in this Police Department," Craig said at a press conference at police headquarters, adding that he thinks more Detroit citizens feel safer, thanks in part to a seven percent drop in violent crime in 2013." (January 2014)

It is my belief that, in most mid- to large-sized agencies, in a controversial shooting or serious use of non-deadly force, the administration is more likely to charge the officer with policy and procedure violations or charge them with a crime and make them prove their innocence, than support and defend their actions.

CASE STUDY

Bill is a patrol officer for a small middle class rural

community. On a sleepy Sunday morning a suspect goes on a shooting spree, shooting his girlfriend and then killing seven others including an 11-year-old boy he hunted down in a basement and killed. Bill responded, got a good description of the suspect from a witness and deployed with his AR15 patrol rifle. When Bill encountered the suspect with his pistol still in hand, he ordered him to stop. The suspect then turned and began to raise his handgun. The officer fired three times, hitting the suspect with his 5.56 rounds twice. The suspect ran a few steps then collapsed and died on scene.

In the aftermath the officer, working with his union representative refused to give a voluntary statement to the county prosecutor. The union rep asked that the officer receive limited immunity for any statements he gave. The county prosecutor refused and threatened to subpoena the officer into the Grand Jury. The experienced union rep stated that the hero officer would invoke his 5th Amendment rights in the Grand Jury and then they would have a press conference outside the courthouse.

Eventually the officer was cleared of any wrongdoing by the prosecutor without the officer making a statement. The officer would later receive a presidential award at the White House for his actions.

CASE STUDY

The primary assistant prosecutor for this office had done the following after officer-involved shootings: doodled on a notepad and asked arcane questions during interviews; told the room full of police detectives and police union reps and lawyers that they "needed to hurry up, I have a picnic I have to get to"; told police investigators that the only time she gave Miranda was when she thought there was a problem with a shooting, and then gave Miranda to the next officer involved.

The actual prosecutor has waited over six months to clear an officer of any wrongdoing because of the political fall-out, cleared an officer even though she incorrectly interpreted the law by stating in one shooting, "although an officer cannot shoot a fleeing subject in the back," and criminally charged five sheriff's deputies in an in-custody death.

The above sad state of affairs and the fact that I've worked on numerous cases where officers were charged with crimes by incompetent investigators and supervisors based on ignorance of use of force law, botched investigations, or even worse political motivations was the reason why I wrote my book Use of Force Investigations: A Manual for Law Enforcement (2012, Responder Media). These are

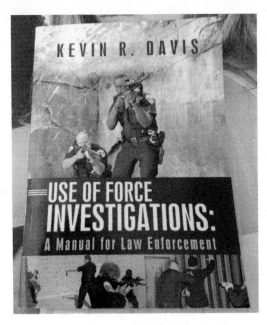

the same politicians and police investigators who may investigate your shooting.

Think it won't happen to you as an armed citizen and you'll be hailed as a hero? I'll bring you back to reality by invoking one person's name – George Zimmerman.

I've written about the "politics of force" several times and have lectured on the topic at the ILEETA conference. Make no mistake about it, carrying of a concealed weapon or armed home defense and the use of or threatened use of deadly force carry political implications you may have not considered. Let's examine how the investigation will unfold and what you can do to protect yourself.

ON SCENE

We have already talked about the danger of "spontaneous utterances" such as, "I didn't mean it," or "it was an accident" and similar. There is a tendency to experience "diarrhea of the mouth" on-scene post incident, having just gone through a fight for your very life and looking for vindication through the responding officers. Make no mistake, you should assume that everything you say is going to be recorded by the officer/agency via "body-worn video and audio cameras" on the officers or at least in a written report. These statements made on the scene will be compared with any statements made later on or at trial. If the statements don't match or there are differences, the prosecution may infer that you are lying.

What should you say? Limited statements about being the victim, witnesses to the incident, the location and description of any evidence that may be missed or lost, suspect(s) description and direction of travel, then make the statement that you are willing to speak more to them but would like your attorney present.

As I mentioned earlier, expect to be treated as a suspect in a homicide versus the victim of an attempted murder, homicide being defined as "death at the hands of another." This is how police officers are treated, by and large, and you should not expect to be treated any differently.

> *Your use of force must be within the*
> *parameters of what a reasonable person*
> *would do in like or similar circumstances.*

As we have already stated, expect to be handcuffed. Expect to be searched and have your firearm, spare magazine and any other self-defense related items taken, as well as your cell-phone. If you are handcuffed you will be searched. If your vehicle is involved in the incident it will be searched as well. If the shooting takes place in your house, the house is a crime scene. You may be asked for a consent search of your car or home but regardless police officers will be looking as they investigate and possibly process the "crime scene." Prior to any "consent" searches, I would recommend you consult with an attorney. Of course, the police may just get a search warrant, but consenting to a search is a different matter entirely.

CASE STUDY

A well-known firearms writer and gun magazine editor used a military style large-bore rifle to shoot and kill a suspect who had threatened him at his home. Both victim and suspect had been drinking. The armed citizen was taken to trial for second-degree murder twice, both trials ending with jury deadlock. The charges were eventually dismissed.

This case which lasted several years cost the armed citizen his editor's job, work with a longstanding publisher and a tremendous amount of money. It is simply not enough to be right you have to be able to prove you were right. Proving you're right is composed of several different parts:

♦ Compliance with self-defense law
♦ Totality of the circumstances
♦ The physical evidence
♦ Video evidence
♦ Independent witness statements
♦ Your companion's statements
♦ Your statement

Compliance with the law is the most important part. Excessive force, whether deadly or non-deadly, is outside the limits of the law. The legal investigation post-incident will examine the need for force and the relationship between the need and the amount of force used. Your use of force must be within the parameters of what a reasonable man would do in like or similar circumstances. Deadly force is reserved for incidents in which you believed that your life or the life of another has been threatened with death or serious bodily harm. It is up to you to articulate or make the case that what you did was within the law, not excessive, and what a reasonable man would do in similar circumstances.

This is accomplished by making a statement working in conjunction with your legal counsel that adequately establishes "totality of the circumstances." This is not an easy thing to accomplish while at the same time protecting your rights. On scene comments, as we have discussed, should be limited to identifying physical evidence that may otherwise not be collected or lost, and identifying witnesses that LE can interview.

CASE STUDY

While working uniform patrol, my partner and I responded to the scene of a local neighborhood carry-out where a police captain had been involved in a shooting. This incident was not widely broadcast; the suspects had driven away after pointing a pistol at the supervisor and him returning fire. The captain of that shift had called my captain and we were dispatched to write a written report. The scene was not secured or evidence techs called out. The carry-out was never closed and customers continued to walk through the lot and in/out of the front door. I had walked into the business to ask the owner for the phone number and some other info for the report when I saw a female customer walk out and heard her kick what sounded like a shell casing along the ground. I followed the sound with my flashlight and found a 9mm casing. Fearing it would be lost, I picked it up and returned to my patrol car to fill out the evidence report. A short time later a detective sergeant arrived and after conversing with the captains, walked over and asked me, "Are you the officer who found the casing?" I said I was and that I picked it up because I was afraid it would be lost. He said, "Why wasn't the scene secured?" I looked over at the two captains and said, "Sarge, I'm not in charge of the scene." He looked over his shoulder at them, nodded, said, "You're right," and walked away.

Now this was over twenty years ago, but even for the time the investigation was not done correctly. Is it possible that police investigators who respond to your shooting scene, in your city or town might do something similar? Absolutely. Once again, most jurisdictions have not had or do not have that many officer involved shootings and certainly don't have that many cases of legitimate self-defense shootings.

You will be transported to the station. You and other witnesses cannot refuse to cooperate or you may be subject to arrest for obstructing justice. In my state Obstructing Justice is: "No person, with purpose to hinder the discovery, apprehension, prosecution, conviction, or punishment of another for crime or to assist another to benefit from the commission of a crime…Destroy or conceal physical evidence of the crime or act, or induce any person to withhold testimony or information…"

If you have threatened a person with a firearm, have fired at them in a self-defense situation, shot and wounded an assailant or shot and killed them, you are not free to go and must cooperate with police in terms of their investigation.

Investigators will undoubtedly transport you to the station for more. You do not have the right to refuse. Investigators may ask for clothing if they believe it is evidence, i.e. bloodstain, ripped or torn indicating a struggle. If you don't supply these items, they may take them with a search warrant. They may photograph you for evidentiary reasons, e.g. bruises, bloody face, scratch marks, scuffed knuckles, etc. Remember George Zimmerman and the allegation that his injuries were minor until police evidentiary photos and video of the police sally port were examined and his bloody face and head indicated the true extent of the severity of the attack and Zimmerman's injuries. These evidentiary issues – photos, clothing being seized as evidence, gun shot residue (GSR) tests – all will aid establishment of the totality of the circumstances and you should cooperate. If you don't, the investigators will simply get a court order anyway.

CASE STUDY

A veteran homicide detective confirmed all of the foregoing points except he stated that uncooperative witnesses will probably not be arrested (witnesses, not participants). This is not to say that there are some jurisdictions where this might still hold true. He did confirm that a citizen claiming self-defense who refuses to comply with photos, GSR and clothing seizures casts doubt on their own innocence.

Photos should be made before you are cleaned up by E.M.S. at the scene or in the Emergency Room. A bloody face, torn or disheveled clothing, all make more of a case than a small scalp laceration with a Band-Aid on it.

If you are injured, if you have a history of physical disease, i.e. heart disease or previous heart attack, or if you don't feel well (parasympathetic backlash after a violent, dynamic encounter), then ask to go to the emergency room. It is often recommended that police officers go to E.R. to be checked out by doctors after a shooting. Over the years, numerous officers have had heart attacks during traumatic incidents and died because they did not seek medical care. It is recommended that if you believe any of the foregoing is true that you seek medical treatment. It is also true that documentation of any injuries will be made right after the event versus days later.

As injuries progress, e.g. bruises get more colorful, etc. have your attorney or someone else with a time stamp camera or smart phone document these as well.

Sometimes a bruise looks just like a red mark versus days later when it is black and blue and covers a wide area.

During this entire time at the station, and with every contact with police, you should assume that everything you say is being recorded – either in written form, audio only or video/audio together. There are no "off the record" statements made to police officers.

THE INTERVIEW

As eminent police psychologist and fellow ILEETA member Dr. Alexis Artwohl, Phd. has stated, "the goal of use of force investigations is: 1) Maximize the thoroughness and accuracy of the investigation while; 2) Minimizing the trauma to the officer and their families. Dr. Artwohl expounds that the investigator is not getting a statement about what really happened but is rather getting a statement of witness "perceptions." Determining the reality of the case or the facts of the case is based on physical evidence and these witness statements. Witnesses interviewed can be participants – the officer(s) and suspect(s) as well as observers. Their perception-based statements are based on what they: saw, heard, felt, smelled, their beliefs, attitudes, biases and expectations. Of course the more you are able to learn about the person the better your ability to ascertain their influence on the person's statements. "The person may be telling the truth and they may be lying. We define a lie as they are deliberately and consciously telling you something that is different than what is in their head." Dr. Artwohl states that oftentimes police officers are disciplined based on an investigators "interpretation of their intent.")Dr. Alexis Artwohl, ASLET Seminar, Buffalo, NY, 1997)

The investigators will want to get a statement from you, without your counsel present, as soon as possible after the incident. There may be tremendous pressure by investigators for you to make a statement after the incident. You should never give a statement without the presence of your attorney. Police officers empowered by the law to use force, would not make a statement post-incident without their attorney present. You must be steadfast and state, "As a victim, I wish to cooperate with this investigation but I will need to meet with my attorney and have him present before any questioning."

What you actually want is to delay questioning for one to two days. For years an immediate statement was required of police officers after a shooting. Over the last ten years or so, we have learned more and more about memory and the effects of stress, SNS response on memory and the need to wait until after a couple of sleep cycles to improve memory.

The investigators have two choices:

1) They release you based on lack of probable cause and make an appointment to bring you in with your attorney for an interview, or

2)They arrest you.

CASE STUDY

A young man and his girlfriend are at a local university area bar enjoying themselves when three drunken males began harassing them. The three drunks were thrown out by the bouncers for their behavior. Later the man and his girlfriend left the bar and while walking down the street saw the three drunks from the prior incident hiding behind bushes next to the sidewalk. One of the three suspects jumps out and attempts to assault the male half of the couple. The innocent citizen throws one punch, knocks out the suspect on his feet. The suspect falls backward, hits his head on the sidewalk and dies from the impact. The "victim" who did nothing wrong, was arrested by investigators too lazy to find out the facts.

Charges would later be dropped but the victim was arrested and incarcerated until he could make bail and had his very freedom threatened.

This case is a sad example of:

1)In a self-defense situation anything can happen and death can result regardless of the mode or method of force including, non-deadly force such as the Taser or pepper spray, and

2)Regardless of your innocence it is entirely possible you may be arrested because most investigators have little experience with true self-defense shootings.

In truth, the investigation does not stop because you won't make a statement without an attorney present. My experience is that the investigators are in a much better position to conduct an interview after a day or two versus right after they've left the scene. During this time they've been able to examine the scene in detail, the physical evidence, take witness statements, find out more about you, etc.

REFUSING TO MAKE A STATEMENT

Are there times when you would want to refuse to make a statement? Yes. Even police officers may want to refuse to make a statement (invoke their right to remain silent) in a criminal investigation. Why? We have talked about the "politics of force" and the inherent dangers involved in a controversial shooting such as the media, "community activists," politicians, political prosecutions, etc. We need only look at the George Zimmerman case to see that despite police investigators not finding probable cause, the investigator was removed from the case, the chief of police removed from office; the prosecution not revealing exculpatory evidence, but the case was still prosecuted an example of politics at its worst.

I have had discussions with attorneys who represent cops in shootings about this topic. Their take tends to be: 1) A voluntary statement is best because the officer did nothing wrong; 2) The investigators are fellow officers who are just doing their jobs and attempting to ascertain the facts; 3) If the officer doesn't comply the prosecutor will simply subpoena them in front of the Grand Jury.

Refer back to the Case Study of "Bill" I listed earlier in this chapter, the officer who stopped a mass killer. Despite all the evidence that clearly indicated that Bill was a hero who had done nothing wrong, the county prosecutor refused to offer him immunity for his statement and his own department would not compel his statement under Garrity, which they could do.

Why? Because, despite the evidence leading to his innocence they did not want to take the potential political fall-out from offering him immunity from prosecution, they threatened to take this valiant officer into the grand jury rather than establish he did nothing wrong based on a professional investigation. It was only the threat of a press conference from his union representative that staved off their threats.

In a political prosecution, innocence is irrelevant because it is not about the facts; it is about appeasing the political machine. Truth be told, the community activists and politicians did not want to hear why George Zimmerman was innocent. They only wanted him prosecuted.

YOUR LEGAL REPRESENTATIVE

Getting the right attorney is paramount to successfully defending yourself in any criminal investigation and possible prosecution, but also for the possible civil suit to come. You should "preload" your legal defense now, instead of waiting until after the fact.

CASE STUDY

Soon after becoming a Deputy Sheriff I attended an Officer Survival course where the topic of post-shooting investigations and liability were addressed. It was recommended that I line up an attorney who I could call in the middle of the night, after a shooting or similar incident. I did so and have retained legal counsel through my police union or other means ever since.

This is not to say that every attorney is familiar with criminal law or self-defense in particular. Lawyers specialize and they may do more work as divorce attorneys, estate management, bankruptcy and other law rather than criminal. Even those lawyers who work as criminal defense attorneys may not know much about self-defense and traditionally only defend guilty criminal suspects. In my own experience working as an expert witness, I have dealt with numerous attorneys who didn't know the first thing about self-defense, shootings, stabbings, use of force and related. They know the criminal justice process but they do not specialize. I have faced expert witnesses in court who were police officer and attorneys acting as experts, as well as prosecutors who didn't know use of force law.

The officer was acquitted. The expert witness the prosecution was using was a sergeant from a police department in my state who was an attorney.

COUNTY PROSECUTORS OR DISTRICT ATTORNEYS

These folks are politicians through and through. That is not to say that there are not some highly competent and ethical prosecutors or assistant prosecutors in office, I've worked with some great ones, even prosecutors who later became common pleas court judges of high-repute. That said, a prosecutor is an elected official and most want to stay in office until they retire, term limits force them out, or they move to another political position or posting. Because of this they are more susceptible to the political winds that blow or the forces of local and national politics. If there is a case that garners national attention, i.e. the George Zimmerman case or a local self-defense case with a lot of community backlash, look for an indictment. Certainly don't look to the prosecutor for a lot of knowledge on self-defense law or an understanding of the dynamics of deadly force confrontations.

Even as a police officer I've joined an association, the Armed Citizen's Legal Defense Network, Inc. Why? Because in the advent my agency determines that an off-duty shooting was not duty related or that I was not acting as a police officer, I'm on my own. The Armed Citizen's Legal Defense Network will help pay for my defense following a self-defense shooting.

According to the Network website, the key points of their program include:

◆ Network members are educated to the highest standards, with new members receiving eight educational DVDs containing lectures by well-recognized subject-matter experts. Members receive a new educational program DVD each year with membership renewal.

◆ A fee deposit paid by the Network to the member's attorney if the member has been involved in a self-defense incident. The deposit gets the legal defense immediately underway, with representation during questioning, and arranging for an independent investigation of the incident.

◆ Network members are eligible for additional grants of financial assistance from the Network's Legal Defense Fund if they face unmeritorious prosecution or civil action after a self-defense incident occurring during their period of membership.

◆ Available expert witnesses – including internationally known trainers, experts and shooting industry professionals, attorneys and recognized leaders

◆ A unique, nationwide network of attorneys and legal experts which the member can draw upon after acting in self defense.

◆ A monthly online journal.

My local attorney is someone with whom I have worked on numerous police shooting cases. He is a strong advocate for officers. I just spoke with him about this very topic of armed self-defense and he concurred that the system (investigations and criminal justice) is certainly not prepared to deal with legitimate claims of self-defense by armed citizens.

MAKING A STATEMENT

If your attorney believes it is appropriate based on the circumstances, you may elect to make a statement. You should never make a statement without your attorney being present! In times of stress, post-incident, an attorney's focus will be on protecting your legal rights. It is a naïve notion that just because you did the right thing and acted within the law that you will be vindicated by the criminal justice system and no amount of explanation by you will change attitudes or protect you. Are there times when such statements would benefit you? Absolutely, in most cases of legitimate self-defense a statement would benefit you. The police are not looking to arrest you for defending yourself and since you've done nothing wrong, your statement can oftentimes aid in your defense.

That said, more and more today the politics of force arise and cloud the issue. The investigators may conclude you acted in self-defense and even sympathize with you but the prosecutor may still decide to seek an indictment. Further, the prosecutor may attempt to take the case away from the city and give it to the county or state investigators.

> ### CASE STUDY
> Five law enforcement officers are indicted by a county grand jury after the death of an inmate at a county jail. The investigation was taken over by the state Bureau of Criminal Investigation at the prosecutor's request. The primary investigator used statements of each individual officer against the other showing inconsistencies and differences. These inconsistencies were used to allege that officers were lying. A suppression hearing was held on the admissibility of these statements in the prosecution. Only the fact that these statements were compelled under Garrity kept them from being introduced.

The statements, made under duress right after the incident, were flawed based on SNS perceptual narrowing and inattentional blindness. The officers simply reported what they were paying attention to, based on their flawed memory.

WHY A VOLUNTARY STATEMENT CAN HELP

Establishment of the totality of the circumstances

There are many other factors that constitute totality of the circumstances other than "I was in fear for my life." Establishing your need for using force / totality of circumstances, include but are not limited to: communications from the suspect to you and you to the suspect, non-verbal communication, postures, body movements which you perceived as threatening, distances, environment, location, what you heard, felt in terms of emotions, lighting, perceptions, locations of participants and witnesses, etc.

Understand that you want to avoid making specific statements such as exact distances and rounds fired. The reason is that during an encounter you're thinking with a different part of your brain, the part that does not deal with things like time, round count and specific distances. You are better to clap out the cadence to the gunfire and indicate distances by placing yourself at the distance from an object for reference, i.e. "If the chair was the suspect, I was standing here," then position yourself.

> ### CASE STUDY
> Because of perceptual distortions – time, spatial, tunnel vision and hearing, as well as cognitive issues based on an

SNS response – police officers are frequently wrong in the number of shots fired and other specifics. Dr. Alexis Artwohl has reported a case where an officer in a dynamic gunfight recalled "beer kegs with .45 ACP on them, flying through the air." Clearly these were shell casing but it is indicative of the perceptual and cognitive impact of the SNS."

Without a voluntary statement, especially if it were just you and the suspect, establishment of the totality of the circumstances may be more difficult and take longer for the investigators. With advice and consultation from counsel, it can certainly be easier to prove your case.

Articulation

"Explaining to the best of your ability, working with your attorney the totality of the circumstances of the incident including: time, environment, distances, lighting, suspect(s) words, actions and body language; your perceptions of pending deadly attack based on suspect's words and actions; your words and actions; your attempts to avoid the confrontation or encounter and the suspect's responses; attempts at verbal warnings or commands to the suspect(s) to back off, move away or stop and his responses; injuries and follow-up care; communication with police dispatch; potential witnesses"

MIRANDA

Most of what you know, or think you know, about Miranda and your right to remain silent is wrong. Like most people, even many attorneys, you have been educated by watching TV cop shows, where an officer handcuffs a subject out on the street and starts saying, "You have the right to remain silent…" Knowledgeable street officers and investigators would never do such a thing because once it is done, it cannot be undone if the suspect asks for his attorney. In proper interview and interrogation, an entire set-up leads to the point where the investigator finally says, "Okay before we talk, I need you to understand your rights…"

"Simply described, Miranda could be said to be warnings to a suspect administered during a custodial interrogation. For Miranda to be applicable to an interrogation, it must meet two criteria. First, the setting must be custodial in nature. The court has defined custodial to mean that the suspect's freedom of action has been curtailed in some significant way. Second, the individual conducting the interrogation must be a law enforcement officer or acting as an agent for a law enforcement officer." *Practical Aspects of Interview and Interrogation, David Zulawski and Douglas Wicklander (CRC Press Inc.; 1993)*

If I were investigating you for a homicide, regardless of the circumstances, unless you are under arrest, I would not read you Miranda. Matter-of-fact, I would probably say, "I appreciate you coming in here today to speak with us. You understand that you are free to go at any time?" After that, I would conduct an interview and everything you said could be used against you in a court of law. After a suspect has given a complete interview which then establishes probable cause of the crime(s), I would then say, "Sir, you're under arrest." Only then when the suspect is no longer free to go, does a "custodial interrogation" setting exist under which I would have to read Miranda.

If you have been placed under arrest on scene or at the police station, you should be read Miranda before any questioning. In such a situation, remember that prior to any questioning or interview that any statements made to any police officers can be recorded and may be used against you.

But understand that, even if Miranda is given, "everything you say can be used against you." This is why it is so important to work with your attorney and have him present before and during any questioning.

> ### CASE STUDY
>
> Routinely police officers are not given their Miranda rights after an Officer Involved Shooting. They don't "need" to be given the rights against self-incrimination because it does not apply, it is not custodial interrogation. However, there are reasons why an officer and his counsel may want them read. The reason for this is that it makes invocation of the right to remain silent easier and compulsion for officers then required.

Is there a benefit to being read your Miranda rights before making a voluntary statement? No.

If you are placed under arrest, Miranda applies and the investigator must advise you of your rights. Cooperation and a voluntary statement after arrest is a decision your attorney should advise on. However, the fact you have been arrested is an indication of the investigator's belief that you are guilty.

IMPEDIMENTS AND ISSUES WITH MAKING A STATEMENT

Human memory is an interesting subject. To get a better understanding of how the brain works and specifically under stress I would suggest Robert Sapolsky's excellent Why Zebras Don't Get Ulcers (Third Edition, Owl Books, 2004). When an officer (or for that matter any witness) has experienced an SNS (Sympathetic Nervous System – fight or flight) response their memory is substantially impacted. The autonomic nervous system is compared to the voluntary nervous system. From Sapolsky's book, "the voluntary nervous system is a conscious one. You decide to move a muscle and it happens. The set of nerve projections to places like sweat glands carry messages that are relatively involuntary and automatic. It is thus termed the autonomic nervous system, and it has everything to do with your response to stress. One half of this system is activated in response to stress, one half is suppressed." If/when an officer is involved in a dynamic event he may go from the higher functioning Parasympathetic Nervous System of his brain to the SNS. The brain literally changes the way it does business with the limbic system (amygdala, hypothalamus, hippocampus and more) or the emotional centers of the brain taking control. This is responsible for perceptual distortions such as tunnel vision, auditory exclusion, or time distortions. Short-term memory versus long-term memory and emotionally charged memory are apparently stored in the brain differently. Sapolsky states that in studies the SNS improved memory retention up to a point, "People in the learning and memory business refer to this as an "inverse-U" relationship. As you go from no stress to a moderate, transient amount of stress – the realm of stimulation – memory improves. As you then transition into severe stress, memory declines."

Thrown into the mix of the SNS response and the perceptual distortions that may occur is the issue of inattentional blindness. Brought to the law enforcement community through the fine works of Bill Lewinski, PhD and the research conducted by his Force Science Research Center, www.forcescience.org inattentional blindness is oftentimes explained by the Gorilla experiment conducted by Christopher Chabris and Daniel Simons which is detailed in their book The Invisible Gorilla (Broadway Paperbacks, 2009). Chabris and Simons engineered a videotaped experiment in a hallway at Harvard University. Chabris and Simons had graduate students in white t-shirts and black t-shirts moving around and passing basketballs back and forth to each other. When viewing the tape volunteers were asked to count the number of passes by the white clad participants and ignore the people in the black t-shirts. You can and should view this experiment right now at www.theinvisiblegorilla.com before you read on.

After viewing they were asked how many passes were made by the participants in white. Varying answers are given but the truth is that it doesn't matter, the sole purpose of the experiment was to see if those volunteers tested saw the person in the gorilla suit walk into the middle of the screen, stop, thump its chest and then walk off.

According to Chabris and Simons in their book, "Amazingly, roughly half of the subjects in our study did not notice the gorilla! What made the gorilla invisible? This error of perception results from a lack of attention to an unexpected object, so it goes by the scientific name "inattentional blindness."

Kevin R. Davis, Use of Force Investigations: A Manual for Law Enforcement (Responder Media; 2012)

Do most police investigators know about the SNS, perceptual distortions under stress, inattentional blindness, or how human memory works? No. Sadly much of the science of human conflict, performance and recall post-traumatic incident is not widely known in law enforcement. Also remember that in most agencies a detective assignment is not a promotion based on performance or knowledge but rather an assignment based on seniority. A detective or investigator this week may have been a patrol officer last week. There are certainly exceptions and this is not meant to impugn the abilities of detectives. It is simply telling the truth.

CRITICAL INCIDENT AMNESIA

Lt. Col. Dave Grossman and Bruce Siddle from Warrior Science Group, penned an article entitled, "Critical Incident Amnesia: The Physiological Basis and the Implications of Memory Loss During Extreme Survival Stress Situations" which was published in Issue 31, August 2001 issue of The Firearms Instructor: The Official Journal of the International Association of Law Enforcement Firearms Instructors. From that article:

"Officers who encounter an extremely stressful situation will consistently exhibit difficulty in transferring information into long term memory. Particular memory related phenomenon in traumatic situations include:

1. During the actual incident there is usually a "sensory overload" combined with a "fixation" on some particular aspect of the critical incident, often to the exclusion of all else.

2. Immediately after the incident, "post-incident amnesia" will often result in a failure to remember the majority of the information observed in the incident.

3. After a healthy night's sleep there is usually a "memory recovery" which will result in the remembering the majority of what occurred, and this memory is probably the most "pure."

4. Within 72 hours the final and most complete form of memory will occur, but it will be at least partially "reconstructed" (and therefore somewhat "contaminated") after the inevitable process of integrating available information from all other sources (media).

…there is a body of research which indicates that intense stress will result in a failure to recall anything learned in a situation (Duncan, 1949; Squire 1986). McGaugh (1990) and Khalsa (1997) indicate that this effect is due to the flood of stress hormones in the brain which occurs during intense trauma. The combination of these factors will very often result in "post-incident amnesia" in which, immediately after a critical incident, the majority of information will not be remembered. (This can explain, for example, the common process by which most mothers tend not to remember the intense pain of childbirth, and are subsequently willing to have more children.)

The greater the trauma, the greater the impact of post-incident amnesia is likely to be. Key factors which will increase the stress include: the perception of threat or danger, the suddenness of the threat and the available time to respond or prepare, the amount of sensory input needing to be processed, and the degree of physical effort (aerobic and anaerobic output) that was engaged in during the incident. If the individual is physically wounded or injured the effect will be even greater, and the effects of post-incident amnesia will be greatest if the wound or injury results in unconsciousness."

The perceptual narrowing of the SNS response as well as its impact on memory and recall mean that there may be lapses in recall, or segments of the event in which you simply cannot recall.

SCIENTIFIC STUDIES ON MEMORY IN TRAUMATIC EVENTS

How does all this relate to a post incident statement or interview? You can only report what you were paying attention to and within the ability of your recall or memory.

Let me refer to research completed by Dr. Andy Morgan psychiatrist from Yale University on more than 500 soldiers completing escape and evasion training at Fort Bragg. After being interrogated (simulated military enemy interrogation but high stress) one in three of the participants (Special Forces personnel, some pilots and Marines) were unable to properly identify their interrogator, often even getting the gender wrong, this despite being in the room alone with the interrogator for over half an hour. Live line-ups resulted in a (26%) accuracy rate, photo spread (33%) accuracy and (49%) in a photo sequence. From the study, "These data provide robust evidence that eyewitness memory for persons encountered during events that are personally relevant, highly stressful, and realistic in nature may be subject to substantial error."

(Accuracy of eyewitness memory for persons encountered during exposure to highly intense stress; Morgan, Hazlett, Doran, Garrett, Hoyt, Thomas, Baranoski, Southwick; International Journal of Law and Psychiatry; 27 (2004) 265-279)

VIDEO

"Use of force is like making sausage. Even when it's done properly, it still doesn't look good."

~Ed Nowicki (Chicago PD ret., legendary trainer and founder of ILEETA)

I began this chapter with the real life story of a police officer who was indicted based on a video that did not even capture his actual shooting. It is entirely possible that your event may be captured on video. With the proliferation of cell phone video and surveillance technology, the violent encounter may be captured by a camera on a storage unit a half a block away. The problems with video are two-fold:

1)Investigators improperly interpreting what is seen on the video
2)Comparison of your statements with what is seen

CASE STUDY

Officers are captured on a gas station video surveillance system apprehending what we are later told is a suspect in possession of a stolen car. The suspect is handcuffed behind his back, and leaned over the trunk of a police patrol unit. All of a sudden one of the police officers is seen reaching over and punching the suspect in the face/head area.

Two of the officers involved are disciplined. The officer who punched the suspect is fired. During the disciplinary hearing we find out that what was not captured on video was the suspect, though handcuffed behind his back, reaching back and grabbing the officer's testicles. The officer was forced to punch the suspect to get him to let go. The officer was reinstated, subsequently sued and won sizable damages against the agency.

Since the Rodney King video and into the YouTube age, we have been inundated with police use of force videos. As more and more incidents of armed citizens defending themselves are occurring, we are beginning to see these incidents captured on tape. But what we see is not the whole story and the two dimensional aspect of video can distort the "facts." We should never make a decision on a use of force based strictly on the visual image provided by video.

Even in the State Court trial of the officers involved in the Rodney King case, Sgt. Charles Duke a legendary L.A.P.D. use of force instructor defended the officers with the tape by breaking the video down frame by frame. Sgt. Duke testified that only reasonable force was used against King. Regardless of your opinion on that case, my point is that videos of use of force incidents that look bad may in fact be completely reasonable.

As graphic or seemingly encompassing as video images are on use of force incidents, they are not the whole picture. All of the other facts and evidence of a solid investigation must be considered before reaching a conclusion.

Dr. Bill Lewinski from Force Science had this to say about videos of police use of force: "People tend to think that a video is an accurate reporter of any particular incident. But I would like you to look at the number of cameras that are necessary for referees to look at any football game. The more cameras they have the more angles they can see things from the better their judgment is about whether or not the action their judging is portrayed accurately and completely. So we know that one video camera from a particular perspective is very limiting in its ability to see anything. Even for instance there's a camera that officers are wearing that sits just in front of the officer's ear. And this reportedly has a view of the officer. It does not. If you close your left eye, for instance, you will see what your right eye sees and your right eye sees a different field of view than your left eye. And your body links both of those. Now imagine you're a camera far behind your right eye, what does that see? It's seeing what's directly in front of the face not even what the right eye is seeing. It really doesn't show the field of view on the left. No camera records things as an officer's eye and brain is recording it that's really embedded in the situation. Just as a quarterback is seeing a different field of view than the viewer sitting at home watching the camera capture the action on the football field." (Dr. Bill Lewinski, Lane County I.D.F.I.T. (Interagency Deadly Force Investigation Team) video, Lane County, Oregon District Attorney's Office)

The danger exists that investigators will obtain a video that looks different or depicts events differently than what you state occurred in your statement. This creates a problem because you are stating, A) your perspective of what occurred, when the video looks like B) what actually happened. As we have stated above when dealing with memory this is completely understandable. The problem arises when the video is compared to your statement and the conclusion made that you are lying or covering up. This is such a problem with law enforcement officer involved shootings that it is recommended that officers and their counsel watch the video before they make a statement!

This luxury will probably not be afforded to you and your attorney. Your attorney may ask if any video evidence exists but it may not be shown to you until later. If you are charged with a crime, it will not be shown but will be available through motions of discovery by your attorney.

Once again we can draw parallels between an officer involved in a shooting and a citizen. The officer's police union and/or attorney can ask to see the video or it may be allowed per policy. The private citizen's attorney will have to negotiate or ask.

Just understand that video evidence has gotten many police officers in the jackpot based on perceptions of untruthfulness by their agency when compared to written reports, and police investigators may have trouble interpreting what they see.

PRELIMINARY HEARING

The preliminary hearing is where the State, and only the State, provides evidence at a "probable cause" hearing to show that there exists sufficient evidence to bind the person over to the grand jury. In some locates this may mean that you as victim may be forced to testify in front of a judge. This will entail a local prosecutor presenting the basics of the case to the judge to establish probable cause. This may also mean that just the responding uniformed officers or detectives testify and not you as prosecuting witness. There is the chance for the defense attorney to question witnesses as well. I have had contentious preliminary hearings from some attorneys in the past where they basically accused me of falsely arresting their client. The right to hold a preliminary hearing can be waived by the defense attorney.

CASE STUDY

Years ago while working uniformed patrol in a high crime district and then street narcotics, I had occasion to appear at preliminary hearings on a weekly basis. Sometimes

> defense attorneys would want to hold a full hearing,
> sometimes they had their client sign a waiver to the hearing
> after finding out what the evidence against their client was,
> so the next step would be having the case sent to the grand
> jury. In some cases the attorney would have a hearing just
> to show their client they were doing something.

In many busy jurisdictions they have televised preliminary hearings as well as Direct Indictment Programs. In DIP programs the DIP investigator presents the case to the judge from the police reports, which eliminates the need for the officers, investigators or witnesses to testify at the preliminary hearing.

THE GRAND JURY

If you have signed felony charges against the perpetrator you will be called in to testify at the grand jury.

As the victim, you are the "prosccuting witness" against the suspect. In order to have the suspect indicted for the felony, the grand jury must vote and reach a True Bill (versus the grand jury voting no or a No Bill). Having testified in front of countless grand juries over the years, the process is pretty simple. You walk into the grand jury room with jurors seated at tables usually to your front on either side of the witness stand (which is a table with microphone for recording the case). A grand jury foreman administers the oath, "Please raise your right hand…" in which you promise to tell the whole truth under penalty of perjury and then take your seat. An assistant prosecutor will read the case, "Mr. Davis is here today reference case 14-0981, State of Ohio vs. John Doe. Mr. Doe is charged with Felonious Assault… Mr. Davis why don't you tell us what happened." The prosecutor may ask leading questions to flesh out the probable cause and totality of the circumstances of the crime committed against you. Grand jurors may ask questions as well. Keep in mind that neither the prosecutor handling the case or the grand jury has much, if any, experience with legitimate self-defense cases. They may have handled the case of a doper who shot another doper and claimed self-defense but not of an innocent citizen with a concealed carry permit or gun in the home who shot and killed, shot and wounded or shot at a criminal suspect.

Can you appear in front of the grand jury as a prosecuting witness and invoke your 5th Amendment right against self-incrimination? Yes. If you or your attorney believes that this case is turning against you and there is the possibility of you being indicted exists, then you may want to invoke your right to remain silent.

You may take your attorney with you to the grand jury but they may not be in the room with you while you testify. If a question is asked that you feel may incriminate you or that may lead to a political indictment, ask the prosecutor if you may step outside and speak with your attorney.

Attorney Muna Busailah, writing in: Vol. IV, Issue No. 3 of the Michael P. Stone, P.C., Lawyers "Training Bulletin" (May, 2001) on "Taking the Fifth" – Part IV: "When Might An Answer To A Question Tend To Incriminate Me?"

"The privilege against self-incrimination inherent in the Fifth Amendment "extends not only to answers that would in themselves support a conviction… but likewise embraces those which would furnish a link in the chain of evidence needed to prosecute claimant…it need only be evident from the implications of the question, in the setting in which it is asked, that a responsive answer to the question or an explanation of why it cannot be answered might be dangerous because injurious disclosure could result."

POST-INCIDENT BEHAVIOR

CASE STUDY

In a shooting in which I was involved in on Sep. 11, 2001, I was lying in bed with the mental "video" of the incident playing in my head. As I was laying there, I can actually remember at one point thinking, "Did I really see a plane fly into the World Trade Center today?"

Over the years I've talked to numerous officers involved in shootings. The biggest thing I can say is that this mental video will play in your head for a few days, whether awake or sleeping. You may have a good night's sleep and then wake up and the first thing that happens is the video will play. This will usually only happen for a few days and then you'll "shake hands with the event" as your brain assimilates the event. PTSD occurs when you get "stuck" in the event and are not able to assimilate it into everyday life.

There are several things I recommend to folks right after a traumatic event:
- Avoid alcohol. Alcohol is a depressant and you're already dealing with some pretty serious emotions.
- Avoid caffeine. Do you really want to throw kerosene on a raging fire?
- Exercise. Even a simply walk can help burn off the residual stress chemicals.
- Don't talk about the incident. Only talk specifics with professionals who have legal confidentiality, i.e. spouse, minister, attorney, and mental health counselor. This includes refraining from Facebook® or similar social networks or forums, even those like gun forums which you post under a user name other than your own. In these incidents, you don't know who your friends are.
- Seek a CISD – " critical incident stress debriefing" or similar with a qualified and certified counselor who is covered by confidentiality. Having gone through several of these as both an officer involved and helping to conduct a debriefing, I would state that these debriefings help.

As a psychologist and veteran police commander has stated, "You are only as sick as your secrets." Be careful when picking an attorney, if you can find who does this for the safety forces in your area, they are more in tune with the issues involved versus a standard psychotherapist. Many psychotherapists and even many clergy members are anti-gun and may not be the best source.

◆ Understand that these are normal reactions to an abnormal situation. You may experience insomnia, appetite loss, depression and a variety of other reactions. If you seek help, work it out and talk it out, you'll be okay. Once again, a victim advocacy group may be able to help.

◆ Many times reactions to a traumatic event have to do with what other stressors are going on in your life. A multitude of other issues – money, marital, etc. – may compound your stress. Once again, it's natural, just work through it.

◆ Understand that this event may change you forever but you can grow from the experience. It is up to you and how you work through it.

◆ Expect to feel an increased level of precaution and threat. You've been through a life threatening experience, this is natural. Remember it's not paranoia or an unreasonable fear. Your fear, based on your experience, is completely reasonable.

◆ Use your autogenic breathing and deep relaxation techniques.

CASE STUDY

At one stressful time in my life, I was being investigated by Internal Affairs; I used autogenic breathing to relax on a regular basis. When I.A. cleared me and "spanked" my accusers (the investigation was used as retaliation), I had my blood pressure taken for a routine physical and it was 120/80. I credit relaxation techniques and regular walking for exercise with keeping my stress levels down.

◆ Be careful about talking to the media. A simple, "This is under investigation and I've been told by my attorney that I should not make a statement at this time," plays better than a stern, "No comment!" or covering up your face and pushing through the cameras.

◆ Don't read the press or watch the news about your event. Understand the old news catchphrase "If it bleeds, it leads." I've worked on cases defending officers that made headline news when they were indicted or charged. Once the charges were dropped or they were vindicated, no mention by the media.

Work your case; actively work on your defense: When working with attorneys, understand their caseload may be extreme and that "the squeaky wheel gets the grease." Don't be a pain but don't let them relegate you to the back burner.

Successful self-defense strategy takes time and work. Your attorney must be focused on your case!

> **CASE STUDY**
>
> I once had a meeting with an attorney on a Saturday morning about a prospective civil case. The man was a former prosecutor and extremely competent in that job. However, I had to call him at home and wake him up; he arrived late to his office in a wrinkled polo shirt with the sticker from an apple stuck to his shirt. He hardly inspired confidence…

Training as part of a defense strategy: Training offers a win/win proposition. First of all, you are more likely to survive the encounter and win the day with solid training under your belt. Next, training may be introduced into your defense as well as your trainers or instructors taking the stand as expert witnesses explaining to the jury why what you did was reasonable.

This is why you want to attend vetted training programs with competent instructors who can both offer professional testimony and survive a close examination into their background! Unfortunately there are some good instructors out there who are all but pathological liars. Convictions for crimes of violence, fraud, YouTube video rants threatening government agents, etc. will all be easily found out and used to impeach your instructor.

> **CASE STUDY**
>
> I was retained on a case to defend a police officer in a use of force. The attorneys asked if I knew the plaintiff's expert. I checked into him and found he had been fired from his last agency for surfing the internet for porn while on duty. He ran a landscaping business as his full-time profession.

> **CASE STUDY**
>
> One instructor who has even taught at a state police academy on contract has fraudulently represented his background for years and years. Among other things, he once claimed he was a member of Delta Force and a small arms, demolitions and hand-to-hand expert, all while serving three years in the Army!

In police search and seizure, evidence obtained improperly or not within the law, i.e. evidence obtained when a search warrant should have been obtained, is known as "Fruits of the Poisonous Tree." This means that since the search was illegal, all evidence obtained from that search cannot be used in prosecution of the case. I liken the training received from frauds, convicted persons or easily impeachable instructors, as "fruits of the poisonous tree." Meaning that the training may have been good but the instructor cannot take the stand because of credibility issues.

Vet your instructors! Even police officers and trainers succumb to the "cult of personality" accompanying many "internet" wonders and "high-speed-low-drag" instructors. I've had the opportunity to meet some of the real deal guys. Most are very low key and don't walk around bragging about their exploits.

SUMMATION

If you are claiming self-defense, then it will be up to you and your attorney to prove that case, to police, to prosecutors, to the grand jury, possibly even to a state court jury if you are tried for homicide, that you acted as a reasonable man would have in like or similar circumstances. Sometimes that is not necessarily easy to accomplish.

Having an attorney, on call, one who has a working knowledge of these types of cases and is willing to roll out of bed at zero-dark-thirty is vital. Understand that you want to cooperate with police as much as possible without endangering your case. You are the victim of a potential murder, felonious assault or other crime! But you must protect your rights! Remember, the system is not set up to deal with legitimate cases of self-defense and you will be most likely treated like a suspect. You want to point out where evidence is located, who and where the witnesses are, point out that you are the victim of a crime and are willing to sign charges. Then make the statement that, "I am willing to cooperate but I want to speak with my attorney before any other questioning and to have him present before I make a statement." Veteran defense attorneys have made the statement, "When in doubt, shut up and ask for your attorney."

You can win the case just like you can win on the street in a violent gunfight. It just takes training, preparation and attention to detail, just like your firearms training and street concealed carry!

Note – I've dealt with some of the issues dealing with the criminal aspects of the use of deadly force, i.e. the criminal investigation with you as victim, suspect and possibly as the focus of a criminal prosecution. What I have not dealt with is the civil case that may arise out of your use or threatened use of deadly force, seeking monetary damages in municipal or state court for injuries and other alleged loss. The groundwork that you lay working with your attorney in the criminal investigation will only help you in a possible civil case. Put simply, a good solid defense and proper statement will seriously reduce the probability of a civil action. Although I've worked on civil cases as an expert witness, it is vital to get the proper competent and knowledgeable attorney for any civil action as well. You can be completely vindicated by the investigators and prosecutors in a criminal investigation and still be sued in state court. Keep in mind, the standard is much lower in civil court – preponderance of the evidence, versus the criminal court standard of – guilt beyond a reasonable doubt.

CHAPTER NINE:

LADIES, GUNS AND ARMED DEFENSE

Women can defend themselves, and with proper training, mindset and awareness, can stop violent attacks against them.

CASE STUDY

Cindy was the office manager for a trucking company who had arrived at a local bank to make a deposit in broad daylight. As she sat behind the wheel of her SUV in the parking lot afterwards, she was approached by a suspect who began by asking her directions and then opened up the door of her truck and forced himself on top of her. Cindy scrambled to grab her .38 Taurus revolver she carried in the center console of her vehicle. Once she got her hand on it she fought against her attacker's attempts at grabbing her arm, and was able to fire a shot which went through her vehicle door but was enough to cause her attacker – a registered sex offender who had just gotten out of prison earlier that year – to run away. He was apprehended by police a short distance away.

Good outcome, certainly a success story. Cindy went home, and her attacker, who was making sexual comments as he lay on top of her, went to jail and then back to prison. It certainly could have ended much worse. This 40ish-year-old lady had recently gotten her CCW permit and, except for firing her revolver at the range for the course, had never fired her gun before.

"If you consciously tell yourself, 'This person is trying to charm me,' as opposed to 'This person is charming,' you'll be able to see around it."

Like most encounters, we can and should learn from Cindy's. Let's examine some of those learning points:

- Carrying concealed can and does save lives. We have no idea what could have happened had Cindy not had a gun. Nationwide from mothers in Detroit to the streets of mainstream America, armed female citizens are saving lives with their guns.
- Cindy was not prosecuted. She was the victim of a crime and was treated as such.
- She did not curl up into a fetal position and submit to being a victim, she acted decisively and that made a difference.
- The suspect began by "interviewing" Cindy. She didn't even realize his intent was nefarious from the start and he was using dialogue to attempt to disarm her and lower her guard. Gavin de Becker in his excellent book The Gift of Fear (Little, Brown; 1997) states, "The capable face-to-face criminal is an expert at keeping his victim from seeing survival signals, but the very methods he uses to conceal them can reveal them. Charm is almost always a directed instrument, which, like rapport building, has

motive. To charm is to compel, to control by allure or attraction. If you consciously tell yourself, "This person is trying to charm me," as opposed to "This person is charming," you'll be able to see around it." We are reminded of serial murderer Ted Bundy and how he would disarm and charm his victims.

◆ "Having a gun" is different than being ready. The mere presence of a firearm in a home or in a vehicle is not enough. We must be ready and prepared to act.

◆ Cars are not holsters. Carrying a handgun in the car (in this case in the center console) is tantamount to being disarmed, as seldom will the perfect opportunity to access the gun be possible, and what happens if you are separated from the gun by circumstance?

CASE STUDY

An off-duty officer was shot and killed in a convenience store parking lot while refueling his vehicle at the pumps. An armed robber approached him between his vehicle and the gas station. He had left his firearm in his truck.

Basic CCW training in no way prepares anyone to effectively defend themselves. It is the start, but we cannot imagine that Cindy's training prepared her to draw and fire within these circumstances. But our very survival is based on our training. It must address and prepare you to win the day in situations other than on flat ranges at 21 feet, which is the average distance and conditions that most instructors work at.

There were the trend setters, those trainers who dealt with this important topic years ago such as the first firearms book for women by a woman (and I'm proud to say I own an original copy…) was Self-Defense Requires No Apology by Jan Jones (Security World Publications; 1985). From Jan's book we read:

"When people learn of my interest in self-defense and guns, they typically respond, "But you look like such a nice girl." I may not be a girl any longer, but I do think of myself as nice, which is exactly why I do have this interest. A belief in my own self-worth has enabled me to make the decision that no one has the right to harm me. With this as the basis of my thinking, I have learned to be more assertive, self-reliant, and confident.

Jan Jones and her excellent book Self-Defense Requires No Apology was a trendsetter in armed defense for women.

We have the right to live unmolested lives, and preparing to do so is a positive rather than a negative."

Other early writers and trainers are: Paxton Quigley author of Armed and Female (Dutton Adult; 1989); Vicki Farnam and Diane Nicholl Teaching Women to Shoot: A Law Enforcement Officer's Guide (D.T.I.; 2002); Gila May-Hayes with her titles – Effective Defense, (Firearms Academy of Seattle; 2000), Personal Defense for Women, (Gun Digest Books; 2009), and Concealed Carry for Women, (Gun Digest Books; 2013); Clint and Heidi Smith from Thunder Ranch with their excellent DVD Ladies Basic Guide to Concealed Carry (FMG Publishers; 2009). Massad Ayoob has championed the cause of the female armed citizen and has trained and focused articles about distaff shooters for years in his courses, books and columns.

Additionally, concealed carry issues specific to women, such as holsters and training, have been getting more attention from gun manufacturers, holster makers and firearms instructors. But we still have a long way to go.

CASE STUDY

Patty was a friend who had gone to a gun store and was talked into purchasing a little .25 acp semi-auto pistol more than 30 years ago. She asked me if I would take her to the range. At that time there was no decent ammo but hardball for the little guns. One trip to the range was enough to convince her the gun was not suitable for her armed defense. She invested in a two inch .38 Chief's Special, which was at that time the most reliable of the smaller guns, and learned to shoot it effectively.

CASE STUDY

A young female teacher was a student in an armed teacher and school staff program. Her husband insisted that she use his full-sized .40 caliber Glock pistol for the course. I'm sure he was all impressed with its "stopping power" and that any pistol less than the .40 didn't have the kinetic energy needed to drop a suspect in his tracks. The problem was that his petite wife was not him and she was very conscious of the felt recoil and failed to qualify with that pistol during the final test. The following week, she came back with a 9mm Glock and had no problems.

CASE STUDY

A young female police officer was a student in an "Officer Survival" class. The double stack 9mm pistol she was issued by her agency was simply too big for her hand. Despite installing a trigger designed by the factory for smaller hands, to fire the first shot she had to compromise her grip and come around the frame. Her agency would allow male detectives to carry pistols with single column 9mm magazines but not uniformed officers. This was done out of an outdated concept of "uniformity" in the patrol officer ranks.

GUNS AND GEAR

There is no "cookie cutter" approach to female armed defense. Just like what works for men (as indicated by the case study above) may not work for women, what works for one woman may not work for another. Age, size, hand strength, upper body strength, build, experience level and much more are determinants of how a woman (or a man, for that matter) can carry concealed, as well as how they can shoot and operate other firearms.

Michelle Cerino from the Chris Cerino Training Group on concealed carry for the ladies:

"Personally, I almost always carry my firearm in a purse. When carrying a gun in a purse or bag, never allow it to mix with the contents inside. Keys, pens, and other small objects can find their way into the trigger guard and can cause an unintentional discharge or render the gun inoperable. A purse specifically created for concealed carry is the best option. This keeps the gun in a separate compartment. Often these specially designed purses offer multiple access points for retrieving your gun.

"Making the decision to carry your pistol in your purse doesn't limit you to having to draw before firing. Outside the box thinking and training will prove that you can shoot from within your purse. A quickly approaching threat may cause this to become necessary, especially if the target threat is in close proximity. Firing through the purse if the suspect is close and time is of the essence. Although I'm a proponent of sighted fire, sometimes it isn't going to happen. Possibly, when you get that strange feeling that something isn't right and you reach into your purse to orient the gun in your hand in preparation, there may be no time to remove it and fire.

"At times, I choose to carry my handgun on my person. There are three criteria I look for in a holster: comfort, conceal-ability and access. Trying various types of concealed carry holsters I came to find the outside the waistband, cross draw holster to be the most comfortable. Cross draw didn't poke me or rub my side when seated. Conceal-ability came simply by untucking my shirt. With the empty gun I practiced drawing while seated in my car. Certainly ready at hand and easily acquired.

"Remember, the body won't go where the mind hasn't been, so if you think you will improvise a new tactic when your life depends on it, you are probably wrong. You have to open your mind and train. Whether you chose to carry in your purse or on your body, practice is essential.

"The decisions are many once you commit to carry concealed. Mental preparation, situational awareness and honing instinct are paramount and continuous pursuits. All of which are done by training in classrooms and reading. Regardless of how or what you arm yourself with, it is important to train. Train the body, mind and warrior spirit. Before you walk out the door, practice a draw, orient your gear and prepare yourself for the unthinkable. Place your mind where your body needs it to be."

CASE STUDY

For years female officers have dreaded "shotgun qualification." Based so much on poor equipment (stocks which are entirely too long, and full charge 00 buck), as well as instructors who taught them poor technique, the ladies would literally hate shotgun training and quals. Give some of them better training on isometric pressure and buttstock placement, reduced recoil 00 buck loads or even low-brass birdshot for training and a reduced sized stock so the officer is not so stretched out and angled, and the results can be impressive. Give them (and male officers as well) an AR-15 or M-4 and they love it.

Strong-side outside the belt holsters which may work great for one female shooter may be incredibly hard for another lady to draw from, as the flair of her hip presses the grip panel into her side. Appendix, actually inguinal channel or inguinal crease, may work for some but not for others. A blue jean wearing lady permit holder from the country may need an entirely different type of holster than a female officer worker from the city.

Guns are as diverse as holsters, with some ladies loving smaller-barreled 9mm single stack pistols, while others like .45 autos of a 1911 design. It is flawed thinking to believe that ladies cannot handle full-size pistols. I've trained enough female officers with Glock 17 semi-auto pistols to know that, with the right hand size and training, they can be quite effective with that 18-shot capacity pistol. That said, off-duty that full-size pistol may be all but impossible to conceal as the weather gets warmer and we start dressing lighter and tighter.

The inherent problem with carrying smaller pistols and revolvers, for both men and women, is that they are harder to shoot. The sight radius – distance between front and rear sights – is usually a couple of inches (my Glock Model 19 with HiViz front sight is 5½ inches, as is my G26, but my Smith and Wesson M&P340 is about 3¼ inches) and that makes them harder to shoot.

Further, many small-frame pistols and revolvers have long and heavy trigger

Size, body type and attire have a lot to do with what and how a woman can carry concealed.

pulls. It is hard to manipulate and accurately fire a handgun when trigger weight is heavier than the actual overall weight of the gun. In my experience as an instructor, female shooters have a tough time holding the handgun on target as they work through the trigger press. This is certainly caused by a longer trigger press (in some cases close to half inch of trigger "take up or slack") that is gritty and around ten pounds in some cases. This is one of the reasons, for both men and women, that double action/single action pistols, known as "trigger-cocking" pistols, which require a long double action first press of the trigger (causing the hammer to cock and then release) are not as popular as striker fired pistols such as the Smith and Wesson M&P and the Glocks (the late great Jeff Cooper called double-action/single-action pistols "crunchentickers"). The harder and heavier the trigger pull, the more prone the shooter is to move the barrel, i.e. slap or jerk the trigger, causing a miss.

We don't want "hair triggers" in defensive handguns, but we want a trigger we can manage successfully to maximize accuracy on target.

Over the last few years, manufacturers have focused on smaller and better-designed handguns for the CCW market. The Smith and Wesson Bodyguard 380, the new Glock 42, Springfield XD-S, Beretta Nano, Bersa BP, Ruger LCP, Taurus models as well as others offer compact packages for female concealed carry. Just make sure that the trigger and sights are acceptable to you. For instance, if your .380 pistol is stoked with 80 grain DPX from Cor®Bon or 50 grain Civil Defense® from Liberty Ammunition, you can maximize the performance from

these smaller framed pistols. In terms of smaller .380 pistols, we have come leaps and bounds in ammunition performance today versus the round-nose ball ammo of yesterday.

A recent informal poll I conducted of female law enforcement officers and CCW permit holders showed that many ladies struggle with the same issues – how and what to carry concealed. Many ladies love their full-size pistols but opt for .380 pistols or five shot revolvers when carrying concealed. Fashion dictated by circumstances, such as while at work or in a more formal setting or function, often makes concealed carry on the person a tough proposition. This often results in many ladies relegating their handguns to purse carry, with one CCW permit holder commenting, "They (the purses) are ugly, by the way…"

So what we seek is a balance, we want to carry as much gun as we can manipulate, operate, shoot well and conceal effectively.

My recommendation is to shoot a variety of different pistols and revolvers before settling on "the one" that you want to purchase. Same thing with holsters, look around and try different rigs before spending your hard-earned money. Do understand though that anyone who has been carrying for a few years has a bag of holsters sitting around that are unused, and that we all have a couple or three holsters that we tend to use on a regular basis.

Don't go into a gun store and get talked into buying something you'll regret

LEFT TO RIGHT: Young woman's hand holding a 1911 semi-auto pistol, Smith and Wesson 5906, Glock 26, Smith & Wesson M&P 340, Glock 42.

later, "Come on little lady, let me walk you down to these pretty pink little pistols…" Don't feel pressured to purchase a firearm that has deplorable sights, a long and weighty trigger, and doesn't reliably function, a firearm you may be able to conceal but can't shoot accurately or operate smoothly. This is a purchase or selection that may have tremendous impact on your survival. Do your homework, try out different handguns, shoot them if possible before you buy. I would recommend Emily Miller's Emily Gets Her Gun for a look into how she went about selecting her home defense handgun. (Unfortunately in Emily's case she is unable, based on Washington D.C. law, to carry concealed, but at least she can own a firearm for home defense now…).

YOU GOT WHAT IT TAKES

CASE STUDY

Paxton Quigley in her excellent book Armed & Female (Dutton; 1989) recounts this story, "Kate Petit's car sputtered to a stop on the interstate highway between Lake Kissimmee and Tampa…Kate was stranded, all right. What looked to her like a mixture of smoke and steam was pouring out the top, bottom, and sides of the engine compartment." She thinks a good Samaritan motorist has come to her aid, the vehicle was driven by, "respectable looking gentlemen who stopped an expensive-looking car on the highway and backed all the way up in front of me and my burning car." What Kate didn't know was that she was being "interviewed" by a suspect who, like Gavin De Becker has written, was an expert at hiding his intent. "After being polite and sympathetic, the man took a knife from the inside pocket, of his suit coat and pressed it sharply into Kate's ribs, telling her that if she didn't cooperate he would push the knife into her heart.

Kate was forced into the suspect's trunk and driven to a remote location. During the drive the suspect yelled at her, telling her what he was going to do. But during the drive Kate physically positioned so that her head was away from the trunk opening and armed herself with a revolver she carried in her purse. "Kate doesn't remember when the man stopped yelling at her in the trunk, and doesn't remember what he said as he opened the trunk. All she remembers is the flood of daylight momentarily blinding her when the trunk lid popped open and an almost slow-motion sight of the bullet holes being made in the man's chest by the .38-caliber revolver she took out of her purse. She had planned to shoot every bullet in her gun at the man when the trunk opened, but after three shots he slumped into the trunk on top of her, dead."

Kate had carried her revolver for years, stating, "But I frequently recognized a feeling of being safe or being less vulnerable when I had my gun with me. You're not going to believe this, but when he put me in the trunk with my purse I was very relieved."

Author Quigley writes, "The suspect was a twice-convicted felon who had previously been found guilty of eleven counts of sexual assault, including sodomy, child molestation, and rape." He was on parole after being recently released after serving 22 months for raping a woman and her 12-year-old daughter.

A potential victim was turned into a victor after using a gun in self-defense and saving her own life.

Most violent encounters are ambushes.

I will state as a husband, father of two beautiful daughters and the trainer of countless ladies, you have the ability and capacity to learn to defend yourself with a firearm. Don't let rampant testosterone persuade you that you are incapable of winning the day in a violent and armed encounter. There are some amazing stories of armed female citizens confronting and overcoming hyper-violent criminal suspects.

STACY LIM

"Officer Stacy Lim of the Los Angeles Police Department would get involved in a shooting on June 9th, 1990, off-duty and far removed from her law enforcement job. Stacy had played softball with her partner and his family and then they went to a restaurant to get something to eat. At 1:45 a.m. she began to be followed by five gang members after the 14-year-old girlfriend of one gang banger saw Stacy's SUV and said to her gangster boyfriend, "If you love me. You'll steal that car for me." Stacy would usually drive with her semi-auto pistol under her right thigh and when she got out of the vehicle would place the pistol under her left armpit, as she walked up to her house. But this time as she stepped out unaware, the gang member had approached her driver's side door pointing a .357 magnum revolver at her. She states, "I saw the barrel of the .357, it looked like the size of a canon. As I raised up my gun, we were probably five feet from each other. He fired one round. He shot me just left center of my chest, went through my chest out my back, nicked my diaphragm, my liver, my intestine, shattered my spleen, put a hole in the base of my heart, and left a tennis ball sized hole in my back as it exited. But I think I was just more mad than hurt at the time. I figured I could feel it later. As he turned, I fired one round, then he turned and ran, I hit him in his shoulder, as he went across the corner (of the car). I came back from behind him, I slowed down, I didn't know where he'd gone. As I got about here (rear driver's corner of the car), I started coming out, I saw him come back at me with his handgun. I fired three more times. I hit him in the shoulder, the back, and the base of the neck. He went down. He fired five more rounds, that went high left (missing Stacy). When I saw him hit the ground, I knew I was bleeding bad, so I had to get back."

"Stacy checked her own wound and knew she was bleeding badly. She attempted to walk up her driveway to the house, she knew she was going to pass out. She states however, "It was a survival thing for me. I wasn't scared because I knew I'd been shot and I knew it was bad, there was something inside of me, that I knew I wasn't going to die."

Her roommate called EMS. Paramedics lost her pulse once on the ride and they brought her back to life with the defibrillators. She was on 70% life support in ICU. She went through 101 units of blood after surgery. The second time she went to surgery she went into full arrest. After massaging her heart for 45 minutes, they sewed up an artery the doctors had missed the first time. Now on 100% life support she was given no chance to survive but, "My parents and family yelling at me to 'Survive! Survive!' Because of my strong will and desire to survive, and that it wasn't my time, I basically starting fighting back and then after 15 days in the hospital, I walked out on my own, with no restrictions. Eight months after my shooting I went back to work. For me, I did what I had to do to survive and that was it. There was nothing heroic about it. I did what I was trained to do. What I was taught to do." (From LAPD: Life on the Beat (TV series))

We don't examine these incidents and tragedies to criticize, but we can learn from Stacy's encounter to avoid similar confrontations.

Awareness and intent coupled with skill at arms can save the day.

- Most violent encounters are ambushes. We can avoid these by maintaining our awareness levels and monitoring who is around and behind us in traffic as well as on foot.
- Driving with a gun under our thigh versus in a holster is dangerous. If intentional contact is made with the suspect(s) we can lose our firearm. Sadly in the infamous Miami shootout with suspects Platt and Matix, one of the FBI agents lost his revolver when his vehicle collided with the suspect's. He spent the entire shootout unarmed and was wounded as a result.
- Prior to getting out of the car, check your surroundings. Getting into and out of cars we are vulnerable, and if an ambush is perceived we can drive out of it.

Stacy Lim was not acting as a cop when she was attacked. Sadly, California prevents concealed carry by anyone other than law enforcement, the politically connected or celebrities, but here we see in Stacy Lim, an ultimate survivor who is a shining example of what a female can do with the will, training and tools to win.

JENNIFER FULFORD-SALVANO

Jennifer Fulford-Salvano was assigned to the patrol division of the Orange County, Florida, Sheriff's Office in May of 2004 when she and the rookie who she was training that day responded to a residence after an 8-year-old boy called 911 to report that strangers were in his home with his mom.

PoliceOne.com quotes the officer:

The woman told her there were three men in the house and she didn't know what they wanted or why they were there. She wouldn't give any more details. The officers told the woman to wait by the street. "I was trying to get to the kids. Everyone else was saying 'pull back, wait for K-9.' But all the intruders had to do was put a hand out and put down the garage door."

She entered the garage door through the open door and crouched down on the driver's side of the van. She could see 2-year-old twins but she couldn't see the little boy who made the call. The door handle was locked so she couldn't get in.

A black male, George Jenkins, came around the back of the garage, positioned himself behind the van and began firing out through the garage. Then he spotted Fulford-Salvano and began firing directly at her. The deputy returned fire and ducked behind the van. Jenkins fell against the garage wall.

Fulford-Salvano then heard movement from the front of the van. Another man, John Dzibinski, began to fire at her from the hood. She fired back and began oscillating between firing at Jenkins and firing at Dzibinski. She emptied her magazine and reloaded.

I kept on thinking, "I need to keep them away from me."

The last time she leaned out to fire at Jenkins, she landed a head shot, but not before one of his rounds hit her in the right shoulder. She didn't notice the injury until she was done firing. With her right, dominant hand out of commission, she picked up the gun with her left hand.

At this point, Dzibinski popped out again from the front of the van and Fulford-Salvano fired, hitting him in the head as well.

Knowing for sure that Dzibinski was done fighting, but not sure the status of the other gunman, Fulford-Salvano took a minute to check her own injuries. When she looked at her body she saw blood coming from lots of different places. She knew she needed to concentrate, control her breathing and focus on staying conscious.

According to PoliceOne.com, only 47 seconds passed. She said her recent training was the key to her making it out alive. "Training in off-handed shooting really, really helped me. I just reacted."

"In her weak hand development training she held a tennis ball in her strong hand and learned to use her off hand to do everything, including reloading using her shoe or the ground."

Fulford-Salvano stated ten bullets hit her. Three hit her equipment and didn't injure her. She recovered and returned to full police duty.

The suspects were at the house to rob the female occupant of 341 pounds of marijuana and $60,000 in cash from her illegal dope trade.

Lessons to learn:
- Oftentimes things are not what they appear to be. In this case it was an armed home invasion robbery of a residence used for dope dealing.
- Don't overextend yourself. By entering the garage, alone, Deputy Fulford-Salvano had to contend with two armed suspects by herself. Could she have just as easily protected the children in the garage from an outside corner versus entering?

Once again we see that heroes are not made, they are cornered, but when Jennifer Fulford-Salvano sprang into action, she took care of business!

Here a female officer learns to properly utilize cover while shooting. *And rolls out to successfully engage her target.*

JEANNE ASSAM

2007: Jeanne Assam had left the State of Minnesota where she had served as a police officer and relocated to Colorado Springs, Colorado. She had been attending services at New Life Church for about six months when she answered a spiritual calling to join the volunteer-plainclothes security team. On the 9th of December she was at home not planning on going to church that day when, after surfing the net, she had come across a news blurb which stated that a Christian mission – "Youth with a Mission" had been attacked in Arvada, Colorado 70 miles north of Colorado Springs. A white male suspect had killed two mission staff members and two others were wounded. The suspect had escaped. Jeanne Assam made the decision to go into church that day.

Around 1 p.m. Assam was in the lobby area when someone alerted her to something going on at one of the entrance doors. She recounts her experiences:

"I was standing in the front lobby, still very crowded, and a volunteer behind the big round volunteer desk, says loudly, "Security!" So I turn around at him and he points towards the front doors "That guy says there's something weird going on outside." So I go talk to this man and he says, "Yeah, there's like a smoke bomb outside the steps." So I was just thinking, should I call the fire department? Or what is this device, is it a dud? Is it going to explode? And still trying to keep everybody back, some people said it was one white male in a

Jeanne Assam wrote about her violent armed encounter in her church in her book God, the Gunman & Me.

red car, and another couple people said, it was three white males in a white car. I was going to make note of both and so I went inside and before I could start writing down the names, before I'd forget, the volunteer said, "There's another smoke grenade outside the cafeteria doors," which was far from where I was standing. Before I could even see another one, I hear this muffled – pop, pop, pop – coming from the east hallway, which was on my left. The east hallway is over 100 yards long and 30 feet wide. It is the busiest hallway in the church. I immediately go over there and as I'm making my way to the beginning of the east hallway, these loud thundering cracks of a high powered rifle just start ringing out and I hear everybody screaming and someone's like, "Get down he's got a gun!" And I thought the gunman was inside our church. A security guy behind me says, "There he is Jeanne, he's coming in the doors right now." Well, the gunman's entering the complete opposite end of the hallway from where I stood, so he had been shooting through the doors of the church. He'd been shooting into the masses of people. So I pulled my gun out of the waist of my jeans where I keep it and just sprinted down the hallway toward him.

And all of a sudden everyone's gone. There was no one left in the hallway except for me and the gunman. And he's pulling open the second and last set of these heavy glass doors. So, I took cover in this hallway on the right that was perpendicular to the east hallway that he was walking down. I put my gun in the high-ready and I was just going to wait for him to come up to me and I was going to shoot him. You know perpendicular and then I'd shoot him. I stepped up to the corner of the hallway and I shouted at him, "Police Officer drop your weapon!" And he turns toward me and I shot rapidly five times and knocked him back, completely on his back. And he sits up and I walked toward him and I said, "Drop your weapon or I will kill you!" And he's shooting at me now, so we're shooting at each other. Obviously I'm gonna keep shooting at him if he's shooting at me. And then he tried to duck behind this hallway and I couldn't let him, couldn't lose sight of him because then I'd have another situation. So I shot him again, for a total of ten times. And I told him you know, "Drop your weapon!" I gave him fair warning and I just knew he could kill me and then he'd kill those other people, so I had to take his life."

According to news reports, Mathew Murray was on a mission to kill many more before Jeanne Assam stopped him that fateful day in December.

Learning points:

- ◆ Even "quiet" Sundays in December in church can result in violent encounters.
- ◆ More and more churches are asking parishioners to volunteer to arm themselves for security purposes. Churches can be the target of anti-religious fanatics as well as the mentally ill or even terrorists.
- ◆ Jeanne Assam states that during her police interview she couldn't remember everything because she was taken downtown immediately afterward for a statement.
- ◆ The Detectives collected Assam's clothing for evidence because they had the suspect's blood on them.

Jeanne Assam would meet with President George W. Bush who told her "Good job, I'm proud of you."

Three amazing women who faced death and, based on their intense will to win and their training, overcame hyper-violent criminal suspects.

You can too.

HOME VERSUS PUBLIC ARMED DEFENSE

Handguns

CASE STUDY

T.K. is an old friend, now retired from her fiscal job at the local sheriff's office where she also held a commission as a deputy sheriff. She and I and a few others worked together for years. Recently asked about what she carried she responded, "Smith & Wesson .357 in purse. In the barn I use an inside the belt holster."

CASE STUDY

A young recently hired female officer was asked what she carried off-duty (on duty it is a Glock 17). She said she carries a Glock 26 in an inside the belt holster.

Ideally we want the same pistol or operating system carried outside and inside the home. If you need a smaller version to conceal while in public, try to obtain a smaller version of the pistol you may use for home defense. In this way, you only have to master or operate one system in an SNS response, versus making the mental switch from a striker fired pistol to a manual safety handgun when someone is kicking in your front door. In the home you do not have to limit yourself to a possibly smaller barreled pistol or revolver. Though these handguns are easier to carry and conceal, they are not necessarily easier to shoot and by design have less ammunition than their full-size counterparts. There are certainly benefits to having a pistol with more ammo onboard. We must remember though, as trainer Clint Smith states, "We don't have a higher capacity firearm to shoot more. We have it so that we have to reload or mess with it less during an encounter."

There are other items, besides our handgun, carried openly on the belt or secured in a weapon safe, that we may want to consider for home defense. These include weapon-lights and lasers, which increase the girth of the pistol in concealment, but may be useful in the home.

Having a white light affixed to your pistol for home defense makes extreme sense as we have indicated in the section of this book dealing with lights and low-light shooting. Red or green lasers can certainly aid you in home defense (attached or as part of a white light) as well.

If you are responsible for protecting your children or homestead, carrying a handgun on your person certainly reduces response time to a threat. When all your instincts are calling for you to run toward the children to protect them, running upstairs instead to access a firearm is counterintuitive.

Long-guns

As we have noted, the ballistic performance of a rifle or shotgun on target (even pistol caliber carbine) is certainly better than a handgun. With four points of contact – both hands, cheek-weld and upper pectoral/shoulder – a long-gun can certainly improve accuracy on target.

Shotguns

Very few female officers I've worked with over the years enjoy shooting the 12 gauge pump or auto-loading shotgun. With 00 buck or other substantial high-brass fodder such as slug, #1 or #4 buckshot, the kick or recoil of the smooth-bore shotgun is just not pleasant for them to shoot. Yes, we can train with bird-shot in practice, but uncomfortable recoil makes it less likely we'll train or more likely we'll flinch. The recoil is even more pronounced due to the longer length of pull (LOP), which tends to be designed more for men than women. A standard 12 gauge pump shotgun may cause the female shooter to have to absorb more energy into her shoulder based on her arm length. By shortening the LOP, the female shooter can oftentimes get more of her body in line behind the stock to absorb felt recoil, versus taking it all in the pectoral/deltoid tie in area, an area with a lot of nerve lines. A better-fitting shotgun that allows the female shooter to square off on the target a little better, and proper technique of leaning into the shotgun by distributing weight forward onto the balls of the feet, does much to mitigate recoil. As pro-shooter and instructor Todd Jarrett has instructed, both pushing and pulling the shotgun (the support hand pushes forward away from the body on the forearm, and the strong hand pulls back toward the pistol grip

– it is as if the shooter were trying to break the shotgun in two at the receiver) helps to further absorb or compensate for recoil.

We can downscale to a 20 gauge shotgun. Older male shooters of my acquaintance have done this because, at advancing age, they simply can't take the stout recoil either. Mossberg, for instance, makes several 20 gauge shotguns, such as the 500 Special Purpose, with: Ghost Ring Sights, compact stock, extended magazine (eight round capacity) which is highly suitable for home defense, as well as the 500 Special Purpose, 20 gauge "Muddy Girl" model which features a kinda cool forearm and pistol grip adjustable paint job which is black, white and pink. Remington also has the Model 870 Express Compact Jr. with a LOP – length of pull of 12 inches might be just the ticket in 20 gauge for the ladies. There are even .410 shotguns for even less recoil.

Though many trainers don't recommend long-guns for home defense based on their contention that manipulation is a problem, I believe this is a training issue, as is clearing a home or structure with a handgun for that matter. I would recommend shotguns and carbines with 18- or 20-inch barrels for this role, however. A 28-inch barreled shotgun is just too hard to move with and is relegated to static home defense in my opinion.

Carbines

Here are excellent choices for home defense that are just plain fun to shoot as well. Carbines of the 5.56, .223 or .30 caliber M-1 carbine varieties have virtually no felt recoil, yet provide accurate fire on target with the ballistic performance that has made them sought after by modern law enforcement.

Easily upgraded or purchased direct from the factory in packages – lightweight, with white lights and adjustable stocks that improve shooting and handling characteristics – modern carbines offer an excellent choice for home defense and allow you, with training, to be effective in both static and moving/ clearing roles.

CASE STUDY

"Sheri" was a very petite police officer of some seniority. Weighing only 90 lbs. soaking wet on her five foot frame, she "suffered in silence" at her agency's shotgun qualifications. She just didn't like it, the recoil hurt her but she knuckled down and did it because she had to. When the agency picked up some surplus M-16s from the federal government and she shot one, she immediately liked it. If a shorter adjustable stocked model M-4 had been given to her, she could have really improved and excelled with her long-guns skills while improving her performance on target and on the street.

SHOOTING SKILLS

There are professional female shooters who shoot 9mm, .40 or .45 caliber pistols and who can smoke me on the range (heck, there are some good amateurs who can as well). Certainly I look at Stacy Lim, Jeanne Assam and Jennifer Fulford-Salvano and the intense gun battles that those three ladies won, and as Wayne and Garth used to say, "I'm not worthy..."

So what have those pros mastered that I need to continually work on? The same thing they work on with diligence on a regular basis, the fundamentals of marksmanship. The FOM – grip, platform, trigger management, sight alignment, sight picture, breathing, follow-through and recovery applied to solve problems – is what they mastered (of course, my bet is that if you asked them, they would say that they have yet to master these, but rather work on them on a regular basis...).

The next thing that is vitally important is to take those FOMs off the static target line and "pressure test" them. By engaging in competition, shooters are forced to deal with and overcome match nerves, which are a milder but still stressful version of an SNS response. On a regular basis, they practice and learn to breathe to reduce their stress, and focus on their task. The "myelination," which is so important to build successful motor programs, is practiced on a regular – daily – basis. Their training is not one time, in time, it is continual and regular.

We see female shooters use the weaver stance promulgated by Jeff Cooper and the Gunsite Academy as well as the modern isosceles stance. We see ef-

This officer came into the author's "use of cover" course with marginal abilities with her handgun. After training in the fundamentals, she ran a scrambler with a partner from 25 yards in, using different cover positions. She is very happy with her target.

ficient use of grip, with a solid 360-degree grip with both hands controlling the handgun, and platform – with proper weight shift used so that the entire body is controlling the pistol and its recoil.

Trigger management has been honed so that sight picture (based on kinesthetic awareness of where the sights are in relation to each other as well as the target) is not disturbed while efficient pressure is exerted straight back on the trigger. Follow through on the sights and trigger is maintained through the break of the shot before another target is shot or transitioned to. Recovery is fluid and consistent without compromising a 360-degree situational awareness.

This mastering of the fundamentals is no different for women than it is for men. It takes time and attention and is not arrived at easily and not maintained without practice. But we are not talking about making shooting your life. We are just talking about receiving proper fundamentals through solid instruction and practice. This does not require daily practice of long duration. It simply takes a few minutes after the fundamentals are learned to hone and maintain the skills.

And it can be a heck of a lot of fun, something that you can enjoy with family members or friends.

WRAP-UP

CASE STUDY

Two Indiana grandmothers, aged 52 and 57, have started a new shooting club called WAR – Women Armed and Ready. Both women have been robbed in the past. According to news reports (Cincinnati.com; Hannah Haney; 5 August 2014), Konnie Couch, one of the founders of the club, which formed in May of 2014, stated, "The thing of it is, bad things happen to good people all the time, and, if something bad is going to happen, it's gonna happen without warning," Couch said. "It's gonna be very quick, and you've gotta be prepared for it." According to the same news report:

Gun ownership among women is on the rise. A 2013 Gallup poll revealed that 15 percent of gun owners are women, up from 13 percent in 2005. Indiana alone has issued 123,536 firearms licenses to women in the first quarter of 2014. (Ohio and Kentucky don't break down concealed carry permit holders by gender). There are numerous female gun groups nationally, including Armed Females of America, Women & Guns and The Well Armed Woman.

"(Our main objective is) to get women trained and where, if they have to… they would be able to react and save themselves. Or at least make a valiant attempt to save themselves," Couch said.

According to a report at News21 by Lauren Loftus and Natalie Krebs, "Women emerge as a forceful voice in the business of defending firearms" - Nearly 79 percent of firearms retailers reported an increase in female customers between 2011 and 2012, according to the National Shooting Sports Foundation. From this surge in popularity comes classes, specialized apparel, custom firearms, shooting-group memberships and conferences for women.

Women have already hit societal and economic milestones: More women than ever before are living alone, marrying later and earning more than their husbands. Firearms are arguably another part of the equation. As Carrie Lightfoot (founder of The Well Armed Woman) put it, owning a gun as a self-protection tool mirrors this shift of women from "being the protected to being the protector."

"Women are taking on that role — they have to," she said, "And they're taking it on pretty fiercely."

It has been my good fortune to be able to train stout-hearted persons of both sexes in both law enforcement and private citizen's firearms training programs. There are differences in the sexes, and we appreciate those differences, by the way. But there are differences within the sexes as well. What firearm a 6'2" 220 lb. man can conceal, shoot, move with and operate may be different than what a 5'5" 110 pound female can, but it is also different for a 5'7" 150 lb. man.

Now there are those ladies who are just tougher than most men. They are strong and aggressive and easily pick up physical skills, period. I can think of three ladies, right off the bat, who have better empty-hand striking skills than 90% of the male police officers I've trained. All three were taught by their fathers at a young age to box, so they learned to develop power through correct body mechanics. All three have and do work hard to maintain these skills. These same

learning principles can be applied to shooting as well. Correct tutelage and practice can allow any shooter to learn and master the fundamentals as well as control over their fight or flight (sympathetic nervous system) response.

Violence, in its many

Women are purchasing and training with firearms like never before.

forms, may be foreign to you. Don't wait until after an incident to learn and train. You can and should do it now! Fortunately now is a great time, based on the many professional instructors, books, DVD's, equipment and firearms geared just for the ladies. Go learn the fundamentals through a qualified and professional instructor. Then expand that training with pressure testing in confrontation simulations. Learn to take that SNS response and allow it to improve and strengthen you versus over-stimulating you in a hyper-vigilant state and caught like a deer in the headlights.

There is no time like the present and no place on earth more conducive to developing the skills and attributes of the female armed citizen. Armed self-defense is not just for men, everyone can empower themselves, take control of their own safety and security, and protect their loved ones from violent criminal attack, and that is true equality.

CHAPTER TEN:

THE ARMED CITIZEN'S RESPONSE TO THE ACTIVE KILLER

San Ysidro McDonalds; Luby's Cafeteria; Case Western Reserve; Columbine H.S.; Columbus, Ohio; Trolley Square Mall; Cleveland Success Academy; Virginia Tech; Ft. Hood, Texas; Aurora, Colorado; Sikh Temple, Wisconsin; Sandy Hook Elementary; the Washington D.C. Boatyard shooting and more. Each of these incidents was stopped by a gun. Either the suspect committed sui-

Police officers engage in scenario during active killer response training.

cide or was wounded or killed by police. Only in one case – the Aurora, Colorado theatre shooting – was the gunman apprehended without a shootout or him committing suicide.

Police tactics have changed over the years. As a police SWAT trainer prior to Columbine, I had my team doing active killer response versus locking the building down and waiting. After Columbine, tactics were developed and implemented recommending four officer "Contact" teams. These teams would enter the structure and hunt for the shooter based on dynamic intelligence developed on the fly, such as gunshots and wounded victims who could provide suspect description and direction.

As time went by we modified tactics, understanding that waiting led to more casualties and that when pressed by an armed response the killer often took his own life, thus ending his continued killing.

Critics of an armed citizen response to the active killer have called CCW permit holders "Jack Bauer wannabes" (from the TV show 24). But if we examine these types of incidents we understand that someone with a gun has always stopped the killing – either the suspect with his gun by way of suicide or others. I would submit that when a law abiding citizen or police officer stops the carnage a lot less people get shot and killed.

CASE STUDY

When Officer Ken Hammond was at the Trolley Square Mall in Salt Lake City, Utah, on 12 February 2012, he was not acting as a police officer for the Ogden Police Department. Celebrating an early Valentine's Day dinner with his wife, he reacted when a suspect armed with a shotgun and handgun entered the mall and started shooting, killing five victims and wounding four others. Hammond's gunfire pinned down the suspect until on-duty officers could respond and shot and killed the perpetrator.

Compare that incident with the sad testimony, in front of congress, by Suzanna Gratia Hupp about her experiences in Luby's Cafeteria:

CASE STUDY

After the suspect drove his truck through the front windows of that restaurant and then started shooting, Ms. Hupp stated that it took her about 45 seconds before she realized that this was not a robbery. Ms. Hupp and her father took cover on the floor behind an overturned table and reached for her purse for a handgun, which she was given for personal protection by a friend and which she had training to use. Unfortunately a couple of months earlier she had decided to take her handgun out of her purse and put it in her car because at that time (1991) it was sometimes a felony to carry a concealed handgun. Ms. Hupp's father rushed the man and was shot and killed by the suspect. Ms. Hupp took an opportunity to run and grabbed her mother to run away with her but her mother refused to leave. Ms. Hupp's mother crawled over to her husband and cradled him until the suspect walked back around and shot her in the head, killing her.

Ask Ms. Gratia-Hupp about her feelings on whether an armed citizen could possibly stop an active killer and she might echo her testimony before congress (which you can see on YouTube). By the way, Dr. Suzanna Gratia Hupp went on to have a very successful career in politics representing the State of Texas and the 2nd Amendment. Suzanna Gratia Hupp wrote From Luby's to the Legislature: One Woman's Fight Against Gun Control (Privateer Publications; 2009).

Suzanna Gratia Hupp was interviewed on CNN recently and said, "Let me point something out that is so painfully obvious to me. Where do all these mass shootings occur? These creeps go to places where they know they can shoot people like fish in a barrel… Until the cops, bless their hearts, finally arrive."

Could you or can you make a difference in such a situation? Ken Hammond did. Jeanne Assam did. Suzanna Gratia Hupp believes that, had she been armed on that fateful day in Texas in '91, she could have.

What can you do? What is your role? Let's take a look at the threat and then look at response tactics for the armed citizen.

THE THREAT

In 2013, J. Pete Blair, Ph.D, from Texas State University, along with M. Hunter Martaindale, published United States Active Shooter Events from 200 to 2010: Training and Equipment Implications through Texas State University. From that report we read some key research findings:

◆ 84 Active Shooter Events (what the authors refer to as ASEs), occurred between 2000 and 2010.
◆ The frequency of ASEs appears to be increasing.
◆ Business locations were the most frequently attacked (37%), followed by schools (34%), and public (outdoor) venues (17%).
◆ The median number of people killed during ASEs is two. The median number shot is four.
◆ The most commonly used weapon was a pistol (60%), followed by rifles (27%), and shotguns (10%).
◆ Attackers carried multiple weapons in 41% of the attacks.
◆ Body armor was worn in 4% of cases.
◆ Improvised Explosive Devices (IEDs) were brought to the scene in 2% of cases.
◆ Some shooters attempted to deny police access to the attack site through the use of barricades.
◆ The attacks ended before the police arrived 49% of the time. In 56% of the attacks that were still ongoing when the police arrived, the police had to use force to stop the killing.
◆ EMS entry to the attack site is often delayed because the police must conduct a thorough search of the scene in order to declare it secure.

Key training implications (modified by the author for the armed citizen):

◆ Expect a fight – Training must not assume that the attacker will be dead or give-up without offering any resistance.
◆ Medical – Training will allow those present to stabilize victims long enough for either EMS to enter the scene or for officers to transport victims to the EMS casualty collection point.

Other recommendations from the report include: medical equipment for officers, hard body armor, and patrol rifles issued to police officers.

The authors identified 14 incidents out of 84 events studied where solo officers made entry. In six of these 14 events, the killing had stopped before the officer made entry. In four cases the attacker stopped himself (two times of suicide and two incidents where the attacker left the scene). In two cases citizens stopped the attacker. In the other eight incidents after the officer arrived, two suspects then committed suicide, and in the remaining six incidents force was used against the suspect with five shootings and one incident where the solo officer subdued the suspect without shooting. Blair and Martaindale state, "If the numbers are put together (57% of the time the attack is ongoing; in 75% of these ongoing attacks the officer uses force to stop the attacks; and in 33% of these use of force incidents, the officers is shot), there is a 14% chance that an officer will be shot when he or she makes a solo entry into an active shooter attack site."

These events are certainly extremely dangerous for armed citizens as well, but what are the alternatives? We are not recommending that you respond to a neighborhood school if you hear of an active shooter event, but what if you are on scene outside a school or it happens at your place of business or other public location such as your church where you have been authorized by your minister, priest or rabbi to carry concealed? How should you respond?

BUSINESS AND PUBLIC ACTIVE KILLER INCIDENTS

Are you expected to be able to hunt down an active killer like a SWAT team member would do? No. But understand that being armed and trained puts you at a distinct advantage to an unarmed citizen in the same circumstances. It gives you a fighting chance. Here are some tactics that might improve your odds:

◆ Understand that the active killer wants nothing but a high body count. They don't want money, they don't want to negotiate, and they don't want hostages. They want to kill and maim as fast as they can.

◆ The active killer wants an apocalyptic ending. They want to go out in a blaze of glory with the police or at their own hand after being cornered.

◆ They are hunting.

◆ They don't want a fight. Standing toe to toe with an armed citizen or police officer is not what they want.

◆ Active killers count on their victims going into shock, curling up in a fetal position and being an easy target.

◆ The active killer can be detected on approach or during preparations for attack. Most carry handguns because they can more easily conceal them. Those with rifles often hide them in cases or under their coats as they approach their intended target zone.

◆ If you do not witness the killer's preparations, the only warning you may have is the presence of an armed man, shooting.

◆ You must overcome your Sympathetic Nervous System reaction and act aggressively and decisively.

◆ Draw your firearm and if the threat is close and direct, move off the "X" and neutralize the suspect with accurate gunfire.

◆ If the threat is at a distance, seek cover. Move your family, friends or companions to a solid covered position and then move away from them to a covered position. Understand that the suspect will begin firing at you and you do not want to draw gunfire toward your family or companions.

- ◆ You can bunker and then ambush. Jeanne Assam's first thought was to take cover in a hallway and wait until the suspect came within view and engage. For an armed citizen, this is a sound strategy.
- ◆ If you move toward the suspect to get a shot, move from covered position to another covered position. This could mean a doorway, pillar, tree, car, fountain, the list is endless.
- ◆ Don't challenge the suspect. Remember, they have no plan to surrender, they want to kill. Challenging the suspect will only expose you to incoming fire. If you go down, others will die as well. If they have presented a deadly threat, shoot.
- ◆ If you have the chance to shoot them in the back or side or snipe them from an unseen position, then the tactics gods have smiled down on you. You do not need to face them or have them point or shoot at you to present a deadly threat.
- ◆ If you have fired, do not approach them. They could be only wounded and playing opossum or lying in wait for your approach. If you are not behind cover then get behind some.
- ◆ Be careful of multiple suspects. Remember there were two shooters at Columbine and two in Las Vegas. Maintain your 360-degree awareness including looking for responding police officers.
- ◆ Start identifying yourself, "I am an innocent armed citizen! Someone please call 911!" Repeat it several times. If you have a "Don't Shoot Me Banner" then this would be an excellent time to deploy it.
- ◆ Follow the recommendations given earlier regarding responding officers. Remember the police are coming hot and heavy, and anyone with a gun who appears in any way to be a threat may get shot.

We haven't talked yet about first-aid, but many armed citizens are now carrying combat first-aid items such as an Israeli battlefield dressing, Quick Clot or other hemostatic agent, and a CAT – Combat Applications tourniquet. Consider these items for family and friends who may be wounded, innocent citizens, and yourself. My friend Eric Dickinson has written a book, The Street Officer's Guide to Emergency Medical Tactics (Looseleaf Law Publications; 2013), which gives valuable insights into dealing with gunshot wounds and other injuries the armed citizen might encounter.

OUR SCHOOLS

Colonel Dave Grossman, author of On Killing and On Combat is also an international lecturer to police and armed citizens on hyper-violent suspects.

According to Grossman, the children in our schools represent America's greatest vulnerability to domestic and international terrorists as well as to demented individuals. Yet, we as a nation refuse to accept this threat and continue to fail to secure out schools accordingly.

Unfortunately even off-duty police officers may be restricted in some states from carrying concealed in "school safety zones." This was true in my state until a couple of years ago when the law was changed, but CCW permit holders are still forbidden by state law from carrying concealed into a school. Fortunately state law in Ohio allows teachers authorized by their school district to carry concealed. Many districts cannot afford to provide "school resource officers" or uniformed officers to work at each school. Even those districts that provide officers to work at high schools cannot provide officers for middle or elementary schools. Some districts provide security guards but most of these guards are unarmed, many don't even carry pepper spray, and those who may be armed have marginal training (I know, I played the "security" game while in college).

A law enforcement officer of my acquaintance has testified at the state level against the armed teacher or school staff program. What's his plan? To allow retired officers in marked polo shirts to carry concealed on school property. Now, I'm not too far from retirement as I write these words, but let me state that some – certainly not all – retired LEOs are capable of securing schools. At this point most officers who retire continue to work until in their 60s. Having worked off-duty in a school for a few years, I can tell you that it is not the type of job I would want to do in retirement. Further, as we age and the further we get from the street, we certainly don't have the abilities we once did. It is also faulty logic based on this police supervisor's opinion that armed staff members don't have the same skills and abilities as retired police officers.

Some training programs recommend "bunkering" i.e. to conduct a lockdown of the school and await police response. As a member of a county-wide school violence committee, I pointed out that in many school shootings, the killer heads to the largest concentration of potential targets present – cafeterias, libraries, etc. to maximize body count. In these environments, hiding or bunkering makes no sense. We therefore recommended a lockdown or evacuation plan depending on where you were. Locking down and piling furniture by the door and throwing books at the armed suspect may be a plan, but it is far from ideal. Oftentimes school districts want to portray that they are doing something, but sometimes it's just feel-good training. It is also true that many schools have "policies," but most teachers are unaware of what they are and there is little to no actual training. In addition, few schools conduct drills. Colonel Grossman points out that schools do fire drills and tornado drills each year and have for decades, but the actual incidence of school fires is virtually nonexistent. Yet, schools don't want to drill in their response to an active killer.

Teachers train in the F.A.S.T.E.R. program designed by John Benner and implemented by the Buckeye Firearms Association.

The F.A.S.T.E.R. program as implemented in Ohio provides excellent instruction – in the classroom, on the range and in dynamic confrontation simulation – to teachers and school staff members. As a prerequisite, all of the applicants must already have their CCW permit. In my state this requires both classroom and range activities. This is not to say that these programs are the end-all, just that this is the minimum standard for entrance into FASTER training.

Having conducted several of these programs, I can state that I did not teach these educators and school support personnel any differently than officers and SWAT personnel. They learned the skills in a repetitive fashion and then were tested in multiple scenarios.

I found that these teacher/staff students were extremely motivated and hard-working, dedicated professional educators from colleges, high schools, school boards, elementary schools, even private academies. I would certainly feel more relaxed knowing that an armed citizen educator was walking the halls of my child's school, than training my child, to "run away from the sound of the guns!"

THOUGHTS ON ACTIVE KILLER RESPONSE

As these incidents have occurred during my police career, I have seen the evolution of police tactics to deal with them. We have gone from a lockdown and SWAT Team deployment to a four-man rapid deployment philosophy. Time being the crucial issue, my friend and law enforcement trainer Ron Borsch refers to this as "The Stopwatch of Death®". Law enforcement has modified its approach to the active killer even more with the recommendation that a solo officer

Some FASTER students complete the Ohio Peace Officers pistol qualification at a higher score than police officers.

should make entry if back-up is not present. One officer aggressively attacking the threat can make a difference and save lives.

CASE STUDY

In Columbus, Ohio, the heavy metal band Damageplan featuring guitarist "Dimebag" Darrell Abbott was playing at a local nightspot when a lone gunman open fired, killing Abbott, security man Jeff Thompson, employee Erin Halk and audience member Nathan Bray. A band support team member, John Brooks, was taken hostage after he attempted to disarm the assailant. Columbus PD Officer James Niggemeyer entered through a back door armed with a Remington 870 12-gauge shotgun and killed the suspect with one shot to the head.

Of course, this is dependent on training and competency. General George Patton said, "Untutored courage is useless in the face of educated bullets." Sadly, police agencies across the U.S. have cut staff and are operating below authorized manpower levels due to the economy.

I have also seen the widespread issuance of concealed carry permits throughout the United States. Sadly, but maybe fortuitously, these two will meet.

There are no magic tactics in dealing with an active killer. You just need to apply the basics and fundamentals, aggressively, to solve the problem.

This is not about being a "Jack Bauer" wannabe. It is about contemplating, planning and preparing for the unthinkable to occur and saving your family, friends or your own life. This is not just a police problem. Ron Borsch's "Stopwatch of Death" concept clearly indicates that as seconds tick away an armed hyper-violent active killer is going about his business. He will not be talked to, negotiated with, cajoled, or rationalized with. He may find perverse pleasure in the pleadings of his intended victims as they beg for their lives only to execute them with headshots while laughing. Someone who is capable of such an evil and unfathomable act as shooting their way into an elementary school classroom and slaughtering five-year-olds is incapable of negotiation. Law enforcement has learned that, the armed citizen must come to accept and understand it as well.

CASE STUDY

On 16 April 2007, Professor Liviu Lebrescu, a survivor of the Nazi Holocaust, was shot and killed as he barred the door to a classroom from the active killer attempting to enter. While holding the door with his body, he shouted to his students to hurry as they escaped through the windows. Though shot through the door and killed, his actions saved a reported 20 innocent lives that day.

We can only imagine how many lives might have been saved had one trained CCW permit holder in class or on staff been in that area on that day. Yet colleges, universities, elementary schools and malls don't see the logic that survivor Suzanna Gratia Hupp has said "is so painfully obvious to her," that these active killers seek gun-free zones with many "fish in a barrel" to shoot. Let us hope that things change and common sense finds its way before other innocent lives are lost.

"All that is necessary for the triumph of evil is that good men do nothing."
– Edmund Burke

This chapter is dedicated to Professor Librescu and all those who have stood up to active killers while empty-handed.

Note – I have intentionally avoided using the names of the perpetrators involved in these atrocities. They have gained enough attention in their infamy. Let us hope we can cleanse their names and the memories of their acts from history as we prepare for and stop those yet to come.

CHAPTER ELEVEN:

CLOSING THOUGHTS

As I write this, just yesterday Detroit Police Chief James Craig made this statement according to The Washington Times (July 16, 2014):

"Criminals are getting the message that good Detroiters are armed and will use that weapon. I don't want to take away from the good work our investigators are doing, but I think part of the drop in crime, and robberies in particular, is because criminals are thinking twice that citizens could be armed."

The 2nd Amendment guarantees your right to keep and bear arms. But with rights come responsibilities.

"I can't say what specific percentage is caused by this, but there's no question in my mind it has had an effect."

Detroit has experienced 37% fewer robberies than it did last year, 22% fewer break-ins of businesses and homes, and 30% fewer carjackings in 2014.

CASE STUDY

A nurse in Milwaukee thwarted a carjacking attempt by two teens, ages 15 and 17. When the two male suspects confronted the nurse telling her they wanted "the keys, car, everything" and then threatened to "Go get the cannon." She pulled a handgun out of her gym bag and opened fire, hitting the 15-year-old. Turns out intercepting the two suspects helped stop a ring of criminals who had committed another carjacking and other crimes. The wounded 15-year-old, police believe, shot a Milwaukee man during an attempted carjacking. (Milwaukee-Wisconsin Journal Sentinel; 06/12/14)

CASE STUDY

An off-duty police major was robbed at gunpoint as she was walking with a friend at night. The police supervisor handed over her purse containing her handgun, police badge, debit and credit cards. The officer's friend's purse was taken by the robber who then ran off.

Two different incidents and two different outcomes, both are citizens of this country. One was armed and prepared, the other was not. Sadly the second incident involved a trained police officer, sworn to protect. The police were quoted as recommending that you give the robber what they want and get a good description, to be a good "victim." What would have happened if the robber, like so many others, had shot both of the women? Or how about if he had run around the corner, robbed another person and then shot and killed them? Sure, these are tough decisions when facing a suspect's gun, and taking action has its risks as we have repeatedly warned, but not being mentally aware or prepared to take action has its risks as well. The nurse by virtue of her mindset and armed capability dominated the violent encounter. The trained police officer chose by her lack of mental awareness and preparedness, and lack of firearm access, to be a victim. We are reminded of another incident involving an off-duty police officer years ago in a barbershop.

CASE STUDY

An off-duty sheriff's deputy was inside a beauty salon with his fiancé when two hold-up men entered and removed wallets and personal effects from victims and ordered them face down on the floor. When the suspects found the deputy's badge in his wallet, they executed him with a shot to the head. The couple was planning their wedding at the time of the incident.

Compare the foregoing cases with this incident out of New York:

CASE STUDY

A drugstore was robbed by two armed suspects demanding OxyContin and Percocet by name. The robbers ordered everyone in the store to lie face down on the floor. Police responded to the 911 calls and ordered the suspects to come out. One suspect responded by trying to fire on the officers, but his gun failed to fire. One of the three officers fired on the suspect but missed. The suspect then ran across the street, still pointing his handgun at the cops. A retired police lieutenant who was getting gas at the convenience station across the street drew his concealed handgun and responded. From a distance of 55 feet, the retired officer hit the suspect twice in the head killing him.

Here we have a "retired" police supervisor, i.e. an armed citizen who still carries concealed and responds to a violent encounter, in which on-duty police officers could have been shot and killed, by shooting and stopping the armed suspect. I have used many off-duty or retired police officer incidents in this book for several reasons. These incidents tend to be better reported, are more easily accessible, and the public incidents have been going on for years, even in states and cities where concealed carry has been more tightly controlled. But make no mistake, off-duty and retired officers are just armed citizens since they are citizens of the Republic first and police officers second. Law enforcement officers, by and large, are not gun-savvy people. There is an old quote from Francis McGee, the late commander of the NYPD's Firearms and Tactics Unit, "Most police officers would rather have a custom Parker pen set than a custom Smith & Wesson." There is a lot of truth in that (although brand new smart phone could be substituted for the pen set in today's world).

CASE STUDY

8 July 2014 – WSVN Channel 7 News in Miami reports that budget cuts in Miami-Dade County could result in hundreds of police officers losing their jobs. The news station reports quotes John Rivera, president of the Miami-Dade Police Benevolent Association, "If the mayor's not going to provide security, then my recommendation, as an experienced law enforcement officer for nearly 40 years,

> is to buy yourself an attack dog, put bars on your windows
> and doors and get yourself some firearms, because you're
> going to have to protect yourselves. We won't be able to."

Although alarmist talk made to provoke citizen support for maintaining police staffing levels, I concur with Mr. Rivera. Of course, I would agree with all or most of his recommendations. Sadly many of our cities and communities have gotten to the point where troubled areas or high-crime districts get a lot of police service but the nicer parts of town don't. When was the last time you saw a police vehicle just patrolling your neighborhood? When was the last time you were walking to your car in a darkened parking lot and looked over to see a police patrol car standing guard over you as you walked through the night?

CASE STUDY

The "average" time for police response in this country is 11 minutes. Now, there are certainly times when police may arrive in a couple of minutes or less, but as the saying goes, "When seconds count, police are minutes away..." Couple this with the fact that violent encounters, even home invasions or burglaries, are often over well within that time and the police often arrive late, with the suspects gone and the oftentimes the victims left in a pile on the floor.

Let me state that I am exceedingly proud of my profession and its commitment to protect communities. Officers rush, often at their own peril, to help the innocent and apprehend the guilty who would prey upon society. Most enjoy nothing more than arresting some bad guy who has preyed upon their communities. This is what most of them live for. But their numbers have been cut over the years and they are strapped to get the back-up they need to enforce the law. They also, by an overwhelming majority, believe in the 2nd Amendment, armed defense and concealed carry by private citizens.

Police officers would tell you, as I am now, that you must plan, prepare, train and arm to defend yourself and protect your loved ones. Law enforcement is by its very nature reactionary, and because of the current state of the economy manpower deficient and training impoverished. There are exceptions but few and far between. Many law enforcement officers must go to the range on their own time, at their own expense and pay for training out of their own pockets.

THE ARMED CITIZEN

CASE STUDY

News Flash (CBS/AP News, 25 July 14) – Darby, Pennsylvania: A psychiatric patient open fired in a psychiatrist's office, killing his caseworker and grazing the doctor. According to reports, the doctor drew his own concealed handgun and returned fire, hitting the gunman three times, wounding and stopping him. "The shootings occurred on the third floor of a wellness center attached to Mercy Fitzgerald Hospital in Darby, just southwest of Philadelphia." AP quotes Yeadon Police Chief Donald Molineux, "Without a doubt, I believe the doctor saved lives. Without that firearm, this guy (the patient) could have went out in the hallway and just walked down the offices until he ran out of ammunition." The Philadelphia Inquirer (Philly.com, 25 July) quotes an ultrasound technician, "There's a sign on the door that says that you have to check your weapons at the front. But you can't expect every crazy person to do that."

USA Today (25 July) reports that according to a hospital spokesman interviewed by the Associated Press, "Hospital policy allows only on-duty law enforcement officers to carry weapons on campus." Indeed, it is standard practice among most hospitals and wellness centers that I'm aware of to restrict even off-duty law enforcement officers within their jurisdiction from carrying onto hospital property. I had the occasion to go to a wellness center for a work-related M.R.I. once on-duty and the technician wanted me to secure my firearm with the unarmed guard in the lobby rather than lock it in a locker where my clothing was secured. It is obvious that the doctor involved in this incident made the conscious decision to violate hospital policy. Lives were saved because of this doctor's decision and his actions.

It is interesting to note that, according to Heidi Smith of Thunder Ranch, "leading occupation for students in all classes are doctors…2-5 in every class we teach."

We have seen an explosion in the number of concealed carry permits nationwide. The Crime Prevention Research Center (CPRC) recently published (July 9, 2014) a report Concealed Carry Permit Holders Across the United States. In that report we find the following:

"CPRC collected the most recent data available for each state and the results showed that there are total of 11,113,013 Americans who currently hold concealed carry permits representing 4.8 percent of the total population.

"The number of concealed carry permit holders is likely much higher than 11.1 million because numbers are not available for all states that issue permits, such as New York. Additionally, four states and the majority of Montana do not require that residents have a concealed handgun permit to carry within the state so the number of residents who carry a concealed weapon is not recorded.

"The report also examines the violent crime rate in relation to the rising percentage of the adult population with concealed carry permits. Between 2007 and the preliminary estimates for 2013, murder rates have fallen from 5.6 to 4.4 per 100,000 – a 22 percent drop in the murder rate at the same time that the percentage of the adult population with permits soared by 130 percent. Overall violent crime also fell by 22 percent over that period of time."

When examining crimes committed by permit holders or instances where permits were revoked, the CPRC provided this data:

"Consider the two large states at the front of the current debate, Florida and Texas: Both states provide easy web access to detailed records of permit holders. Over two decades, from October 1, 1987 to May 31, 2014, Florida has issued permits to more than 2.64 million people, with the average person holding a permit for more than a decade. Few -- 168 (about 0.006%) -- have had their permits revoked for any type of firearms related violation, the most common being accidentally carrying a concealed handgun into a gun-free zone such as a school or an airport, not threats or acts of violence. It is an annual rate of 0.0002 percent.

"The already low revocation rate has been declining over time. Over the last 77 months from January 2008 through May 2014, just four permits have been revoked for firearms-related violations. With an average of about 875,000 active permit holders per year during those years, the annual revocation rate for firearms related violations is 0.00007 percent – seven one hundred thousandths of one percentage point.

"For all revocations, the annual rate in Florida is 0.012 percent.

"The numbers are similarly low in Texas. In 2012, the latest year that crime data are available, there were 584,850 active license holders. Out of these, 120 were convicted of either a misdemeanor or a felony, a rate of 0.021 percent, with only a few of these crimes involving a gun."

YOUR RIGHTS AND RESPONSIBILITIES

Those numbers are pretty clear, just like in Detroit. But with rights come responsibilities. It is simply not enough to go through a CCW permit training program and devote no more study or preparation to your armed defense. These programs are meant as minimum entrance level training programs, not all that you'll ever need or all that you should do to properly prepare.

Time after time in my police career I have had officers tell me that they responded just like they had trained or that training saved their lives. In the violent armed encounters in which I have been involved, most started and were over in seconds, with no time to "think" about what to do, only time to respond to threat cues or suspect actions – stimulus/response as we talked about earlier.

Your responsibility then is to train and practice.

Our Second Amendment rights are guaranteed by our Constitution. A Constitution which placed the Right to Keep and Bear Arms second only to "freedom of speech, or of the press, or the right of the people peaceably to assemble." But as Thomas Jefferson so eloquently stated, "The price of liberty is eternal vigilance." So too, the price of safety, security and self-defense is eternal vigilance.

Obtaining the correct firearm(s) under your American right to keep arms is only one part of the equation. Knowledge, training and practice will improve your performance under stress when those who would attempt to take your "life, liberty and the pursuit of happiness" as our nation's founders wrote are our unalienable rights in the Declaration of Independence.

Evil exists in our world, our country and society. And as Rev, Charles Aked (1916) is quoted as saying, "It has been said that for evil men to accomplish their purpose it is only necessary that good men should do nothing."

I compliment you that by purchasing or reading this book you are doing something. I hope that you will continue on your quest to train, prepare and plan. Training has saved my life and countless men and women I know. This guide is a testament to the lifesaving power of knowledge, training and practice.

"I pray that the Good Lord blesses you with the strength and will to train to win!" ~ Kevin R. Davis

BIBLIOGRAPHY AND SUGGESTED READING

Siddle, Bruce K. (1995). "Sharpening the Warrior's Edge." PPCT Research Publications

Artwohl, Alexis; Christensen, Loren W. (1997). "Deadly Force Encounters." Paladin Press

Goleman, Daniel (1995). "Emotional Intelligence." Bantam Trade Paperback

Artwohl, Alexis (2003). "Deadly Force Encounters: Preparing to Survive, Coping with the Aftermath."

Patrick, Urey W.; Hall, John C. (2005) "In Defense of Self and Others...Issues, Facts & Fallacies – the Realities of Law Enforcement's Use of Deadly Force." Carolina Academic Press

Chabris, Christopher; Simons, Daniel (2009) "The Invisible Gorilla: How Our Intuitions Deceive Us." Broadway Paperbacks

Sapolsky, Robert M. (2004) "Why Zebras Don't Get Ulcers: The Acclaimed Guide to Stress, Stress-Related Diseases, and Coping – Third Edition" Owl Books

Adams, Ronald J.; McTernan, Thomas A.; Remsberg, Charles (1987) "Street Survival: Tactics for Armed Encounters." Calibre Press

Grossman, Lt. Col. Dave (2008) "On Combat: The Psychology and Physiology of Deadly Conflict in War and Peace." Warrior Science Publications

Ayoob, Massad F. (1987) "The Semiautomatic Pistol in Police Service and Self-Defense." Police Bookshelf

Ayoob, Massad F. (2007) "The Gun Digest Book of Combat Handgunnery: 6th Edition." Krause Publications

Ayoob, Massad F. (2012) "Gun Digest Book of Concealed Carry." Krause Publications

Schmidt, Richard A.; Wrisberg, Craig A. (2008) "Motor Learning and Performance: A Situation-Based Learning Approach." Human Kinetics

Federal Bureau of Investigation: Uniform Crime Reports (2012) "Crime in the United States 2011" Criminal Justice Information Services Division

U.S. Department of Justice (2013) "Firearm Violence, 1993-2011" Bureau of Justice Statistics

Tom Aveni (2005) "Officer-Involved Shootings: What We Don't Know Has Hurt Us." The Police Policy Studies Council

Williams M.D., Dr. James (2005) "Tactical Anatomy Instructor Manual." Tactical Anatomy

Kilgore, Kristie (2001) "Eyes Wide Open" Clinetop Press

Givens, Tom Lessons From the Street DVD, Personal Defense Network

Brooks, Pierce (1975) "...officer down, code three." Motorola Teleprograms, Inc.

Byrnes, John D. (2002) Before Conflict: Preventing Aggressive Behavior Scarecrow Press

Branca, Andrew (2013) The Law of Self-Defense: Second Edition Law of Self Defense Publishers

Davis, Kevin R. (2012) Use of Force Investigations: A Manual for Law Enforcement Responder Media

Lee, Cynthia (2003) Murder and the Reasonable Man New York University Press

DeBecker, Gavin (1999) The Gift of Fear Dell

DePorter, Hernacki (1992) Quantum Learning Dell

Cooper, Jeff (1998) To Ride Shoot Straight and Speak the Truth Paladin Press

Wasdin, Templin (2011) SEAL Team Six: Memoirs of an Elite SEAL Sniper St. Martin's Press

Rogers, Bill (2010) Be Fast, Be Accurate, Be the Best Rogers Shooting School Publications

Rogers, Bill Reactive Pistol Shooting Panteao Productions training DVD

Daniel, Rich Legitimate Training with Airsoft DVD FFKG.com

Murray, Ken (2004) Training at the Speed of Life Armiger Publications

Jones, Jan (1985) Self-Defense Requires No Apology Security World Publications

Quigley, Paxton (1989) Armed and Female Dutton Adult

Farnam, Vicki and Nicholl, Diane (2002) Teaching Women to Shoot: A Law Enforcement Officer's Guide D.T.I.

May-Hayes, Gila (2002) Effective Defense Firearms Academy of Seattle; (2009) Personal Defense for Women Gun Digest Books; (2013) Concealed Carry for Women Gun Digest Books

Smith, Clint and Heidi (2009) Ladies Basic Guide to Concealed Carry DVD FMG Publishers

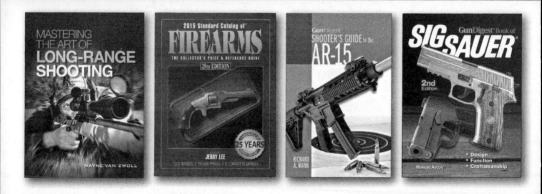

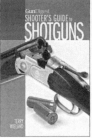

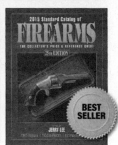
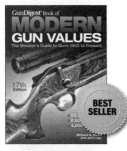
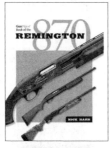
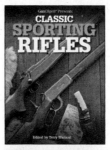
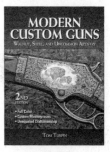

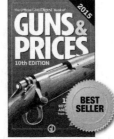
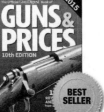

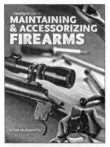

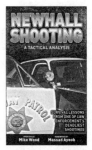

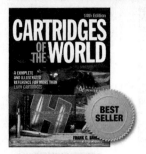
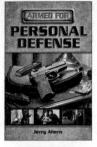

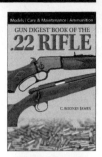

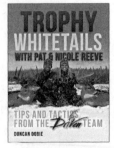

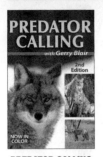

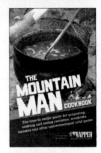

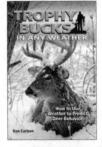

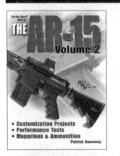
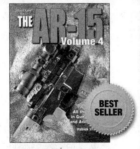
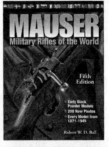
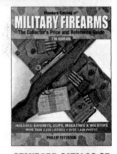
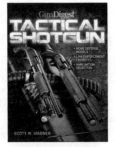
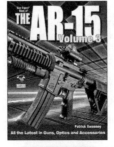
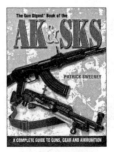

ANTIQUES & COLLECTIBLES

STANDARD CATALOG OF COLT FIREARMS
U5560 • $34.99

STANDARD CATALOG OF SMITH & WESSON
FSW03 • $42.99

FLAYDERMAN'S GUIDE TO ANTIQUE AMERICAN FIREARMS
Z0620 • $39.99

RELOADING

HANDBOOK OF RELOADING BASICS
T1864 • $19.99

RELOADING FOR SHOTGUNNERS
RFS5 • $24.99

RELOADING FOR HANDGUNNERS
W0932 • $27.99

ABCs OF RELOADING 9TH EDITION
Z9165 • $27.99

BEST SELLER

SURVIVAL

GUN DIGEST BOOK OF SURVIVAL GUNS
U1060 • $24.99

BUILD THE PERFECT SURVIVAL KIT
U6487 • $18.99

LIVING READY POCKET MANUAL: FIRST AID
U8353 • $12.99

FOOD STORAGE FOR SELF-SUFFICIENCY AND SURVIVAL
U8352 • $17.99

BUILD THE PERFECT BUG OUT VEHICLE
U7403 • $17.99

THE UNOFFICIAL HUNGER GAMES WILDERNESS SURVIVAL GUIDE
U1956 • $17.99

PREPPER'S GUIDE TO SURVIVING NATURAL DISASTERS
U3133 • $21.99

SURVIVAL SKILLS YOU NEED
W1803 • $22.99

BUILD THE PERFECT BUG-OUT BAG
W6554 • $16.99

BEST SELLER

HANDGUN TRAINING FOR PERSONAL PROTECTION
U2147 • $21.99

GLOCK DECONSTRUCTED
V9707 • $29.99

GD BOOK OF CONCEALED CARRY, 2ND EDITION
V9337 • $27.99

GUN DIGEST BIG FAT BOOK OF THE .45 ACP
Z4204 • $24.99

1911 THE FIRST 100 YEARS
Z7019 • $32.99

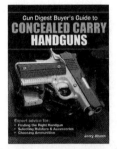

GUN DIGEST BUYER'S GUIDE TO CONCEALED CARRY HANDGUNS
Z8905 • $24.99

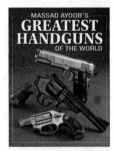

MASSAD AYOOB'S GREATEST HANDGUNS OF THE WORLD
Z6495 • $27.99

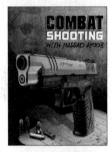

COMBAT SHOOTING WITH MASSAD AYOOD
W1983 • $25.99

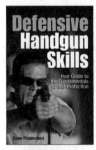

DEFENSIVE HANDGUNS SKILLS
Z8883 • $16.99

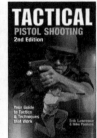

TACTICAL PISTOL SHOOTING
Z5954 • $24.99

GUN DIGEST BOOK OF THE REVOLVER
W1576 • $22.99

GUN DIGEST BOOK OF THE GLOCK
Z1926 • $27.99

DEFENSIVE REVOLVER FUNDAMENTALS
U4713 • $22.99

GUN DIGEST SHOOTER'S GUIDE TO HANDGUN MARKSMANSHIP
U3674 • $19.99

GUN DIGEST BOOK OF COMBAT GUNNERY
Z0880 • $24.99

PERSONAL DEFENSE FOR WOMEN
Z5057 • $22.99

CONCEALED CARRY FOR WOMEN
U3668 • $22.99

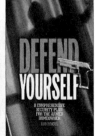

DEFEND YOURSELF
U7396 • $24.99

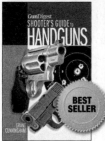
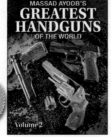
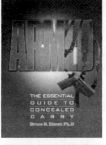

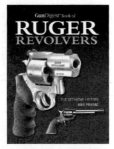
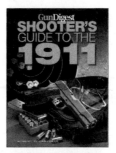
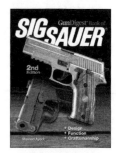
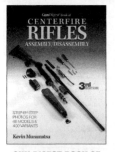

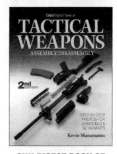
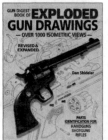

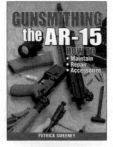
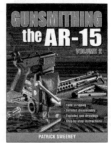

GUNSMITHING

**CUSTOMIZE THE
RUGER 10/22**
NGRTT • $29.99

**GUNSMITHING:
PISTOLS & REVOLVERS**
Z5056 • $29.99

**GUN DIGEST BOOK
OF RIMFIRE RIFLES
ASSEM/DISASSEM**
W1577 • $34.99

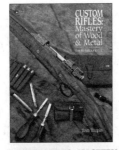

**CUSTOM RIFLES: MASTERY
OF WOOD & METAL**
V8196 • $59.99

**GUN DIGEST BOOK
OF THE AR-15**
GDAR • $27.99

KNIVES

**101 KNIFE
DESIGNS**
U1059 • $29.99

**SPIRIT
OF THE SWORD**
Z7241 • $24.99

**WAYNE GODDARD'S
$50 KNIFE SHOP**
WGBWR • $19.99

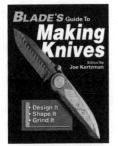

**BLADE'S GUIDE
TO MAKING KNIVES**
BGKFM • $24.99

HOW TO MAKE KNIVES
KHM01 • $14.99

**KNIFEMAKING WITH
BOB LOVELESS**
Z7240 • $24.99

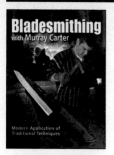

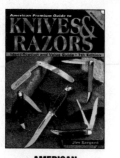